G000161329

C. P. MEAD

Hampshire's Greatest Run-maker

Best wishes
Neil Jenkinson

by
Neil Jenkinson

Published by
PAUL CAVE PUBLICATIONS LTD
74 Bedford Place, Southampton

Printed by
BROWN AND SON (RINGWOOD) LTD.
Crowe Arch Lane, Ringwood, Hants. BH24 1PD

To Jilly and for Phyllis

ISBN 0-86146-086-3

First published November 1993

"You don't take up cricket, you think you do but you don't; you get taken up. You think you are going to do what you please with the bat, but the fact is the bat does what it pleases with you; you think it's your servant, but in reality it's a master."

Norman Douglas

London Street Games
(Chatto and Windus, 1931)

CONTENTS

Introduction 1

Chapter One — Philip Mead 1887-1958 — Battersea 5

Chapter Two — Southampton 9

Chapter Three — Consolidation 13

Chapter Four — To the top of the tree 18

Chapter Five — With Warner and Douglas in Australia 24

Chapter Six — Fry and Hampshire — Hampshire defeat the Australians 29

Chapter Seven — The Business of Batting 34

Chapter Eight — At the Cape and After 42

Chapter Nine — Standing — at the wicket and among cricketers 50

Chapter Ten — 1,100 runs in Two Days 54

Chapter Eleven — 1921 65

Chapter Twelve — The new record by Mead 74

Chapter Thirteen — Tate's Ball and another Tour 78

Chapter Fourteen — Success is not enough 86

Chapter Fifteen — Need for Renaissance 90

Chapter Sixteen — Out of the Rough 96

Chapter Seventeen — Success to Success 102

Chapter Eighteen — 1928 108

Chapter Nineteen — Australian Autumn 114

Chapter Twenty — When Winter Comes 120

Chapter Twenty-One — Age can Wither 128

Chapter Twenty-Two — West Indian Summer 132

Chapter Twenty-Three — Not with a bang 146

Chapter Twenty-Four — Suffolk Punch 151

Chapter Twenty-Five — Unseen Bournemouth 155

Acknowledgements and Facts and Figures 159

Index 168

Charles Philip Mead

INTRODUCTION

Hampshire cricket was reborn on 1st September 1955 — or so it seemed to the crowds who crushed around the pavilion at Dean Park, Bournemouth.

All day in increasing gloom, with more than a hint of drizzle, they had watched Donald Kenyon, of Worcestershire, fighting a rearguard action against the Hampshire bowlers. At last he was left high and dry on 103, as after a frustrating delay caused by light rain the last wicket fell. Hampshire's victory took them to third position in the County Cricket Championship table; they had never finished as high before; indeed, only four times in the previous 30 years had they occupied a single-figure position and then never higher than seventh.

The Hampshire captain, Desmond Eagar, led his players onto the balcony of the little pavilion to acknowledge the enthusiasm of the crowd. Then he went downstairs, soon reappearing with a tall spare figure in raincoat, trilby and dark glasses. Eagar's career with Hampshire had not begun until 1946 but his sense of history was always highly tuned and he knew that the elderly man sitting in the downstairs dressing room should not be left out.

Eagar introduced to the excited crowd, Philip Mead, who briefly expressed his thanks that they had remembered 'an old has-been' amid the success of the season.

Nineteen years after his last match for Hampshire, Philip Mead's name was still familiar to many of the supporters at Dean Park; he continued to hold almost all the County's batting records and was recalled in a wider sphere for what had been his record-breaking score in a Test match against Australia in 1921. Little was seen of him now; he himself had not been able to see anything for more than a dozen years.

From that year (1955), Hampshire's cricket has flourished. Winners of the County Championship in 1961 and 1973, they have impressed through the efforts of a succession of brilliant high-scoring batsmen — imports like Philip Mead himself — beginning with Roy Marshall and continuing with Barry Richards, Gordon Greenidge and Chris and Robin Smith, who have been supported by a series of reliable professionals for any one of whom Eagar would have given much in those early post-war years. No one who saw them will forget the electrical effect of the arrival in championship cricket of Marshall in 1955 or Richards in 1968. Yet for consistency, longevity and the will to play, Mead still over-tops them all. He played with at least three generations of Hampshire cricketers. He was a great personality of the cricket field 'noted for his mannerisms at the crease', as Wisden put it, and his place in cricket is not dependent on statistics. Yet figures do show how pre-eminent he was in and after his generation.

1

For a start, see how his record compared with the other leading Hampshire batsmen as late as 1955:

	Career Dates	Matches	Innings	Not Out	Runs	Highest Score	Average
C. P. Mead	1905-36	700	1171	170	48892	280*	48.84
G. Brown	1908-33	539	900	46	22962	232*	26.88
J. Arnold	1929-50	396	710	45	21596	227	32.92
A. Bowell	1902-27	474	806	43	18467	204	24.20
N. McCorkell	1932-51	383	675	63	15835	203	25.87
N. H. Rogers	1946-55	285	506	25	15292	186	31.79
A. S. Kennedy	1907-36	596	916	110	14925	163*	18.51
J. A. Newman	1906-30	506	786	121	13903	166*	20.90
Lord Tennyson	1913-35	347	553	20	12626	217	23.68
E. M. Sprot	1898-1914	265	452	28	12212	147	28.80

By the end of the English season of 1990, 35 years on, most of the heroes of the past have been swallowed up — but not Mead:

	Career Dates	Matches	Innings	Not Out	Runs	Highest Score	Average
C. P. Mead	1905-36	700	1171	170	48892	280*	48.84
R. E. Marshall	1953-72	504	890	49	30303	228*	36.03
G. Brown	1908-33	539	900	46	22962	232*	26.88
J. R. Gray	1948-66	453	809	81	22450	213*	30.83
J. Arnold	1929-50	396	701	45	21596	227	32.92
H. Horton	1953-67	405	723	80	21536	160*	33.49
C. G. Greenidge	1970-87	275	472	35	19840	259	45.40
D. R. Turner	1966-89	416	678	73	18683	184*	30.88
N. H. Rogers	1946-55	285	506	25	15292	186	31.79
C. L. Smith	1980-91	222	383	48	15287	217	45.63
B. A. Richards	1968-78	204	342	33	15607	240	50.50
T. E. Jesty	1966-84	340	538	74	14753	248	31.79
R. A. Smith	1982-92	230	390	68	14227	209*	44.18

(* = not out and the figures are for Hampshire.)

Mead was one of a group of fine players who all started in cricket before the First World War, were in their prime in the 1920s and continued to play well into the 1930s. The eldest of their number was George Gunn (born 1879), who played for Notts from 1902 to 1932. Almost every county boasted a representative: Essex, Jack Russell; Gloucester, Alf Dipper; Hampshire, Mead and Brown; Kent, Frank Woolley and Hardinge; Lancashire, Ernest Tyldesley, Makepeace and Hallows; Middlesex, Patsy Hendren, Jack Hearne and Harry Lee; Notts, Gunn and Whysall; Surrey, Hobbs, Sandham and Ducat; Sussex,

Ted Bowley; Yorkshire, Percy Holmes. Herbert Sutcliffe would have been of the number but did not play before the First War. Hallows (born 1895) was the youngest; Woolley, who did not retire until 1938, was the last to play first-class cricket.

Year after year these men scored heavily, retaining their form well into middle age. Of course, their fielding was not tested by competitive one-day cricket, yet few of them were absolute passengers in the field even when nearer 50 years of age than 40 in a period when not as much attention as now was given to fielding agility.

Mead stood out among them, both for his consistency and his longevity. He almost played against W. G. Grace in 1904; he took 100 from the bowling of the Bedser twins and Stuart Surridge in 1938. He earned his living as a professional cricketer from 1902 for 40 years. Indeed, he never made or rather kept money from any source other than cricket. He inspired great affection — except among bowlers.

By the end of the 1920s there was much discontent among spectators and administrators at the huge growth of run-making in county cricket which culminated in the season of 1928 when 414 centuries were scored, a number which was not exceeded until 1990; 23 batsmen achieved an average of over 50 runs an innings and because of the high scoring many county matches were unfinished.

Yet the 1920s were not entirely years of tall scoring in England, even if they were in Australia. With the exception of 1921, the seasons 1920-1925 saw much third rate cricket in a period when many counties still relied on amateurs who were not first-class to make up their numbers. All through this period, Hobbs, Woolley, Mead and the others consistently made large scores against all-comers and when the seasons of big scores arrived, they still bettered the efforts of their rivals and mostly continued to do so well into the 1930s.

The incentive to these men to stay in the first-class game lay in the fact that they were unlikely ever to earn as good a living again once their cricket left them. Survival was made easier for them by the soundness of their technique which enabled them for years to overcome slowing reactions and bodily wear and tear.

Among this group, Philip Mead was for a quarter of a century one of those who were pre-eminent for the way in which they faced all the best bowlers which successive generations had to offer under all conditions with vast and consistent success. By the time of his retirement in 1936, he stood and still stands high in the list of run-getters:

3

	Career	Innings	Not Out	Runs	Highest Score	Average
J. B. Hobbs	1905-34	1315	106	61237	316	50.65
F. E. Woolley	1906-38	1532	85	58969	305*	40.75
E. Hendren	1907-38	1300	166	57611	301*	50.80
C. P. Mead	1905-36	1340	185	55061	280*	47.67
W. G. Grace	1865-1908	1493	105	54896	344	39.55
W. R. Hammond	1920-51	1005	104	50551	336*	56.10
H. Sutcliffe	1919-45	1088	123	50138	313	51.95
G. Boycott	1962-86	1014	162	48426	261*	56.83

This is his position among the century makers:

J. B. Hobbs	197
E. Hendren	170
W. R. Hammond	167
C. P. Mead	153
G. Boycott	151
H. Sutcliffe	149
F. E. Woolley	145

Yet he played in only 17 Test matches spread over 17 years.

The two greatest left-handed run scorers of their generation were born within two months of each other in 1887. One, Frank Woolley, figured in 52 consecutive Test matches between 1909 and 1926. Until around 1923, he had the added advantage of his skill as a top class slow left-arm bowler (a facet which Mead abandoned well before the First World War), a factor which counterbalanced Woolley's many batting failures at Test level. In international matches which, in England, were limited to three days it was natural to select the Kent man with his unique ability to change the course of the match in a few minutes whatever the quality of the bowling, rather than Mead whose approach and technique were more appropriate to games spread over five days — which became commonplace after his prime. As to why there was not often room for the two left-handers in international teams, examination of Mead's career reveals a certain logic for his omission, as this book tries to explain.

At his death, Mead was the subject of glowing tributes and long obituaries, but little has been written about him since. Patrick Murphy gave him his due 'Mead' of appraisal in 'The Centurions' (published by J. M. Dent and Sons Ltd., 1983), but his description of Mead's character and personality does not resemble the man depicted in this book in which I have attempted to bring Mead back into view in the gallery of great cricketers: As one of the greatest.

PHILIP MEAD 1887-1958
Chapter One
Battersea

Charles Philip Mead was born in Battersea, south London on the 9th March, 1887. Forty years before the district was 'cow fields, mud ditches . . . a waste expanse of what attempted to pass for country, where mysterious coke furnaces glowed and windmills stood silent. Ancient women sat in cottage doorways smoking pipes'.

It was also, more attractively, intensely cultivated as market gardens which were famous for such produce as melons, peas and first and foremost, asparagus. The lowest lying portions known as Battersea Fields, described above by Thomas Carlyle, were the scene of a weekly 'carnival of folly'; this became so degraded and objectionable that in 1846 an Act of Parliament was passed to convert part of the fields into a Royal Park which, levelled and planted out, became in the 1850s Battersea Park as we know it today. There were other open spaces — up on the heights, Wandsworth and Clapham Commons.

By 1887, however, the fields and ditches were mostly gone and Battersea was the suburb of terrace houses, shops and tenement blocks packed around Clapham Junction which it still is today. A hundred years ago it was a place of gas lighting, communal privies, ineffective heating, alleyways, dirt and pawnbrokers.

Ashton Buildings where Philip was born (at number 10), was pulled down long ago. The place stood near Battersea Church Road, adjacent to the High Street between the London and South Western Railway and the Thames in what had been before the expansion of the mid-19th century the original waterside village of Battersea.

Philip was the second eldest child, and eldest son of the seven children of Matthew Orlando Mead and his wife, Louisa Hannah, whose maiden name was Mann. Family tradition has it that she was distantly related to the brewery and cricketing family, but married beneath her! There is also a story that the Meads were music-hall artistes. This remains unverified. The family came originally from Bedfordshire.

As the family grew the Meads moved first to 35 Duffield Street, nearer to the railway, where they probably lived with Matthew's father, and then via Shaftesbury Park Chambers to 214 Eversleigh Road, both of these addresses being on Shaftesbury Park Estate, a little to the north.

To be granted a tenancy on this estate was a great piece of good fortune for a working man in the 1880s. A company set up with the encouragement of the Earl of Shaftesbury had built around 1,200 houses for occupation by skilled artisans, beginning in 1872. The neat tree-lined streets, lying down the slope from Lavender Hill have now for years contained the homes of the reasonably prosperous — Battersea is only four miles from the City of London for the commuter — but when built the estate was considered a revolutionary development in popular housing; there were three or four types of house; the accommodation included two or three bedrooms, a parlour, a kitchen with a range for heating and cooking and a scullery containing a copper, a larder and a sink supplied by a cold water tap. There was a WC outside in the yard. To contrast this 'modern' housing with the wretched limited accommodation to be found elsewhere in the Borough would remind Matthew Mead and his wife of their great good fortune. The lighting was by gas and drainage was to the mains; there was, of course, no bath. Although there were, and are, no through roads on the estate, 100 years ago the streets would have echoed to the noise of street traders, of horses and carts and to the playing of children. The estate was a fine modern place for a boy to grow up in and was only a few minutes away from the park and the commons.

Rents were under ten shillings a week but on a dock worker's wages, for that is how Matthew Mead earned his living, such a rent with a growing family took some finding. It was, in fact, common for these houses to be shared by two or more families.

If food was not plentiful, the infant Philip's activities did not help. While he was still in petticoats, 'vegetables were not safe from him. He would get hold of a stick and hit potatoes all over the show'.

A little later this early practice was extended in the park and in the street and was put to more constructive use when Philip became a pupil at Shillingstone Street School which is only a boundary's hit away from Eversleigh Road.

It was a proud afternoon when he took his score to 131 not out in the South London Schools Senior Cricket League, earning the presentation of a medallion and chain, selection for his first representative cricket match for the South London Schools, and a reputation as a distinguished son of the school where for many years his portrait hung.

Neither his home in Eversleigh Road, nor his picture may be seen today. The house was bombed during the Second World War and Shillingstone Street School ceased to be a junior school long ago.

Philip Mead cannot have been more than ten years old at the time of this his first batting success, and he finished his formal education and passed into the wide world soon after. He began a promising career in the retail trade with a West End store.

It was not long, however, before his cricket ability brought him to the attention of Surrey County Cricket Club. C. B. Fry, it is said, saw him playing at Surrey's ground, the Oval, as a schoolboy and encouraged him to become a professional cricketer. In 1902 he joined the ground staff there.

Surrey cricket was entering a rare state of decline after nearly 20 years of prosperity; through massive all-round strength they had headed the county championship in 1887 and the five following seasons, and again in 1894, 1895 and 1899.

Even at their peak Surrey had never possessed a top class left-arm slow bowler, and the authorities perhaps saw in Philip the possibility of breaking the pattern. It was as a slow left-arm bowler that he was taken on the staff.

A place at the Oval was highly regarded, as a successful career in sport was one of the few opportunities open for a working class lad to escape the prospect of a life of drudgery and poverty. The successful applicant had to undergo a strenuous trial — scrutiny while batting and bowling in the nets, followed perhaps by participation in a trial game or games; and much of the work was tedious and tiring, involving keeping the ground tidy and the buildings in repair, pushing the roller, bowling to senior professionals and to members, and selling scorecards at matches. The ground and playing staff constituted a substantial and structured body of men and boys in which everyone was expected to know his place.

There was too an opportunity actually to *play* cricket, through games for the Colts and the Club and Ground. In 1902, just 15 years old, Philip played for both XIs and enjoyed as a bowler a fair amount of success. For the Colts in July, he returned figures of seven for 26 against Cane Hill Asylum; less the opposition might be under-rated or the members of their team misjudged, it should be noted that the hospital chaplain, Rev. J. C. Crawford, was a well known club cricketer and Surrey supporter and three of his sons, Vivian, Neville and R. T. played successfully in county cricket. Indeed, Neville gained international fame for England against Australia. Philip Mead's five for 46 versus Whitgift Grammar School and three for 29 against Byfleet also contributed to a promising season's work. In seven matches for the two sides, however, his highest score was four not out!

In 1903, Jack Hobbs (aged 20) was a Surrey trialist. Although an application by him to Essex had been ignored, Surrey had no hesitation in snapping him up although Phil Mead dismissed him in both innings of that year's trial match. Soon after this he added five opponents from his native Battersea to the number of his victims. Here his success ended; apart from figures of 15 overs, 11 maidens, 11 runs and one wicket against Epsom College, he achieved nothing further for the Colts, while six outings for the Club and Ground brought him no reward as a bowler. He played an innings of 38 against St. John's School, Leatherhead, but did not get a turn with the ball in the last two Club and Ground games of the season which suggests that confidence in his bowling had diminished if it had not evaporated completely.

It was not altogether surprising that in September the County Committee decided not to re-engage him. At 16 his career with Surrey appeared to be over.

A fortnight later the authorities changed their minds, but they were too late. He had made alternative arrangements.

7

"But W. G. Grace said I was too young. So I didn't play." Aged about 18, 1906.

Chapter Two
Southampton

On 23rd October, 1903, the Committee of Hampshire County Cricket Club approved 'the engagement of Llewellyn and Mead'. In Llewellyn's case the reference was to renewal of his contract. Born in South Africa, he had been a valuable member of the Hampshire team since 1901 and had some experience of international cricket, though not at the loftiest level, for South Africa against an English touring side in 1895-96; he only just missed greater fame in 1902 when he was among the 14 selected for England against Australia at Edgbaston. After a fine beginning, he had some patchy seasons but was a highly competent left-handed all-rounder.

The terse entry in the Committee minutes does not reveal when, or if, Mead was given a trial.

Denzil Batchelor, in his appreciation of Mead, in 'The Book of Cricket', writes that he tramped down to Hampshire and was taken on by C. B. Fry at the Training Ship *Mercury* at Hamble, near Southampton. Batchelor was a close friend and biographer of Fry and was in a position to know. Fry and his wife made a life's work of the Training Ship but in 1903 Fry was playing cricket for Sussex; on the other hand, Captain C. A. R. Hoare, a staunch backer and sometime President of the Hampshire Club, was also the financial supporter of *Mercury* — and of Mrs. Fry — and a year or two later at least paid the costs of maintaining some of the County's professionals.

The connection between the Club and the training ship was further strengthened by the fact that J. C. Moberly, the Chairman of Hampshire, was one of the Trustees of *Mercury*.

It is likely that Fry showed a continuing interest in Mead's progress and was partly responsible for his acceptance by Hampshire. Certainly he was responsible for Mead being employed in coaching the naval trainees, not much younger than he was, during the necessary two-year period of residence in Hampshire. In those days, a cricketer wishing to join a county other than the county of his birth had to spend two years in his adoptive county before he was qualified to play for it. In Mead's case, the two years would not be up until the autumn of 1905 so that his entry into County Championship cricket would be delayed until the following year.

Hampshire's operations at Southampton were run on a much smaller scale than those at the Oval. Hampshire had only recently appointed a paid secretary, F. H. Bacon. Their professional staff numbered eight, headed by Tom Soar at a salary of two pounds a week. The others received between £1.10.0d (£1.50) and £1.5.0d (£1.25). Mead's pay, which compared well with the wages of his father, was £1.8.10d (£1.45) a week! So sport for the 17-year-old Mead was a paying proposition — but only for the summer months.

Hampshire had been carried into first-class cricket as recently as 1895 by amateur strength, mainly from Service personnel stationed at Portsmouth and Aldershot, and the professional bowlers, Baldwin and Soar. The Boer War and *anno domini* had thinned their ranks (not the most accurate of expressions in the case of Harry Baldwin who was of enormous girth), and the County finished at the foot of the Championship table in 1900, 1901 and 1903. In that year, a great enthusiast, E. M. Sprot, was appointed captain and over the next two or three years the County began to build up a useful professional nucleus.

For Mead the time passed slowly while he worked at *Mercury* and played cricket and soccer, which for a time formed an important role in his life. Whether his enthusiasm for the horses and cards (he became a dab hand at bridge over the years) dates from this time is a matter for speculation. The prospect of his entry into the first-class game arose momentarily at the end of 1904. In those days, the County staged a cricket festival at Bournemouth in September. They put his name forward to play for the Players of the South against the Gentlemen. However, the captain of the opposition, none other than W. G. Grace, objected, saying that he was at 17 too young to play. "So, of course, I didn't play," remembered Philip Mead only too well.

It was different in 1905 when the Australians, led by Joe Darling, were the tourists. On July 6th, 7th and 8th they visited Southampton and Mead was permitted, although not yet qualified for the County, to make his first appearance in first-class cricket. The tourists were at full strength, apart from Darling, as the names and scores testify: Victor Trumper 92; Clem Hill 115; M. A. Noble 101; Syd Gregory 134, total 620.

Fielding out to Trumper and Co. must in itself have been a valuable lesson in batsmanship. In such a score, Mead's own bowling figures, two for 56, were the most economical for the County and his victims were the redoubtable Warwick Armstrong and Hopkins. Then batting at number eight, he calmly faced the bumping bowling of Cotter, one of the fastest bowlers of that era, and led a partial recovery; he and Persse added 34 in 20 minutes for the seventh wicket; then with Stone, the wicket-keeper, he put on 67 in half an hour for the eighth. By the end of the innings, Hampshire had scrambled to 239 and Mead had made the second highest score, 41 not out. At the second attempt, he opened the innings with Stone. Sadly he was run out without facing a ball — the beginning of a long-running, or non-running saga.

Hampshire lost by an innings. However, the County Committee and local papers were impressed with young Mead's performance. In August, the County voted him winter pay. How the boy who had only once exceeded 20 in minor games for the Surrey club had so greatly improved his game remains a matter for wonder. Equally astonishing is the fact that following changes on the staff, only Llewellyn, Stone, Langford and Bowell were now senior to Mead.

Eventually, Mead qualified and in May, 1906 he played his first championship game against, of all teams, Surrey at the Oval. Going in first, his usual position for some years, he gallingly failed in each innings, being caught in the slips before a run was scored in the first innings and bowled for three in the second. He attoned somewhat by dismissing Hobbs, J. N. Crawford and Lord Dalmeny, the Surrey captain, to earn first innings bowling figures of 26-11-50-3.

A few days later, he made up for his batting failure, for against Yorkshire at Southampton when facing the bowling of Hirst, Rhodes and Haigh, he scored 60, helping Sprot to add 120 in the first innings and batted finely in the second for 109.

Beginning the third day on 34 not out, he reached 50 with an on-drive; a square cut from the bowling of Haigh took him to 97 and a drive for two from Ringrose followed by a stolen single took him to three figures in only his second Championship match. The columnist of the *Hampshire Independent* wrote, "He could not have had a more trying ordeal than to face the Yorkshire bowlers, but the strength of the attack served to accentuate the brilliance of the performance. He timed the ball perfectly, kept it on the carpet (only two or three times did he sky the leather) with the full face of the bat always applied to the stroke."

Subsequently, he made 79 against Kent at Tonbridge and 132 in the match with the West Indian tourists at Southampton. By September, his aggregate was 1,014, with an average of 26. So he joined a list of distinguished players who have achieved four figures in their first season of Championship cricket.

Many do not do as well in their second season. In 1907, a wet summer, when batting was more difficult, he maintained his total of runs and his average. By this time, as the great players of cricket's 'Golden Age' had retired or declined, a new generation was pressing forward, many of them amateurs; of the top 15 batsmen in the first class averages only four — J. T. Tyldesley, Tom Hayward, Jack Hobbs and Ernie Hayes (the last three from Surrey) were professionals. Among the amateur heroes were Fry, A. J. L. Hill and Sprot of Hampshire, P. F. Warner, Perrin, Jessop and B. J. T. Bosanquet and three of the seven Foster brothers of Worcestershire. The first 15 bowlers included five amateurs and four of them were googly bowlers touring with the South African team — R. O. Swartz, G. C. White, A. E. Vogler and G. A. Faulkner.

Mead was 52nd in the batting (but 21st among the professionals) and 93rd in the bowling. Hampshire, with six victories to set against 11 losses dropped to 12th in the championship. Nine professionals figured in the XI and the pattern for the future was being laid down. Bowell, Stone, Jack Newman and on a few occasions the youthful Alec Kennedy, as well as Llewellyn and Mead, were all members of the side, as four of them still would be 20 years later. Hill and Sprot were the most successful batsmen and the leading bowler, H. W. Persse, was also an amateur. However, in 24 championship games, his victims number only 60 and herein lay the team's weakness.

For Mead, the season did not open very successfully; scores of nought, 14 and two (the last two against Surrey) were followed by 65 from the Middlesex bowlers at Lord's, in the course of which he put on 113 with Bowell (69) in 110 minutes. Mead's innings, however, lasted for nearly three hours. In the second innings, he made only six and when Hampshire moved on to Chichester, he was one of five victims of E. H. Killick at the cost of only two runs which was the main cause of their ten-wicket defeat.

June started with a remarkable win over the County Champions, Kent, to which Mead contributed significantly by helping Sprot in a stand of 110 in the second innings when Hampshire were set the large total of 306 to win. Mead was dismissed for 43 and Sprot went on to 111. The return fixture was not as distinguished — Kent hit up 596 and won by an innings. Mead followed a score of 95 against Sussex in June (a game in which he also captured five wickets for 49) with 102 against Warwickshire at Southampton on 8th July. In this innings, he hit 11 fours and batted for over three-and-a-half hours and gave only one chance (when he had reached 89). Only one of his colleagues exceeded 30 in the two Hampshire innings, and Warwickshire who had obtained a first innings lead of 89 needed no more than 60 to win.

Mead was frequently, but not invariably, opening the innings. It was in that position that he enjoyed some useful practice in the middle of July for the Club and Ground against E. J. Morant's XI, when he and Stone began with a stand of 243. After Stone's departure at that total for 89, Mead remained until he had made a faultless 287, a total which he was never to beat, which included a six and 49 fours. He increased in consistency as the first-class season progressed. Of the six innings over 50 which he scored in 1907, four came in August. It would be some time yet before he would reach the heights of a score of 200 in first-class cricket.

Chapter Three
Consolidation

As a very young man, Mead played a good deal of soccer. So did the other Hampshire professionals who ran their own side for a time. Few of them did as well as Mead who as a forward played several games for the Southampton Reserves and actually rose for one game to the heights of their league side, in December, 1907, when he played in goal. His career did not advance further but football had, as we shall soon see, a crucial role to play in his life.

Cricket was graced in 1908 by the presence of a team from the USA, the Philadelphians, paying their final first-class visit to this country. Their impact was limited and interest centred largely on the County Championship. Hampshire rose to eighth in the table, thanks principally to the all-round performances of Llewellyn and the arrival of J. R. Badcock, a fast bowler who had a great season. Unfortunately, he could not maintain his success in subsequent years.

The year was one of development for the County and developments for Mead. It began with his by then customary failure against Surrey (scores of eight and 22, although the latter was top score in the team's total of 68) and he did not play a substantial innings until he made 119 not out against Leicestershire at the beginning of June which was the largest contribution to the County's first victory of the season by five wickets. By the end of the month, he had only one score over 30 to add to his 100 and an average of only 22 for 358 runs. Then batting at number five he made a score of 110 in the drawn return match at Leicester, and this led him into a succession of consistent scores, beginning with 55 and 61 in the Surrey game at Portsmouth; his average for the second half of the season was 37 and overall 29.42 for 1,118 runs.

It was his bowling which created momentarily the most attention that year when Northamptonshire visited Southampton in July. Rain so interfered with the cricket that by lunch on the third day not an innings apiece had been completed. No hope of a result? Sprot did not agree. He took a step without precedent in County cricket and declared Hampshire's innings closed at lunch when they were still 24 runs behind. This ensured that lunch and the interval between the innings coincided. Following that novel move, he swiftly put Mead on to bowl and the left-hander carried all before him, taking seven wickets for 18, tumbling Northants out in 80 minutes for 60 runs. Sprot with two sixes and eight fours hit up 62 not out of the 85 to win in less than an hour.

In September, Mead made his initial first-class appearance for a side other than Hampshire: the occasion was historic in more ways than one, as Hambledon played England at Broadhalfpenny Down in a game commemorating the erection opposite the Bat and Ball Inn of the monument to the 18th century cricketers. Again Mead just missed W. G. Grace who had been invited to inaugurate the memorial and play in the match but did not appear.

Mead's horizons were expanding in other directions. Playing football, he met two brothers called Englefield who turned out for the Freemantle Club in Southampton, and then made the acquaintance of their sister, Beatrice. Mead regarded himself as a very lucky man when she agreed to become engaged. They were married on 19th September, 1908 at Freemantle Parish Church. This was a successful partnership lasting over 40 years and bringing the couple two sons and a daughter.

A further engagement for the groom came in November when he accepted an invitation to join the M.C.C. bowling staff. So the 22-year-old Mead began 1909 as a married man. In later years, his indifference, to use a neutral word, to net practice became renowned; Alec Kennedy once queried his early lack of talent money and his reply, "You may lead me in May but I'll catch you in June" was more or less true both in 1908:

	Innings	Not Out	Runs	Average
May/June	18	2	358	21.80
July/August	21	1	748	37.40
and in 1909:				
May/June	17	—	449	26.40
July/August	23	2	957	45.57

The game with the 13th Australian touring side in 1909 proved a non-event, with Hampshire being overwhelmed by Frank Laver who in a low-scoring game took 13 wickets.

The successful phase of the season for Mead began when he carried his bat while scoring 88 runs in Hampshire's second innings against Warwickshire on 3rd July, immediately followed by his only century of the season, 114 at Northampton. Only twice after this was he dismissed for a single-figure score. The totals were not remarkable but the runs steadily mounted up particularly at the end of the summer when he finished with 47, 24 and 86, 89, 25, 84 — and nothing.

This was the year in which C. B. Fry transferred his allegiance from Sussex to Hampshire; he never appeared regularly although in 1911 and 1912 he made runs with regal profusion and in the latter year captained England. There is no evidence that Fry ever directly gave Mead technical advice. Just batting with such a man in a number of long stands must have been beneficial to Mead. Certainly, with the advent of Fry, Mead became a more confident and aggressive and prolific scorer.

In the opinion of a respected critic of the time, J. N. Pentelow, it was in 1909 that Mead went right to the front. Hayward, Hobbs, Rhodes and Sharp, of Lancashire, were the only professionals ahead of him in the first-class averages. Pentelow wrote: 'Not only did he make many runs but he made them in fine

Beatrice Mead around the time of her marriage.

style. Moreover, he was a great run-saver *as he has been throughout his career.* In the revival of Hampshire cricket, the young Surrey-born left-hander has played a great part alike with the bat and in the field.'

The favourable references to Mead's fielding will surprise those who, fortunate as they were to see him play, did so only in the latter stages of his career. Pentelow's assessment of Mead's methods at this stage of his career is informative 'whilst many batsmen neglect the cut, Mead is great at this most charming of strokes; his onside play is very strong indeed and he drives as well as the best man . . .'

The Hampshire Committee agreed. On 4th November, 1909, they voted Mead a grant of £10 in recognition of his services. He had made 1,459 runs at an average of 37.41.

Mead also did excellently in 1910. So did Hampshire. Their position of sixth in the championship was the result of fine bowling by Newman (156 wickets, average 18 in County matches) and Llewellyn (133 wickets at 20) and consistent batting. Eight regular members of the side averaged over 20; Alec Bowell, the opening batsman, who had a poor season finished ninth and Newman and Kennedy (who was making his way into the side at the age of 19 but was only a change bowler with 31 wickets in 19 matches) completed the side. Phil Mead was, of the regular players, third in the batting averages below the amateurs A. C. Johnston and J. G. Greig. He hit only one century, but in 17 innings scored between 29 and 95 and in nine innings exceeded 50. His totals of 81 and 63 not out largely contributed to a nine-wicket victory over Gloucester at Southampton at the end of May. It was not really surprising that Hampshire defeated the weak Gloucestershire side; every member of the home team at some time scored 1,000 runs in a season *and* scored a century.

Mead's only three-figure innings of the season (111) was, with the bowling of Llewellyn and Newman, a major factor in the victory over Warwickshire by an innings in two days in July. He and Stone (79) opened with a stand of 193, a performance which they equalled (Mead 87, Stone 105) against Lancashire a month later. Mead also scored 95 against strong opponents, Kent, at Dover; it was not enough to prevent the home team winning by ten wickets.

The season was a purely domestic one, so opportunities for representative cricket were limited. Mead was fortunate in that his membership of the M.C.C. staff involved him in appearances for the club in their games early in the season at Lord's. Although he did not shine in these games, at least his name became familiar to the authorities and his general performances (he scored 1,416 runs at 31 an innings compared with, for example, Jack Hobbs 1,982 runs in 63 innings, average 33) were good enough to earn him selection for his first major representative match in September for England versus the County Champions, Kent, at the Oval, when he did his reputation no harm with an innings of 63.

England did not have a winter tour but South Africa did. Llewellyn visited Australia with the first South African team to tour there in the winter of 1910-11 and in doing so ended his County career. At the end of the 1910 season, he declined the terms offered him by Hampshire and accepting the offer to join the South African party diverted into league cricket where, to the County's loss, he remained a leading light right into the 1930s. It appeared unlikely that Mead would replace him as Hampshire's left-arm spinner. In 1910 he captured no more than eight wickets, at 54 runs each.

In 1911, there would be no Test matches and only very belatedly was a tour by an Indian side — almost totally unsuccessful — arranged. Perhaps the season would be a fine one for one was certainly due and in the autumn M.C.C. were to send a side to Australia. In 1912, Australia were due to return the visit. A South African magnate, Sir Abe Bailey, was anxious to involve his country in a triangular tournament in England; in 1909 his approaches had been rebuffed by the Australians. He expected to be more successful next time round.

For aspirants for Test selection, 1911 would be one long trial.

Sprot demands more notice at this stage. He had first played for the County in 1898. He had not made a name as a cricketer at Harrow but more than compensated for this during his time at Sandhurst and after, while serving in the King's Shropshire Light Infantry. He became a scratch golfer and excelled at tennis and billiards. Later he was an expert angler. Succeeding Charles Robson as captain of Hampshire in 1903, with his free hitting, he represented the only real element of consistency in the County's batting for a number of seasons before the coming to maturity of Mead and the arrival of Fry and a host of amateur batsmen from the military in the years immediately before the First World War.

He must also have spent sleepless nights over the deficiencies of the County's attack in the early years of his captaincy. As a leader in somewhat depressing circumstances, he rapidly became highly efficient and as an ever present member of the side, maintained a tight hold over his professionals.

A friend wrote, long after his cricket career was over, of his humour and use of detached and ironic comment searing those whom he disliked; 'sham and pretentiousness did not escape his not unmalicious condemnation; arrogance aroused his otherwise infrequent anger. A shy man, he did not readily grant admittance to the small circle of his intimates . . . he had a keen appreciation of the foibles of others', from which we may deduce that he was highly observant, had a tongue which could bite like a whiplash and would, as was usual in those days, have kept his distance from the professionals. Yet he nurtured a whole generation of Hampshire cricketers — Mead, Brown, Kennedy, Newman, Livsey and Tennyson in those years up to 1914.

Under his lead, Hampshire invariably played attractive and enterprising cricket. His name will forever be linked with that of Mead in connection with one match, that against Northamptonshire at Southampton in 1908 (see page 13). The main point of the episode is that Mead, who was not even at that early stage in his career a leading bowler, rose to his captain's demands on that occasion and there can be little doubt that Sprot was just the man to impose his own ardour on his increasingly match hardened professionals. It is fascinating to speculate how the Hampshire sides of the 1920s, containing those same seasoned players, would have fared under Sprot had he not resigned in 1918 and been replaced by Tennyson.

He retired to Farnham where he lived the life of a civilised gentleman, playing golf, fishing, painting and reading until his death in 1945.

Chapter Four
To the top of the tree

The summer of 1911 was one of sunshine, drought, the Coronation, the review of the Fleet with all flags flying at Spithead and the investiture of the Prince of Wales at Caernarvon Castle; the average sportsman would best remember the heat.

Out of 180 county cricket matches only 35 were unfinished. C. B. Fry in eight innings hit six centuries — three in one week. His 258 not out for Hampshire against Gloucestershire was, according to Wisden, made with consummate skill. His batting was not a matter for surprise for who could forget the performances of Ranjitsinghi and Fry for Sussex in the years up to 1904? Now it looked as if a new combination, Fry and Mead, would make a name in cricket history. If some had seen Mead in the top rank in 1909, he set the seal upon his reputation in 1911.

The year began for him with a welcome and flattering piece of publicity. In the 1911 edition of Wisden, P. F. Warner wrote an article entitled 'Our Young Cricketers'. It received considerable publicity and the progress of the players whom he discussed, including George Brown (of Hampshire), J. W. Hearne, Patsy Hendren, F. R. Foster and Major Booth of Yorkshire, was watched with great interest right up to the time of the First World War three years later.

Of Mead he wrote, 'His position at the wicket is rather ungainly, as there is a somewhat awkward bending of the knees, but in actual playing of the ball his style is good, and his defence sound. Like most left-handers he is very strong in all the leg-side strokes and he drives well. He is quick on his feet, frequently jumping in to slow or medium bowling and he is one of the best players of googlies . . . I believe him to be the best left-hand bat in England. Mead is an excellent fielder with a safe pair of hands.'

Encouraged by this warmth of praise from such a source, from first to last he could scarcely do anything wrong that year. He began with 82 for M.C.C. against Yorkshire at Lord's on 8th to 10th May, and followed with exactly 100 against the weak Somerset attack at Southampton on 12th May (and took three wickets); then went on to make 37 and 19 against M.C.C. for Hampshire at Lord's. By this time it was already June, yet Hampshire had played only one county championship match! Mead was getting match practice with the M.C.C.; a score of 127 at Lord's against Leicestershire took two hours and three-quarters and contained 16 fours.

While Fry was scoring 150 against Derbyshire, Mead was absent. Test Trial matches were a prominent feature of the season. Three were arranged specifically, while it was announced that the Gentlemen and Players matches would also count as Trials. On 1st, 2nd and 3rd June, Mead played in the first trial game at Sheffield. Opening the innings with Jack Hobbs, he scored 34 and 24. This was not remarkable, but only Robert Relf, A. R. Litteljohn (neither likely to get an international cap) and Warner, did better. Hobbs compiled 22 and 32. Jack Newman obtained four victims, but that game was the nearest he approached to international selection, and the same could be said for a number of others taking part in the match.

By 5th June Mead was at Southampton for Hampshire's match against Kent, in which he scored 15 and 73. Two records were established in this match — the aggregate of runs (Kent 416 and 359 for five declared; Hampshire 208 and 468 for eight) and Hampshire's score in the last innings. Hardinge scored 175 and 109 for Kent and Fry hit another 100.

Then on to success for Mead in another high-scoring game at the Oval, where his scores were 65 and 53, although Surrey won. After making 70 in the second innings against Leicester at Portsmouth, Mead hurt his hand so badly in trying to catch A. E. Knight that he had to stand down from several games. He did not pick up the threads again until the Test trial at Lord's. For this game, all sorts of people told the selectors (Lord Hawke, P. F. Warner and G. L. Jessop) that they were not available. Perhaps they were wise. Mead did play and was bowled by Woolley for three. Woolley himself went for scores of nought and seven and could do no better than take two for 87. But both were selected for the team to go to Australia. Hardinge who carried his bat through the second innings of the Rest and made 113 not out, was not selected.

By August it was clear that the selectors did not require any more Trial games, and the public were not interested, so the third game, fixed for Manchester at the end of August, was cancelled.

The Test trial at Lord's, was followed by a trial of a different kind, against Lancashire at Old Trafford; the scores, Lancashire 676 for seven declared (R. H. Spooner 186, Jack Sharpe 135, K. G McLeod 101, J. T. Tyldesley 98, A. Hartley 59), Hampshire 102 and 119 (Mead 46) tell all too clearly of a dreadful defeat.

In the drawn return match with Leicestershire which followed, Mead achieved a particular triumph. Opening the batting in the first innings he was at the wickets for three hours and three-quarters for his score of 109, in the course of which with George Brown, he put on 96 runs in an hour. When Hampshire batted again, with a lead of 71 he hit another 100 in quicker time, three hours. The game was drawn inspite of Mead's success. By this time it was clear that the Hampshire attack was not, in the prevailing hot conditions, going to bowl out the opposition, however many runs the Hampshire batsman might score from time to time. Against Yorkshire at Huddersfield, Hampshire suffered a ten-wicket defeat despite Mead batting right through the innings and scoring 120 runs. He had quietly and undemonstratively, compiled three centuries in three consecutive innings.

His scores of 25, 23 and 30 in the Southampton Cricket Week were unremarkable. This was soon followed by another purple patch for Mead. At Southampton, Warwickshire led Hampshire by 137 on the first innings. Hampshire lost Bowell and Fry for 92; Phil Mead went in second wicket down. Twenty minutes later he was joined by A. C. Johnston and in two hours and 40 minutes, by brilliant hitting, they added no fewer than 292 runs, while in the course of only three hours batting with the aid of 32 fours and without a mistake, Mead scored 207. Although, because of injury, Frank Field, their fast bowler, was not playing, Warwickshire, who were to become County Champions that year, were otherwise at full strength and this display of batting created a sensation. A local reporter recorded: 'This has been a memorable week for Phil Mead who played his highest and best innings in first-class cricket and for the first time exceeded the second century. I have been following cricket for many years but have never witnessed a more charming display than that of Mead's. It was exhilarating to watch him draw himself up to full height and with a dexterous turn of the wrist glance good length balls to the leg boundary; to see him jump in and drive powerfully and surely between the ring of fieldsmen . . . and guide the ball so accurately between closely placed slips that before a man could move, the leather had flashed past. He scored with astonishing freedom without a semblance of a chance and the ball rarely left the ground. Jessop and Alletson have made runs more quickly but I doubt if either occupied the crease for so long without an imperfect stroke, at a run a minute . . . his chances of selection should be enhanced.'

Mead was soon associated again with the figure 292. The next day, Hampshire were hosts to Sussex at Portsmouth. Going in first with Bowell, he was at the crease for only three hours and ten minutes for his score of 194, made out of 292 while he was in, and he completely mastered the bowling of Albert Relf, Jupp, Cox and Vine, hitting them for 32 fours. Bowell obtained only 40 out of the opening stand of 163 in 105 minutes.

So, in two days, Mead made 401 runs and was out only once. There was no more high scoring in the match and he missed the second innings because of a poisoned arm, but Hampshire went on to success without him. He was also absent from the following drawn game against Kent at Canterbury, made remarkable by the batting and behaviour of Fry, who hit 100 in each innings, although in the second, according to press reports, he was repeatedly beaten by the bowling of Fielder and D. W. Carr. He irritated supporters by complaining noisily and ostentatiously that Blythe, the Kent and England left-arm bowler, was tossing the ball up into the sun, and Kent notables had to make soothing noises to the crowd.

Mead was fit for the next game, scoring 34 out of a huge total of 594 for six declared against Gloucestershire, to which Fry contributed 258 not out. However, Jessop in turn scored freely, hitting two 100s, neither of which lasted much more than an hour and a half, and Hampshire's George Brown and

Alf Dipper, of Gloucestershire, chimed in with other three-figure innings and another drawn game resulted.

As the season simmered and renewal of the fight for the Ashes that winter became imminent the attention of cricketers was focused on the selectors. The touring side for Australia was chosen in instalments. By the end of July, Fry, Spooner, Warner, Foster, Barnes, Hobbs, Rhodes and Strudwick, followed by J. W. H. T. Douglas had received invitations. Spooner refused his. Soon afterwards S. P. Kinneir, James Iremonger and then E. J. 'Tiger' Smith were also asked to make the trip. Kinneir, a left-handed opening batsman, had had a distinguished career with Warwickshire, beginning in 1898, but at the age of 38 he had no previous touring or international experience. His two innings that summer for the Players against the Gentlemen at Lord's, 158 and 53 not out, were the principle reasons for his selection. Iremonger had long been a good county bat for Nottinghamshire, and in the previous year at his county's need, he had developed skill as a steady medium-pace bowler. Neither Kinneir or Iremonger were an obvious choice. 'Tiger' Smith had only as recently as 1910 taken over behind the stumps for Warwickshire from A. A. Lilley, who had been the England wicket-keeper in 35 matches over 14 years.

At the beginning of August, Woolley, and George Gunn, who had batted so well for M.C.C. on the previous tour in 1907-08, received invitations — and immediately following his successes against Warwickshire and Sussex so did Philip Mead.

Then Fry said that he would not be able to go and Warner was appointed the captain. Hitch, Vine and J. W. Hearne were the final selections.

The end of the 1911 county season for Hampshire was rather unsatisfactory because Middlesex hitting up 544 for nine won by an innings at Lord's; Surrey obtained a comfortable first innings lead at Bournemouth; while Lancashire with 375 won by an innings and 27 runs. Mead's scores in these ventures were 51, seven, 28, 28 not out, and 28 and 85. Hampshire with only seven victories to set against ten defeats dropped five places to 11th in the championship table, largely because of the absence of Llewellyn. Newman especially missed his former colleague's skills and took only 67 wickets at the large cost of 33 runs each, as against his record for the previous year of 156 at 18. Even fine fast bowling by George Brown, who took 87 wickets in championship matches as well as scoring 1,000 runs, could not make up for the left-hander's absence.

There still remained the Festival matches before the adventure of the trip to Australia. Mead's season was by no means over. For the Players against the Gentlemen at Scarborough early in September, he enjoyed a memorable triumph. He was number five when the Players batted first; by the end of the day he had reached 172 not out and next morning advanced his score to 223 before he was bowled by Falcon. Magnificent on-drives formed the majority of his 31 fours, while he made his runs in a little over four hours out of 399. The Gentlemen's attack comprised Douglas, Falcon, Aubrey

C. B. Fry, cricketer, scholar, diplomat and would-be King of Albania.

Faulkner, the great South African leg-break bowler, P. R. Le Couteur (an Australian Oxford Blue and leg-break bowler who had taken 11 wickets in the University match in 1910, and repeated the feat in 1911); another member of the attack was B. J. T. Bosanquet, although he was playing his first first-class game since 1908 and was no longer in the front rank as a bowler. This attack was not as formidable as that of the Players, which comprised Barnes, Hirst, Field, G. J. Thompson and Wilfred Rhodes, but was still powerful.

Mead's next game, also at Scarborough, was for the M.C.C. team for Australia versus Lord Londesborough's XI, against which he scored 11 and 43 in an exciting draw. Finally at the Oval, Warwickshire the champions had the honour of meeting 'England' over four days. It was perhaps a doubtful privilege for the county to face opposition including Hobbs who scored 97, Mead 101, Warner 244, J. W. Hearne 52, as well as Rhodes, Woolley, Hitch and Strudwick, all members of the touring party, and Spooner and Fry (102 not out) who could not go. The side declared at 631 for five and defeated the champions (129 and 137) by an innings and 365 runs. Warwickshire were weakened by the absence of Kinneir, who was kept away by an attack of lumbago, but they were outmatched at every point. Mead went in on the first evening after Spooner had been bowled with 41 runs scored. At the end of the day the total had risen to 162 without further loss in reply to Warwickshire's feeble score, with Hobbs 85 not out and Mead 51 not out. In all they put on 152 before Hobbs was dismissed. Mead and Warner added a further 61. Mead was then caught by Charlesworth from the bowling of Sidney Santall. F. R. Foster had figures of 34 overs, two maidens, 155 runs for one wicket.

Mead's success for 'England' promised well for the winter tour, which was now only a fortnight away.

All the auguries were good; Mead stood second in the batting averages for the season:

Innings	Not Out	Runs	Highest Score	Average
52	5	2,562	223	54.51

The next most successful professionals in the list were Kinneir (1,629 runs average 49.36); Tom Hayward (2,149 runs average 47.75 — he was thought to be too long in the tooth, or weak in the legs for the arduous trip to Australia), and Frank Tarrant (2,030 runs average 46.13); as an Australian playing for Middlesex he was not, in those days, eligible to play for England, and was regarded as not qualified to play for Australia either. Fry headed the table and Spooner and Perrin, of Essex, both amateurs, came after Mead.

It was a particular encouragement to Mead that Warner, who had written so enthusiastically about him in the Spring, was to captain the touring side.

Chapter Five
With Warner and Douglas in Australia

In retrospect, it was a glory to be associated with the side which Warner took to Australia in September 1911. Just as it was for those who, like Mead, travelled there with A. P. F. Chapman in 1928-29, and the names of the individuals who made up the party have acquired a ring of greatness merely from the fact that they made the trip as if the whole was somehow greater than the component parts.

Yet the selection of the team was criticised at that time. The unavoidable absence of Spooner and Fry, as well as Jessop, was regretted, and many of the team were condemned as inexperienced; the younger set were F. J. (Tiger) Smith, Woolley, J. W. Hearne, F. R. Foster, Hitch and Mead, whose ages ranged between 25 in the case of Smith to Hearne, barely 20. No exception could be taken to Hobbs, George Gunn, Barnes, Rhodes or Strudwick, who with Warner (a successful leader of M.C.C.'s first team to Australia eight years before) had all made previous tours. Douglas returned home in the following spring with his reputation as a cricketer and, as it happened, as captain greatly enhanced but it is easy to forget that he had no previous experience of Test cricket and would not have been any informed critic's choice as captain when the team was selected.

Even the most successful touring parties contain odd selections. Kinneir, at 38, was one and those two worthy County stalwarts, Iremonger and Vine, made two more. Those three, Hitch and Strudwick, who was an early victim to his rival Smith's experience in taking the bowling off his County colleague, Foster, eventually made up the 'ground staff', although Vine at least had an hour of glory before the trip was over.

The general features of the tour — how Warner scored 151 in the first match and was then prevented from playing through illness; how Australia won the first Test, thanks to the fine leg-break and googly bowling of H. V. Hordern, but England won the remaining four by increasingly large margins, and the Australian players became increasingly at odds with their Board of Control; with the splendid batting of the English openers, Hobbs and Rhodes, and most of all the bowling of Barnes and Foster, have become a matter of history. Phil Mead did not become one of the ground staff but he did not make history; he played in four Test matches without justifying the high hopes of his supporters.

The journey out in those days before the traveller was numbed by air travel was, initially, a gentle introduction to the heat; Mead always excelled at deck games, although he was socially rather backward in coming forward, so he was a notable member of the party in his quiet way; the team broke their journey at Ceylon, as Sri Lanka was known, and he scored 25 in the customary

24

match there. Eventually, the novelty of the sights and sounds of the voyage gave way to the uproar of arrival at Freemantle and Perth.

Phil Mead was in many ways an uncertain starter. The tour tested him in many ways. It is the glare which the stranger to Australia notices most, not only directly from the sun but reflected from the land. This is especially trying for the games player. The heat, the size and noise of the crowds, the hardness of the ground, the numerous exuberant social functions and the constant curiosity of the public made demands on his stamina; but always the glare, compounded by the pace of the ball off the pitch, made the greatest possible contrast with the cool damp of the English summer. The breakdown of Warner was not encouraging — he had enthusiastically committed to paper his good opinion of Mead. Douglas was a different proposition altogether — tense, tough and an unknown quantity as a leader.

As we have seen, the side contained three left-hand batsmen. Initially, Kinneir was used as an opening bat, while Douglas treated Frank Woolley as more bowler than batsman, sending him in at seven, eight or even nine, as he did in the second match of the tour against Victoria. This left the middle of the order clear for Mead who began moderately with 20 out of 563 against South Australia; after a vilely hot journey from Adelaide to Melbourne — 17 hours in the train, interrupted by a change in the railway gauge at Albury, he followed with 34 and 22ᵗ against Victoria and 46 in a rain-ruined gamed with New South Wales.

By this time, Warner, George Gunn and Foster had all hit 100s — indeed, Foster had reached three figures twice. Against Queensland, not then a power in the land, Mead's totals were 79 and 54 not out. He did not bat in the two-day game at Toowoomba in which the top scorers were Kinneir with 80 and Woolley 99. Against an Australian XI at Brisbane in sticky heat, after another long journey, he was bowled by J. W. McLaren for a duck, but atoned with 50 in the second innings. So far, fairly good — good enough anyway for selection for the first test at Sydney starting on Friday, 15th December 1911.

The game, played in further sweltering heat, was one of even-scoring in all four innings. Victor Trumper alone reached three figures and Jack Hearne with 76 was the top scorer for England. The leg-break and googly bowling of Hordern won the game for Australia; he caught and bowled Mead for nothing in his first test innings. The second promised much and ended in disaster. Gunn and Mead coming together had the makings of a good stand until Gunn played a ball straight to short leg. Mead, whose call it was, went for a single but was sent back and could not make good his ground. The scorebook read 'Run out — 25'. On the sixth morning, England lost by 146 runs.

Christmas was celebrated with a grand lunch in Melbourne, when everyone felt a long way from home, followed by a drawn match against XV of Bendigo (which was of little general interest then and even less now). The second test match followed. It will be for ever memorable for the bowling of Sidney Barnes.

The start makes sensational reading even now. Barnes' first ball hit Warren Bardsley on the heel and rebounded onto the wicket; almost immediately Kelleway was given l.b.w., and when Barnes bowled Clem Hill, the left-hander, with a ball which moved into him through the air and turned away off the pitch to hit the off stump, the score was eight for three which soon became 11 for four when Smith magnificently caught Armstrong. Barnes had to stop bowling through a recurrence of illness and Australia made a partial recovery to reach 184. England collapsed after a second wicket partnership of 127 between Rhodes (61) and J. W. Hearne (114). Only Armstrong with 90 in the second innings exceeded 50 for Australia and the best batting came from Hobbs who hit 126 not out when only four men were needed to achieve victory by eight wickets in the second innings. Phil Mead's contribution was limited to 11 runs in the first innings and one catch, when Australia batted again.

The Test matches now dominated the programme and only a two-day match against XV of Geelong (Mead 65 and 33 not out) intervened before the third Test at Adelaide which started on Friday, 12th January, in beautifully cool weather. This time, Australia began by collapsing for 133 against Foster (5-36); in reply, England amassed 501. Phil Mead, following Rhodes (59), Gunn (29) and Hearne (12) as a partner for Jack Hobbs (187), was not out 31 at the end of the second day when England's score was 327 for four wickets. It seemed that he had a heaven sent chance to excel but on the Monday he increased his score only to 46 before being caught and bowled by Hordern. Batting again 368 runs behind, Australia fought a fine rearguard action led by Hill (98) and seven other members of the side scored between 72 and 25. Nevertheless, England won by seven wickets.

The tourists scored plenty of runs against XV of Ballarat before steaming to Tasmania for two matches. An indication of the Englishmen's attitude to the match at Launceston was that Barnes did not bowl in either innings but opened the batting. He and Mead made a stand for the second wicket and when Woolley replaced Barnes, there was some very swift scoring. Mead was very strong on the leg-side and scored fast in the later stages of a very good innings. He at last pulled a wide ball onto his wicket when only two short of a century which was in the event his highest score of the tour.

The second game against Tasmania at Hobart will always be memorable for the glorious batting of Woolley whose innings of 305 not out was the highest score ever made by an Englishman on tour in Australia and remained so until exceeded by Colin Cowdrey's innings of 307 for M.C.C. against South Australia at Adelaide 51 years later.

Phil Mead did not bat. In his book 'The King of Games', Woolley complains that he was down to bat at number nine but Barnes told him to get his pads on when the openers, Kinneir and Rhodes, went in as he felt that "Mead might be missing" when one of them was out. A wicket fell. There was no sign of Mead. Woolley moved hesitantly to the front of the pavilion not wishing to find a colleague joining him en route for the wicket and reached the gate without interruption, took his place at the wicket and proceeded to play the innings of a long lifetime.

For Mead, the remainder of the tour was an anti-climax in spite of the team's success. Fine victories followed at Melbourne against Victoria and then over Australia, and the Ashes were won. In the State match, Hearne (143) and Douglas (140) were the principal contributors — Mead failed with scores of two, and an early victim to E. A. Macdonald for nought. He fared better in the test but 21, batting at number eight, was only a minority interest in a total of 589. The honours were taken by Hobbs who scored 178 and Rhodes (179) who shared in an opening stand of 323 to head Australia's score of 191 on their own. Rhodes who batted nearly seven hours put on a further 102 with Gunn. Foster and Woolley also exceeded 50 before Foster, Barnes and Douglas then between them took all the Australian wickets but one.

Mead contributed another score of 21 to a further handsome victory over New South Wales but again batted at number eight and cannot have been surprised when for the final test, his place was given to Joe Vine who justified his selection by staying with Frank Woolley (133 not out) while 143 was scored. None of the home side scored more than 61 and England won their fourth successive test match by 70 runs.

By the end, Phil Mead, like Woolley and Rhodes, had missed only one game on the tour and scored 659 runs at an average of 34, a figure lower than that of all the other specialist batsmen except Vine; yet Woolley who averaged 54 and was second to Hobbs in the batting table played one more innings than Mead and would have scored only 11 more runs but for his 305 at Hobart. He had a moderate test series, too, until he scored his century in the final test at Sydney.

The side returned home in triumph but as far as Mead's career was concerned, those two innings of Woolley's were to have adverse effects upon his prospects of selection in the Triangular Tournament in 1912, and in the longer term as well. Warner did not play after the opening game but during his illness and recuperation, with the aid of his 'intelligence department' as he called it, was well informed about the matches which he could not see and by the New Year he was an interested spectator.

His opinion of Mead contrasts strongly with the view he had expressed in Wisden a year before. "Mead was disappointing. He never seemed to hit off the pace of the wicket and seldom timed the ball really well. He was rather clumsy on his feet, did not play the slow bowlers well and seemed to lack confidence." Perhaps all the other characteristics described stemmed from the last one. I have not come across any other writer who describes Phil Mead, even late in his career, as clumsy in his footwork. However, Warner concluded hopefully: "There is no reason why on another visit he should not be successful for after his fine work in England, there can be no doubt of his ability." Woolley, on the other hand was now "a beautiful class batsman" whom Warner would "as soon see bat as anyone in the world."

The team were treated as great heroes on the voyage home which, broken by a stop at Colombo, finished as far as the players were concerned at Toulon from which they travelled overland in time to catch the start of the 1912 cricket season.

Mead was selected as one of Wisden's Five Cricketers of the Year in the edition published that spring. The editor, Sydney Pardon, made a number of neat points in his authoritative style: "By reason of a slight crouch at the wicket, Mead is not such a good batsman to look at as Woolley but he is far more watchful than the Kent player and therefore vastly stronger in defence. He has a fine cut and his on-side hitting, as he showed in many fine innings last summer and especially at Scarborough, is powerful to a degree. Endowed with excellent physique, he has never known what it is to have any sense of fatigue when he is batting. His ambition is to win such a place among left-handed batsmen in England as Clem Hill has held for years past in Australia. Apart from his batting, he is a capital field in the slips or anywhere else he may be placed."

This account, apart from encapsulating the by now inevitable comparison with Woolley and a favourable comment on Mead's hitting powers and fielding, includes a reference to his ambition. His aspiration revealed in a rare expansive moment, he may have felt had not been carried nearer to fulfilment by his experiences in Australia.

A young Mead.

28

Chapter Six
Fry and Hampshire

The summer of 1912 was as different as it possibly could be from its immediate predecessor. Where there had been heat, now there was damp, cool weather, wind, mackintoshes and misery. A season fit to rank in notoriety with 1932, 1950 or 1985. The many breaks from cricket may have enabled Mead to improve his hand at bridge but had no effect at all on his batting; nor did the conditions hold back the success of Hampshire who were setting out on one of their most successful seasons.

Mead began with only two but next scored 111 not out against Yorkshire at Sheffield and followed this with 135 and 37 not out at Worcester. On 27th May, Hampshire were at Canterbury for a match which witnessed remarkable batting. Mead scored 106, Fry also reached three figures (143) and they added 246 in four hours for the third wicket. G. N. Bignell hit up 79, A. C. Johnston 67, Newman 49 and E. I. M. Barrett 42 in Hampshire's mammoth total of 599. Kent replied with 418 and the match was inevitably drawn. Mead scored only 106 in five completed innings in the next three matches but returned to top form in the game with Warwickshire at Coventry on 20th June. Mead (111 and 61 not out) added over 100 in each innings. After the home side had scattered the Hampshire bowlers to the winds and to the tune of 484 for nine declared, Mead and Johnston added 250 for the second wicket. Mead batted three and a quarter hours and hit 11 fours before falling to a fine catch by Charlesworth. When Hampshire batted again, a draw was certain but the two Hampshire men contributed a further 151 while they were together.

In spite of unpleasant weather, there was more spectacular scoring when Cambridge visited Southampton on 24th June. The University scored 484; Hampshire's response at the end of the first day was not encouraging at 28 for two. Next morning, Mead took the attack to the bowlers scoring 140 in two and three-quarter hours with the aid of 17 fours in his fifth century of the season. His total was one of only two scores exceeding 50.

When Oxford in turn visited Southampton at the end of the following week, he contributed 93 to the County's score of 453 for two declared but was overshadowed by Fry (203 not out) and Barrett (138 not out) who added 264 for the third wicket. At this stage, the beginning of July, Mead was one of the only three batsmen to have reached his 1,000 runs (the others were Macartney and Hayes) but Hampshire stood in the lower half of the Championship table. Following two test trial games, the long-awaited Triangular Tournament was well under way. The members of the winter touring party had been home little more than a week when the first trial match took place at the Oval. It was entitled England versus The Rest. Probables v Possibles would have been more accurate as 'England' included eight members of the successful test team as well as Fry, Spooner and Walter Brearley. Mead played for The Rest

Photograph of Phil Mead
taken at Sheffield, 1912.

in company with Douglas, Relf and Strudwick. He scored one and 17 and England won by an innings and 13 runs. Tiger Smith correctly prophesied to Warner how Mead would be dismissed in the second innings 'caught Smith bowled Foster' just as he was in the first. He also fell victim to Foster in each innings of The Rest in the second test trial at Lord's beginning on 23rd May for scores of only four and two, which effectively disposed of his chances of playing for England in the Tournament; not that the 'possibility' can ever have been very strong. In the England side selected for the first test match, only seven members of the winter party survived — Hobbs, Rhodes, Woolley, Foster, Smith, Barnes and Warner, who more or less had recovered from his illness. Spooner and Fry played a major part in the series, by the end of which Woolley's place in the England side was assured.

Fry played the leading role in the management of the England team. He captained the side in all six matches, of which four were won and two drawn. Overcoming the initial suggestion that he be appointed only for one match, he succeeded in persuading the Board of Control that he head a Selection Committee limited to himself and two other members (they were H. K. Foster and John Shuter, stalwarts of Worcestershire and Surrey respectively) which, Fry said, met only once to choose the best XI, and nominate substitutes. Only 17 Englishmen appeared in the six matches and Fry made no call on Mead.

That to be chosen for England in England was a very different matter from selection for a touring party was exemplified by the fact that Warner took part in only two of the games and Douglas who had been so successful when leadership was thrust upon him in Australia played in only one — in which he did not bowl.

There were, as so often, peculiar selections, for included in the side against Australia at Manchester was Schofield Haigh, coming to the end of his career with Yorkshire, while Ernie Hayes, who had been playing for Surrey since 1896, played against South Africa at the Oval. Mead might surely have been considered for that place. Was Hayes really one of Fry's original selections?

The Australian side, weakened beyond redemption by the dispute between leading players and their Board of Control which resulted in the voluntary absence of Hill, Armstrong, Trumper, Ransford, Laver and Carter was no match for England and as for South Africa, they were no match for either.

By the middle of July, the cricket world was astonished by the success of Northants, unbeaten at the head of the Championship table. Hampshire then stood ninth. Yorkshire eventually pipped Northants, while Hampshire could take some satisfaction from rising to the sixth place.

In a season redolent of big matches but in reality devoid of surprises (the wonderful bowling of Barnes could no longer rank as a surprise).

Hampshire defeat Australians

The real sensation was left to mid-July — the scene, Southampton — where Hampshire caused delight to their supporters by defeating the Australians by eight wickets. Mead's batting dominated the first day after he went in second wicket down with the score at 40 (how often did he do that) and with Fry took only 35 minutes to add 62 for the third wicket, then accompanied by the Revd. W. V. Jephson (55), he put on 95 for the fifth wicket in about an hour. No-one else stayed with Mead for long, although Sprot with a six and four fours hit up 29 in ten minutes. When the innings ended at 371, Mead had hit as many as 25 fours and made 160 not out out of 331 scored in four hours while he was in. At the end of the first day, the tourists were 47 for three and on the second, in spite of sound batting by Warren Bardsley who batted two and a quarter hours for 60 and some hitting by Minnett, whose 58 occupied only an hour, they were made to follow-on 174 behind. Kennedy bowled brilliantly and with the aid of two run-outs, worked his way through the Australians who set Hampshire only 84 to win — Mead 33 not out steered the County to victory.

The magazine 'Cricket' commented that after all Philip Mead might force his way into the England XI before the last test was played, adding with great imagination "it is evident that he can score plenty of runs against the Australian bowling".

But in spite of his close association with Fry, the supremo, the nearest he came to selection was as 12th man against Australia at the Oval, a position which he turned down as Hampshire did not wish him to miss the two contemporaneous County games. If this was a touch of sour grapes, it extended more widely in Hampshire than just to Mead.

He failed to impress in Hampshire's defeat by Yorkshire in the next match in which the Southerners' totals were 441 (Fry 186 and Barrett 120 added 246 in 195 minutes for the fourth wicket) and following heavy rain 95! There ensued a spell of truly dreadful weather for Hampshire in which four matches out of six failed to show even a decision on the first innings (but in the wet Hampshire beat Leicestershire and Warwickshire).

The season ended with a visit from the very moderate South African team at Bournemouth in September. Hampshire's 137 left them 25 behind on the first innings; Philip Mead, going in at number four, took out his bat for 64 which included only two fours. Three of his colleagues, Barrett, Sprot and Kennedy, were run out while he was in. Then the South Africans, with Dave Nourse taking particular advantage of the improved conditions, scored 432 at four runs an over. Nourse was at the wicket for four and a quarter hours for his 213 not not. Wanting 458 for victory, the County lost three wickets for 40 but Mead with help from Barrett and Sprot prevented a beating. He was again not out for 77 at the finish. So in four innings — 160, 33, 64 and 77, he made 334 runs against the touring sides without once being dismissed.

He was again a welcome visitor to the Scarborough Festival, compiling for Lord Longsborough's XI scores of 21 and 47 and 23 not out against the Australians and South Africans respectively, and as late as 16th, 17th and 18th September, he was playing for The Rest of England against Yorkshire. The Rest won by an innings but his score was only 15. He could comfort himself with the thought that if he had not made the test team that summer, few other professionals had — only Hobbs, Rhodes and Woolley had held regular places for their batting and he was still very much to the fore in other representative matches.

Hampshire, too, had little cause for complaint; their final position in the Championship table was not bettered until 1955 and unbelievably but true, Hampshire batsmen occupied the first three places in the national batting averages:

	Innings	Not Out	Runs	Highest Score	Average
C. B. Fry	32	3	1592	203	56.85
A. C. Johnston	20	1	1044	175	54.94
C. P. Mead	52	14	1933	160	50.86

I. E. M. Barratt with 1,381 runs at an average of 40.61 was not far behind.

More than that, they were the only batsmen to average over 50 runs an innings. Fry's figures for the County (612 runs at an average of 102) are doubly eloquent as to his continuing skill, and the effect of his frequent absences, for Hampshire often carried a long tail. Mead's not-outs — remember, he was usually batting at number three — provide a telling testimony to his skill, to the uncertainty of the lower orders and to the weather which left so many innings incomplete. Just as significant to Hampshire was the remarkable increase in skill of Alec Kennedy who at the age of 21 improved his figures in Championship matches from 51 wickets at 30 runs each in 1911 to 112 for an average of 17.20. In all games in 1912 his victims totalled 139 for 2,447 runs, that is 17.60 runs each.

On top of all this, the first-class counties all received £2,520 as their share of the test match profits.

The future looked really encouraging — and Mead was still only 25.

Chapter Seven
The Business of Batting

Philip Mead is commonly regarded as a dour defensive batsman. There is nothing so far in the progress of his career to justify that; the year 1913 may be considered an average English summer — whatever that is — that is to say, it was one of those seasons which fall midway between the heat and drought of 1911 or 1989 and the soggy meanness of 1985 and, so, is a suitable one in which to assess in detail the quality of some of his larger innings.

The season was an inconsistent and disappointing one for Hampshire who sorely missed the skills of Fry, who did not play at all, Johnston, who was studying and played in only six games, and Barrett. The weather in April and May was damp which prevented the batsmen getting into form, and to make matters worse, because of illness, Kennedy was unable to play until the middle of June. Too much bowling fell on Newman and when Kennedy, who was perhaps pressed into the fray too soon, did resume his place in the side, he did not recover full efficiency so the County could not get other sides out.

The situation in batting was remedied in mid season when the Hon. Lionel Tennyson and Lieut. C. H. Abercrombie joined the side. Tennyson, ebullient and powerful, became a famous figure in the game; Abercrombie, a well known all-round sportsman in his brief day, made an equally strong impact on Hampshire cricket in 1913, but naval service kept him away in 1914 and two years later he lost his life in the Battle of Jutland. Each caused a sensation — Abercrombie, who had played some Forces cricket in 1911 and 1912, hit up 126 in his first innings for Hampshire on 30th June at Southampton against Oxford University, and subsequently batted superbly for 165 against Essex before taking 144 from the Worcestershire bowlers at Dudley. Tennyson, in turn, created headlines when he played what was described as an 'extraordinarily lucky' innings for M.C.C. at Lord's, also against Oxford, when he and M. W. Payne put on 175 for the first wicket in 90 minutes. This was in the second innings of his first match! He, too, made a century against Essex and followed it with 111 at Trent Bridge. While they supplied a much needed tonic, the inconsistency remained. It was highlighted by the Essex match. The scores — Essex 507 (Newman six for 102) and 102 for two wickets; Hampshire 100 and 534 for seven wickets to which, first, Tennyson contributed 116; then Abercrombie with 165 and George Brown, 140 not out, added 325 for the seventh wicket, which 77 years later remains a County record. The result — a draw with first innings points to Essex and only two to Hampshire.

Surrey (531), Cambridge University (493), Kent (527), Oxford (554) and Middlesex (548 for eight) all plundered the Hampshire bowlers, and the County were grateful for two wins each over the weak Worcestershire and Somerset sides for their final position (tenth) in the Championship table. Phil Mead's performances must be assessed against this background. There were times when he seemed to be affected by the general inconsistency, yet at the end of the season he stood at the head of the first-class batting averages, scoring 2,627 runs at an average of 50.51, only marginally lower than in 1912. For Hampshire alone, his figures were 48.77 for 2,146 runs.

There were no first-class touring sides or Test matches in 1913 but it says much for his standing that he had the opportunity to play ten innings in various representative matches and twice not out in those he scored 481 runs at an average of 60.

In purely County matches, he reached the century eight times, exceeded 50 on nine other occasions and 40 on six more, was dismissed between 20 and 39 in ten innings and played 17 other innings for scores of under 20. Consistency is always relative!

Yet he probably played a greater number of memorable innings in 1913 than in any other season up to 1921, and the rapidity with which he accumulated runs was often noteworthy.

It was perhaps lack of practice which showed in his performances up to 19th May as his initial scores, all made at number three, were one, one, six and nought. Then in the game with Leicester at Southampton, he ran into top form and enjoyed some real practice. Stone, Bowell, Remnant, Brown and Newman were out by the time the Hampshire score reached 104; none of the last six batsmen reached double figures, yet at number five Mead, let off once, received sufficient support to enable him to reach three figures — 102, including 11 fours, in two hours. His principal helpers were Jaques (seven) who stayed while 37 were added, and Rutherford who made eight helped put on 35. When the acting captain, Hesketh-Pritchard, went in he ensured that Mead received as much as possible of the bowling and Mead responded by excelling with skilful placing of the ball on the leg side. Then when the fielders were moved across to fill the gaps, he followed with a succession of powerful off-drives. The pair saw the 200 up and Mead hitting his last 50 in 32 minutes, Hampshire reached 219.

Leicestershire bettered this by 22 runs; Hampshire, to no great effect as far as Championship points were concerned, dominated the rest of the drawn game. In only 90 minutes, Stone (93), with Remnant and Brown, took the score to 153 and Mead followed this lead by hitting quite brilliantly for the last hour of the day. Resuming next morning at 60, he continued at the same rate and took his score to 113 made in two and a quarter hours, when Pritchard, who was again his unselfish partner, declared.

So Mead shared with Llewellyn the distinction of being the only Hampshire batsman to make two separate 100s in a first class match twice. Each time Leicester were the opponents — indeed it is remarkable that of his 14 100s to date, as many as seven were against Leicestershire. He surpassed even that feat of monopoly against Warwickshire at Southampton a week later. It was typical of Hampshire's in and out form at this time that after gaining a lead of 59 on the first innings (to which Mead contributed 25), they lost by 64 after being set 331 to win with four and three quarter hours remaining. Again, Hampshire's early batsmen failed. Four wickets fell for 50. Indeed, only two of the side reached 20. One of them was the Rev. W. V. Jephson, Rector of Whitchurch, who contributed 22, and the other was Mead. The two added 60 runs, an anonymous fielder giving Mead a life when he had scored 34, but soon he was playing in a style which a local reporter described as 'watchful, judicious and bright'. Scoring more briskly as he went on, he reached his 100 in two hours ten minutes. J. S. Rutherford (four) kept up an end while 43 were added in 50 minutes and Jaques remained until Mead reached three figures — out for 156.

To the large crowd the most fascinating feature of the innings was the duel between Mead and F. R. Foster who had had the better of him in such a crucial fashion in the previous season. The locals appreciated the reversal of fortune, noting that Mead's mastery became pronounced; as he picked the ball almost off his toes and hit it clean and hard to leg for four. At one stage, the crowd burst into ironic cheers and shouts and Foster stopped bowling. When he resumed, Mead hit him for three fours in an over. With an off-drive from Foster and a cut from the bowling of Jeeves, he reached 150. His last 70 runs came in about an hour, with the aid of 27 fours, mostly hard drives. At last he was caught one-handed by W. C. Hands, the bowler, stretching up to a hard straight drive — a rare example of Mead lifting the ball. In all he scored 170 at a run a minute out of 266, that is 65 per cent of Hampshire's total.

It was still only the beginning of June when Hampshire met Surrey at the Oval. On this occasion he needed a little luck; he was dropped first ball and shortly after at nine was reprieved again but soon began playing formidably well, confidently placing the ball between the fielders with an accuracy and timing which by then must have become near to proverbial on the County circuit. He reached his 50 in 70 minutes. He and Jack Newman added 152 for the fourth wicket, to which Newman contributed 59. Mead had the great pleasure in reaching his first 100 against Surrey and in all his total of 116 occupied three and a half hours and included 13 fours. An observer noticed that he hardly ever lifted the ball, a tribute to the soundness and economy of his technique and a reminder that during his early years, up to 1910, it was not sufficient for the batsmen to clear the ring to score a six — the ball had to be hit out of the ground. Up to this point, I have not traced a single example of Mead hitting a six.

Hampshire's total of 355 diminished in significance as Surrey took apart their bowlers to the tune of 531. Demoralised by this, Hampshire collapsed in their second innings. Only Mead could stay for long; he batted for close on two hours for 61 out of the Hampshire total of 136. Then to Cambridge and an innings of 160 not out in four hours, which represented the culmination of this period of tall scoring. In the period 12th May to 14th June, he had hit five 100s in nine innings and it is not surprising that on the latter date, he was the first to 1,000 runs and headed the first class averages — his figures: 13 innings, two not outs, eight hundred runs, highest score 170, average 72.72. This is not the record of a plodder. A correspondent to the *Hampshire Advertiser* compared Woolley and Mead at this time. He referred to the former's success in Australia and in the Test matches of 1912 and concluded "Woolley holds the higher position . . . it is a matter not of skill but of temperament." Woolley was supremely confident from the first ball, immediately taking the attack to the bowler. Mead liked to get off the mark with a push to leg which occasionally resulted in his downfall when energetic young fielders were waiting round the corner. It did not take Mead long to get into his stride, but this initial difference in approach points the distinction between the lofty elegant Woolley, who was always likely to be the centre of attraction in any group of people, and Mead, often to be found indifferently standing on the edge of the crowd.

A fortnight passed before Mead again reached three figures in another remarkable display, this time in a drawn game against Nottinghamshire at Southampton. On the first innings, the visitors led by 65; then Bowell, Stone and Sprot (31 in 15 minutes) attacked the bowling before Mead took over and soon dominated the proceedings. He hit most of his 17 fours by hard driving and apart from giving the chance of a catch when he had scored 26, batted faultlessly for his 127 made in only 140 minutes.

Although not required for the Players at the Oval, he was selected for the showpiece of the season against the Gentlemen at Lord's, but he fell victim to Foster for only seven and was not called upon when the Players achieved a target of 123 runs in 105 minutes. This failure could have been unfortunately timed, for the selectors were about to begin the task of choosing the party for the tour of South Africa which was to take place during the winter. Fortunately, the committee were more concerned with general form than the odd failure. By the end of July, summonses had been sent to selected professionals, including Mead. He celebrated on 8th August with 97 in the second innings of Hampshire's game against Somerset, giving himself additional cause for celebration by reaching his 2,000 runs for the season while he hit 13 fours. He and Remnant added 77 in 55 minutes while with Brown he put on 78 in ten minutes under the hour. Only in September was the full composition of the touring party completed or the itinerary agreed. Even then the identity of the captain remained in doubt, the names of Douglas, A. H. Hornby, M. C. Bird, H. K. Foster and G. L. Jessop all being the subject of rumour! After dallying for a surprisingly long time, the selectors plumped for the man who, while enduring a lean time in 1913, had brought the Ashes home two years before — Douglas.

Mead continued his celebrations by hitting his eighth century of the season in splendid style against Sussex. The usual skilled placing of the ball to leg and artful drives between the offside fielders brought him 17 fours as he progressed to his century in 140 minutes. He and Stone added 137 for the fifth wicket in an hour and a quarter.

By August, H. C. McDonnell, on holiday from Twyford School, was providing much needed relief to the bowlers, in which A. Jaques and Brown were also playing an increasingly prominent part to the advantage of the side which was demonstrated by five victories as against three defeats in the last 14 matches; the most emphatic was the defeat of Gloucestershire by 315 runs at Bournemouth on 28th, 29th and 30th August. At the half-way stage of the match, there was no indication that Hampshire would win so easily: Hampshire 278 (Tennyson 83, Mead 51, Abercrombie 65, the future Hampshire captain and Mead adding 116 in an hour for the third wicket): Gloucestershire replied with 230. The second innings showed Mead at his very best. Going in second wicket down, he batted for only three hours and 40 minutes for his score of 171 not out, which included 23 fours. Still no sixes — his technique did not allow him to lift the ball, unless he wished to spray it over the heads of the middle distance fielders. Although the second highest score was only 46 by Tennyson, Hampshire reached 385 for eight before declaring. Tennyson had by then also been selected as a member of the winter touring party (in substitution for P. R. Johnson of Somerset) — not a bad effort for one enjoying (and that is the right word) his first season in County cricket. Kennedy and Newman (six for 52 and four for 20 respectively) soon disposed of the western County for 83.

By 1913, there was a considerble gulf between the stronger County sides and the rest. No victories are to be despised but, at the highest level, the only teams whose defeat was something to enthuse over at that time were Kent, winners of the County Championship for the fourth time in seven years, Lancashire (although they had a lean time in 1913), Middlesex, Northamptonshire, Surrey and Yorkshire. Derby, Gloucestershire, Somerset and Worcestershire, in particular, were all, because of weakness in batting, really easy prey for a reasonably strong County side. This puts into prospective Hampshire's final position (tenth) in the Championship table, but does not diminish Mead's achievements in 1913. His list of hundreds that year, all for Hampshire, reads as follows:

171	not out	v. Gloucestershire (Bournemouth)
170		v. Warwickshire (Southampton)
160	not out	v. Cambridge University (Cambridge)
127		v. Nottinghamshire (Southampton)
116		v. Surrey (Oval)
113	not out)	v. Leicestershire (Southampton)
102	)	
100	not out	v. Nottinghamshire (Nottingham)
100		v. Sussex (Southampton)

By the end of the County season, Hobbs and Mead had each reached 100 nine times (Hobbs achieving the feat before lunch three times), and when the

PHILIP MEAD CARRIES THE HAMPSHIRE HOG ON HIS BACK!
(This man Mead is in too big a hurry. There was not room for the cartoon last week, and since then he has made it a trifle out of date by scoring another century. Let it be supposed that the 127 is branded on the other side of the hog. — Note, Editor.) — *Cricket*, June 28, 1913.

season's swan-song, Kent and Yorkshire against the Rest of England for which both were selected, began on 15th September, it was touch and go as to which of them would finish at the head of the batting averages. Hobbs scored 23, Mead 43, so at the finish the figures were:

	Innings	Not Out	Runs	Most	Average
Mead	60	8	2627	171	50.51
Hobbs	57	5	2605	184	50.09

Mead was now the proud father of two sons, for Ronald born in 1909 had been joined by Frank in 1913.

The fee for the Australian tour had been £300. This time the compensation for a shorter five-month absence from Mrs. Mead and the children was £200, at a time when a farm labourer earned ten shillings (50p) a week and a dock worker 30 shillings (£1.50).

This was an offer which he could not refuse, although in 1913 he had another source of income in addition to his pay from Hampshire and from MCC (where he continued to be a member of the bowling staff) for he had gone into business as a partner of Walter Toomer. Toomer was an unusual combination — Southampton footballer and schoolmaster. His father had for years been a cricket bat maker and Walter enlarged on the theme, setting up on his own as a retailer of sports equipment and continuing from around 1913 with Mead, as Mead and Toomer. This should not imply that Mead was the senior partner. His appearances were, of necessity, spasmodic and his main role was to make his presence felt at peak periods, such as Christmas and the Spring. Then he took an informed interest when cricketers and their young were selecting new bats. Although some said that even when Mead was present at the shop, he preferred to remain in the back room, it is remarkable in 1993 how many cricketers, or more accurately, former cricketers recall buying their first bat under his benevolent gaze. The business still flourishes in London Road, Southampton, in the hands of Walter's son, Arthur.

Neither Walter Toomer nor Hampshire, nor presumably Mrs. Mead, raised any objection to Mead's departure southwards in October for the winter tour.

Back row: E. Remnant, J. Stone, J. Newman, G. Brown, C. P. Mead, A. Bowell, A. S. Kennedy.

Chapter Eight
At the Cape and After

The side led by John Douglas was the third to visit South Africa in the 11 years since the end of the Boer War. The previous two teams had not been strong enough; in 1905-06, P. F. Warner led a party which included only two players, J. N. Crawford and Colin Blythe who might have been expected to play in a test match against Australia, and was duly trounced 4-1, largely because of poor batting on matting wickets. Four years later, of the team taken out by H. D. G. Leveson-Gower, Hobbs and Blythe, his health permitting, alone would have been automatic selections for the best English XI, although the young Woolley, not very successfully, made the trip. South Africa won that series by three games to two.

So in 1913, M.C.C. did their best to send the strongest possible team: they relied principally on players who had done so well in Australia; Douglas, Hobbs, Woolley, Barnes, Rhodes, Mead, E. J. Smith, Strudwick and J. W. Hearne. Albert Relf and Major Booth, all-rounders old and new, completed the professional contingent, while Douglas had the amateur company of Morice Bird, the retiring Surrey captain, D. C. Robinson of Gloucestershire, and, as a late addition to the side, Lionel Tennyson. If Fry and Jessop had accepted invitations, the side would have been truly representative of English cricket.

The home country's strength, which had briefly reached a peak in England in 1907, was not only on but well beyond the wane. In England in 1912, the public had been all too aware of the poverty of their performances and now of that side they lacked both Faulkner and Pegler.

After a slightly hesitant start, Hobbs and Barnes had matters much their own way — on the field at least. Socially the side met with mixed fortunes; there was almost a public scandal when they departed for their hotel from one end of Bloemfontein railway station while the Mayor, red carpet, Boer notables and all waited in vain at the other! There were also problems with the manager, Ivor Difford, a South African, who earned the side a reputation as drinkers by keeping part of their unused hospitality allowance for his own purposes.

Mead was an invaluable member of a touring team, particularly in South Africa where socially and politically the atmosphere was still volatile. Quiet and calm (except sometimes when his score approached the 90s) he could be relied on not to drink too much nor to let the side down. Tennyson could also be depended on — to extract the maximum enjoyment out of any situation. According to Tiger Smith's recollection, the attitude of the professionals was that any combination would be too good for the South Africans, but Douglas was not as optimistic as that. He sub-ordinated everything to the winning of the Test matches; many offers of hospitality were turned down and weak opponents were given no quarter. There were three matches against local XVs before the first test and all were won by an innings.

For Mead himself the early matches created unhappy memories of the Australian tour. The dusty and windy atmosphere at some places was even less like home than the conditions in Australia had been. Then there was the matting. At that time, every pitch in the Dominion was a matting one. The expression 'matting' covered a multitude of surfaces and the pitches varied widely, depending on the nature of the ground under the matting. In some places, at Newlands, Cape Town, and at Port Elizabeth, the mat was laid and pegged down on turf. Elsewhere it was secured on hard bare soil and the soil varied, too, from a hard sandy base to, yes, gravel.

Some grounds were entirely without any turf on the wicket or the outfield. Mercifully this was not true of most of the grounds where the Tests were played, and the South African Cricket Association tried to persuade the cricket centres to adopt a uniform class of wicket, but it was over 20 years before the last Test match on matting took place. In 1913, where the mat was stretched over a bare hard surface, the bowlers were surprised and frustrated by the amount of bounce which was accentuated at higher altitudes. The mat always took spin. Matting which complied with the regulations of the SACA did not extend as far as the popping creases.

The initial first class game was at Newlands played on a wicket of matting laid on grass which had been well watered and was much slower than the practice nets had been.

Facing Western Province's score of 376, M.C.C. collapsed and were put out for 199. They saved the game easily enough in the follow-on, their reputation for the moment severely dented. Mead was dismissed for scores of four and 13 by Budgen, an off-break bowler. He scored 78 and 25 in the next two games against local XVs of the South Western Districts and contributed 42 to a third victory in a more important fixture by an innings over a Cape Province XI at Port Elizabeth on a pitch similar to the one at Newlands. His score of 84 against XV of Grahamstown promised well in a further innings victory.

Amid such sweeping successes, individuals had little chance to atone for first innings failures as Mead found when the two games against Border brought him scores of nought and 26 at the beginning of December. The first Test match at Durban was to begin on the 13th and it was a disappointment for Mead when he failed again against Natal at Pietermaritzburg which was made worse by the fact that the successful bowler was J. L. Cox who was considered to be a certainty for the first Test.

Fortunately for Mead, only Hobbs, who had a wonderful tour, and Douglas really shone against Natal, and as D. C. Robinson, one of the selected 14, had been taken ill on the voyage out and Hearne was smitten with influenza, the side almost selected itself. As it happened, Mead played an innings of 41,

43

adding 63 for the fifth wicket with Douglas. This was encouraging, as was the result: South Africa 182 (H. W. Taylor 109, Barnes five for 57) and 111 (Barnes five for 48) lost to England — 450 (Douglas 119, Hobbs 82, M. C. Bird 61, Tennyson 52) by an innings and 137 runs.

The second Test at the Wanderers, Johannesburg, was almost as one-sided.

The home sides's 160 and 231 (Barnes

26.5	9	56	8
and 38.4	7	103	9
65.3	16	159	17)

failed to equal England's 403 by an innings and 12 runs. Relf and Rhodes led off with 141 runs in under two hours. Hobbs was kept back for the second day and had to sit on his pads while they enjoyed their triumph before he was dismissed for 23, but Mead helped Rhodes in a stand of 152 which carried over to the third day. When Rhodes was caught and bowled by Blankenberg after batting for over five hours for 152, the score was 333 for three wickets. Yet none of the last seven batsmen reached 20 and it was left to Mead to steer the total towards 400. When he, too, was dismissed by Blankenberg, he had batted for three and a half hours, hit 12 fours and reached his first Test century (102), a perfect way to end the old year.

England had to bat twice in order to win the third Test match by 92 runs. Mead was bowled for a duck by Blankenberg when England batted first for a mediocre 238; when they went in again with a lead of 87, he was top scorer with 86. After the dismissal of Rhodes at four, he and Hobbs (41) added 79 in less than an hour and next day, with Douglas (77), he took the score to 177, adding 93 for the fourth wicket. Mead batted finely for 145 minutes hitting 13 fours.

By this stage, only H. W. Taylor of the home batsmen was regarded by the English as a worthy opponent with the bat, although J. W. Zulch now rose to the occasion helping Taylor in a stand of 153; nevertheless, South Africa then collapsed to 217 for seven. Blankenberg, too, surprised the visitors by a valiant 59, but in each innings, Barnes was too skilful for the others, returning figures of three for 26 and five for 102 in the match. J. W. Hearne had five for 49 in their first innings.

After that game, there was major industrial strife in the mines at Johannesburg and fear that the railways would be brought to a halt. The Government called out the South African Defence Force and mounted militia, consisting chiefly of Boers, rode in from the country and picketed the streets. Martial law was then imposed.

The cricketers, in such a disturbed period, played one or two minor matches on empty grounds. During one period of uncertainty, the whole team joined the volunteers and served as special constables, according to Tennyson, who may have found the role useful in avoiding the 9 p.m. curfew.

The South Africans showed greatly improved form at Durban; they led by seven runs on the first innings and at length set England 313 to win. Only Hobbs, with scores of 64 and 97, shone, and when rain and bad light ended the game, England, their five best wickets gone, were still 159 behind. Still Barnes excelled himself — no, not even Barnes could do that — but the South Africans still could not get the better of him and he returned figures of seven for 56 and seven for 88. He was unable to play in the fifth Test for reasons variously stated to arise from a dispute about pay, injury, or an argument about the arrangements for his wife whom he had insisted should accompany him on the tour. An evenly balanced game at Port Elizabeth was expected. 'Evenly balanced' was fortunately the state in which Mead and the others arrived at Port Elizabeth. The mail boat was too large for the height of the tide to allow the team to land on the quay so they were hoisted in baskets by crane and lowered into small boats which carried them ashore.

Back on dry land, only Taylor, Zulch and P. A. M. Hands showed form worthy of the occasion and England won by nine wickets. Mead batted three and three-quarter hours for his second 100 of the series. He hit only eight fours but he and Woolley added 104 for the fifth wicket, while Douglas helped put on 79 for the sixth.

So to the end, with Western Province forcing a draw on 10th March before the tourists made a recuperative voyage back to the United Kingdom.

Hobbs confirmed every golden opinion, scoring 1,489 runs on the tour at an average of 74. Douglas approached him most closely with 827 runs at 51. Mead finished fourth in the averages below Hearne, scoring 745 runs and averaging 39 runs in an innings in first class matches; in the Test matches, his seven innings ran him a good second to Hobbs:

	Innings	Not Out	Runs	Average
J. B. Hobbs	8	1	443	63.28
C. P. Mead	7	0	378	54.00

Of the others, only Rhodes averaged over 40, thanks to his 152 in the first Test. Woolley's figures were 138 runs at an average of 23. He captured seven wickets in the Tests for 39 runs each.

Although the amateurs, Jessop, Fry and Spooner, were absent, the side was considered by good judges to be the strongest available and Mead had fully justified his place in it. Before sailing for home, the team played association football, winning against a local side, although they played in ordinary clothes, a feat under the blazing sun which many of them were glad to remember years later.

Then there was a final hazard. The manager, Difford, tried to 'fine' some of the team. He withheld £5 from Mead on the grounds that he had been unfit for two games at the end of January and Mead was not alone. It needed all the force of Douglas's personality to remedy the ill feeling — and the cash shortages.

Although no one appreciated it at the time, there were to be no more Tests, in a cricket sense, until the autumn of 1920, six and a half years on. Sydney Barnes, who had taken 49 wickets at 10.93 runs each, did not figure in international cricket again.

The 1914 season

They returned home to persistent sunshine. The warm weather had begun in March and continued for many months with a short break at the end of June. There were no tourists and the high point of the summer, apart from Gentlemen v. Players, was to be a week of cricket in June celebrating the centenary of Lord's on its present site. There was sustained interest in an exciting struggle for the County Championship — would Kent retain the title which in 1913 they had won for the fourth time in eight years? No, they would not, but in April no-one foresaw the circumstances in which Surrey would come to be the champions; both actually and metaphorically the sky seemed cloudless.

Mead was soon back into his stride, scoring 76 against Leicestershire (who else!) at Southampton and 82 a week or so later in the return. He eclipsed even his partiality for the Leicester bowlers at home against Yorkshire. On the first day, the visitors were put out for 232, quickly enough for Hampshire to reach 128 for three before the call of time. Remnant and Mead were responsible for most of these runs; next day, after Newman had helped him add 55, Mead found a further assistant in Lieut. G. C. Harrison. By lunch, they had added 105 in 70 minutes, in the course of which Mead completed his century in two and a half hours. In the afternoon, they increased the score by 65 and when Harrison was stumped, the sixth wicket had produced 170 in only two hours. There was no further stand and Mead was last out after five and a half hours' batting, including 26 fours in his score of 213. He had given only one very difficult chance. This was a remarkable feat against the bowling of Hirst, Booth, Drake, Wilfred Rhodes and the young Roy Kilner.

His great effort did not bring victory. On the third day, David Denton and Hirst took only four and a half hours to add 312 and the game was drawn.

Mead's next three or four innings produced nothing worth writing home about, apart from 69 in 90 minutes against Nottinghamshire at Southampton but on 16th June, 1914, he was third in the race to 1,000 runs after Tarrant and J. W. Hearne. He had done enough to earn selection for the big celebration at Lord's — not Gentlemen and Players but the M.C.C. South African XI against the Rest which began the week of celebration of the Lord's centenary. The Tuesday, 23rd June, was THE big day. In the afternoon, the King and his two elder sons, the Prince of Wales (Edward VIII) and Prince Albert, who subsequently became King George VI, visited the ground and were introduced to the teams, and that evening the Hotel Cecil welcomed the cream of English cricketers to the Centenary Dinner. Among the diners were the cricketers playing in the match and Mead, with Hobbs, Rhodes, Hearne and Co. enjoyed 12 courses, accompanied by six different wines and a programme of music ranging from Irving Berlin to Elgar (Salut d'Amour) before the even more serious business of the evening began — the 13 speeches. This last flowering of pre-war oratory produced two jokes at least, both from the Earl of Dartmouth ('Mark Twain has told us that when he was young he could remember everything, whether it happened or not, but when he became old, he could only remember the latter'. The other is not so memorable!). The other speakers included Lord Hawke, the new President of M.C.C., Lord Harris, F. S. Jackson, C. B. Fry and W. G. Grace, who when he rose to speak received a reception which those present never forgot. He at least was very brief.

The match itself was a whitewash, at least partly because the wicket was affected by rain after the first day. The Rest made a consistent assault upon the M.C.C. bowlers and scored 467, E. Humphreys of Kent contributing 117, A. P. Day 79, S. G. Smith 78 and Fry 70. In reply, Mead top-scored for the M.C.C. with 21 out of their total of 94 and they followed on. Then only Rhodes, with 52, exceeded 30 against the fast kicking deliveries of Bill Hitch who followed his seven for 42 in the first innings with a further five wickets for 51 runs. So on 24th June, M.C.C. were defeated by an innings and 189 runs.

The guest most senior in rank at the Dinner was His Highness Prince Albert of Schleswig-Holstein. He was there by right as a cricketer who played for the Charterhouse XI in 1896 and as a member of M.C.C., but it was a mark of the absence of hostility to Germany that he should be so honoured only seven weeks before the outbreak of war. Indeed, the cricket season and the life of Philip Mead were at first unaffected by the outbreak of hostilities on 4th August 1914.

Hampshire certainly missed Abercrombie, serving at sea, and Tennyson who played little, but J. G. Greig, a light of earlier years on leave from India, compensated by playing a good deal, and A. C. P. Arnold proved to be another young amateur prospect. Above and beyond them, the greatest addition to the County's strength was the greatly improved Arthur Jaques. He had enjoyed success for Aldenham School as a bowler but did not get beyond the trial games at Cambridge and had to wait until 1913 before success in local cricket brought him to the attention of the Hampshire authorities. That year he captured 53 wickets at an average of 28, but only in 1914 did he rise to the front rank. A lanky six foot three inches tall, he bowled accurate fast medium out-swingers with a pronounced break back. That these were as difficult to play as they sound was proved by his figures in 1914, when he became one of the characters of the season. He proved immensely difficult to force away and his packed leg trap (one of the earliest examples) snapped up many catches. He and Kennedy earned the following figures:

	Overs	Maidens	Runs	Wickets	Average
A. Jaques	926.4	244	2187	117	28.69
A. S. Kennedy	1289.4	331	3243	162	20.01

with Newman an invaluable third bowler. Whether or not Mead moved over to the leg side, he held as many as 43 catches that year. Jacques was also spoken of as a future Hampshire captain and led the team in some of the early matches.

Britain's entry into the First World War on 4th August came upon Southampton, as it did on most of the rest of the country, suddenly and almost unforeseen. As late as 25th July, the leading articles in the *Southampton Times* were divided between the crisis in Ireland and a dispute over the finances of Southampton Council's electricity undertaking. Even on 1st August, the paper contained only a passing reference to 'the gravest news of the European situation'.

The Oval and the pavilions at Trent Bridge and Old Trafford were soon requisitioned; service players returned to their units, while Territorials were called to the Colours, some with unexpected rapidity. A. T. Sharp of Leicester had to abandon his side halfway through a match. F. H. Bacon, the Hampshire Secretary, suggested that a corps of professional cricketers be formed for home defence.

For the present, M.C.C. counselled 'go on' on the principle that as far as possible the country at home should pursue a normal course. This was not easy in Hampshire. The Portsmouth Week was given up, the games being transferred to Southampton and Bournemouth. Southampton itself and the surrounding countryside were transformed into a vast camp of men preparing to embark for France. The local population were, not surprisingly, diverted from their sport, and following their greatly improved start to the season, the County's performances reverted to mediocrity.

Philip Mead was no exception to all this. In the three weeks up to 17th August, his scores were six and 31, nought, 42 and 97 not out (an innings which combined with rain to save the game against Middlesex), ten and 46, eight and seven and 20 and 12. The last two innings were played at Chesterfield where Hampshire defeated the moderate Derbyshire side by 15 runs. They returned to Southampton to inflict a walloping on Somerset; the scores — Somerset 213 and 226; Braund hit his last first class 100 in their second innings; W. Hyman who in 1902 in a club game had scored 352, largely off the bowling of W. G.'s brother, E. M. Grace, made 60 and 34, and for Hampshire the Twyford schoolmaster, H. C. McDonnell took four for 57 and seven for 47. Hampshire amassed 486 for six wickets declared. Mead played a splendid chanceless 158 in three and a half hours. He hit 24 fours and with Arnold (76) put on 152 for the third wicket. Jack Newman hit his maiden first class 100 and Alistair McLeod, Desmond Eagar's predecessor as Hampshire's secretary, showed good form for his 27. So do the generations overlap. Hampshire won by an innings and 47 runs.

At Southampton, in the game removed from Portsmouth, they also defeated Warwickshire, but in a far more closely fought out match by three wickets. McDonnell took five for 70 in Warwickshire's first innings of 288, which Hampshire exceeded by 75 (Mead 96 in 160 minutes — 12 fours). Warwickshire's good start in their second innings suffered in spite of a subsequent collapse to set Hampshire 189 to win. Only 140 minutes remained; two wickets fell for 15 but Mead and Arnold put on 104. Mead was caught by Jeeves bowled Field for 65 and in the event Hampshire won by four wickets.

Bowell (204) shone in the other game transferred from Portsmouth — to Bournemouth — against Lancashire. Mead scored two and 31 and rain ruined the finish on 26th August.

On the following day, *The Sportsman* published a famous letter from W.G. calling for a cessation of first class cricket. The same day, Hampshire began a game against Essex who were outmatched. Only McGahey in the first innings and Carpenter (99) in the second did anything against the bowling of Kennedy (five for 50 and seven for 25); nine of the Hampshire side reached double figures in their total of 352 (McLeod 87). Mead scored 37 and Hampshire won by an innings and 19 runs. In a third game at Bournemouth, they beat Kent by an innings. Jacques had nine wickets in the match and Mead reached 128 in three hours with 18 fours before he was bowled by S. H. Day. The other famous Kent amateurs were otherwise engaged.

And that was it. The Hampshire professional staff, including Mead, Kennedy, Newman, Remnant and Livsey, who had replaced Stone as wicketkeeper during the season, enlisted in the 5th Hants Territorials; Fry, who had played a few games, Jacques and Arnold were all accepted for active service. Tennyson and Abercrombie were already professional fighting men. Newman, Livsey and others were soon looking forward to broadening their horizons as they sailed to India; Philip Mead was not among them.

Chapter Nine
Standing — at the wicket and among cricketers

The cause of Mead's rejection for active service at the age of 27 was unromantic, and for a professional sportsman, rather disheartening. It was varicose veins, and from this time on, the condition will be as ever present in the dressing room and on the field as were Kennedy, Newman or Brown. The material effect for Mead was not disastrous. The County Committee decided that winter to continue to pay three members of the staff, Jesse Hopkins, the invaluable groundsman, 40 shillings (£2) a week, Mead £1.5.0 (£1.25) and Kennedy ten shillings (50p). They alone were given contracts for the following 12 months up to the autumn of 1915, and in the event, the Committee went on paying Mead for much longer than that, although there was no County cricket at all from 1915 to 1918. So, there was plenty of time to spend with Walter Toomer in the business, and for the only time in their active years, long summers at home with Mrs. Mead and the children, who were now aged five years and 18 months. It was about this time that they set up home at Niton, a newly built good sized semi-detached house in Newlands Avenue, Shirley, Southampton which, in happier times, would have been about 20 minutes walk from the real place of business — the County ground.

Toomer soon enlisted and was away for the duration, so Mead had a more active part to play in the running of the business. In 1916 he again failed to satisfy the medical examiners. As a prominent sportsman who was very much at home, Mead soon became involved in fundraising events for the 'war effort'. The first took place as early as October 1914 — a soccer match between Phil Mead's XI and a theatrical revue company which raised 30-odd pounds for the relief of Belgian refugees. Such football and cricket games were of little importance but provided much needed entertainment as well as helping good causes. The flavour can be obtained from a game at the county cricket ground in 1915 when Mead scored 112 not out against an Australian XI. Most of this grandly-named side, however, were without any proper gear and Mead himself had to keep wicket.

It was not long before the first deaths in the War were recorded and over the next four years, of Hampshire's pre-War players, Abercrombie, Arnold, the Secretary F. H. Bacon, Jaques, Persse and others lost their lives. It cannot have been easy for Mead to retain his customary good humour. Even such a popular cricketer as Jack Hobbs felt it necessary in his autobiography to explain how he came to work on munitions (and play league cricket) before he joined the Armed Forces in 1916. Mead, as a volunteer, had been turned down, but not everyone knew that, and his rejection on health grounds might for him have had ominous implications for the future of his career in cricket.

It was July 1917 before the Hampshire Committee, feeling perhaps that they had done enough for Mead, terminated his wages. However, by then they were turning their attention to the state of the County ground and the possibility of re-starting County cricket after the war.

Before Mead began the task, after a four-year break, of restoring and increasing his reputation, we can consider how that reputation stood at the outbreak of hostilities after almost ten years of first class cricket. Of those cricketers active in 1914, Haywood with an average of 42, J. T. Tyldesley with one of 40, W. G. Quaife (40) and Fry (50) had all begun their careers a decade before Mead. Among his contemporaries, Hobbs with 21,800 runs had scored more than Mead (whose figures at the end of 1914 stood at 15,836 runs) and their averages at around 38 runs an innings were the same. None of his other contemporaries approached these figures. Frank Woolley in 1914 scored 2,272 runs, averaging over 45, but this was the first time he had been so prolific (however, he also took 125 wickets for 19 runs apiece). Phil Mead had ceased to be a serious bowler by 1909. Woolley's lack of success on the matting in South Africa in 1913-14 had, as far as comparisons went between the two, probably balanced out to a certain extent Mead's moderate achievements in Australia two winters before. Jack Hearne, only 23 years old, headed the averages in 1914, scoring 2,116 runs at 60 per innings. He also was a successful wicket-taker, capturing 123 wickets at an average of 22 with his leg breaks. He was still looked on as something of a prodigy. These young men were really in a class of their own — so was George Gunn who in 1914 was aged 35, but people were not quite sure what that class was. Players who were to become household names in the '20s, such as Patsy Hendren and Ernest Tyldesley, were looked on only as promising youngsters (although they were only two years younger than Mead and Woolley) while others like Percy Holmes and Charlie Hallows were barely started. So Mead's reputation stood very high, and we have already seen that there was at that time no element of stodginess attached to it.

The methods by which he achieved his high position are still, 75 years on, capable of analysis. He would appear from the dressing room (by no means always situated in the pavilion in those days) with his strange rolling approach to the pitch, 'like a longshoreman with a purpose' as R. C. Robertson-Glasgow put it. Then, on arrival at the wicket, the shuffle, or little ceremony which he insisted on before each ball was bowled. Batting left-handed he faced towards the square leg umpire and pulled the peak of his cap three times. This done (and many caps were worn out by the action), he turned to the crease, tapped his bat three times in the block hole, and shuffled his feet in three movements up to the bat. Only when this ritual was completed did he allow the bowler to make a start, and any spin bowler operating off a short run who tried to hurry on, or even interrupt the process, would be held up, as Mead backed away and the whole thing was gone through again before he faced up to the attack. The confrontation between Mead and Grimmett of Australia in 1926 and 1930 when that gnomic wizard of spin was so anxious to rattle through his overs that he constantly had to be sent back, was the source of much mirth. Yet, to the viewer of cinefilm of Mead at the crease, the movements are so understated that they would not normally hold up the flow of the game; almost a fetish — certainly an aid to concentration.

But the concentration had begun long before that when the openers went out to bat and every detail of the field-placing was already in his mind's eye before he himself reached the middle. Over the years he acquired a wonderful memory for the field-placings of each of the bowlers whom he faced regularly. The defect of this virtue was that he could be disturbed, especially early in an innings, by some unexpected change in the field or the bowling. At the crease, concentration indeed is his prime characteristic. The stance, a little crouched, the bat, looking unbelievably broad, angled forwards. The head very still. When the ball is delivered, his quickness of foot comes into play. Two or three steps towards the ball which is then stroked away either on the off-side or more probably, turned to some part of a wide arc on the leg-side. His favourite way of getting off the mark was to use his feet to get early to the ball, place it square or fine to leg, and to turn the shot into the beginning of a run. He also liked to complete a 50 or century in this way and it was in these three circumstances that he was sometimes vulnerable to catches to short leg off the ball swinging in to the left-hander. Usually so complete is his mastery, that he has played the stroke to an unmarked position in the field, and started to run all in one movement, from a good way down the wicket. This required an equal degree of anticipation from the other batsman. 'Good luck' he would murmur as he sauntered past his partner who was rushing headlong to the other end. Mead was also a master of the off- and on-drive, as befitted so large, and long-armed a man. But he never appeared to force the ball away and indeed, advised against unnecessary violence on the grounds that it resulted in a raising of the head.

With his skill in placing the ball, and his swiftness of foot, he had no need for violent aggression. He was also a master of little dabs to off and on which, in the opinion of many of his professional colleagues, enabled him, if he wished, to score off any delivery. A feature of his batting which irritated the fielding side was his skill in lifting the ball safely over an inner ring of fielders but well short of any on the boundary, something at which Leslie Ames was also adept. How often the ball, deflected fine, just beat square leg to the fine leg boundary; sent to fine leg, the fieldsman then found himself chasing fruitlessly square! It was methods such as these which had enabled him by 1914 to take such a high position among his contemporaries, with 2,000 runs in a season four times running to his credit and, as a spectator expressed it some years later, the ability to defend all day for 280 not out.

Mead must greatly have missed the County circuit during these quiet blank seasons, but by April 1919 the long summer days behind the neat hedges and stained glass of home were over.

Hampshire 1914

Chapter Ten
1,100 runs in Two Days

The authorities did the game a good service when, in the autumn of 1918, they made arrangements for the first season of peace. They decided that County championship games would be played over two days only instead of three. This proved so unpopular over the one season, that cricketers have not been troubled by the suggestion since. The season of 1919 should not detain us much longer than a drunk who accosts us from the gutter asking for a fiver for a cup of tea. The daily playing hours, 11 a.m. to 7.30 p.m., were described by a wit of the time as likely to prove unsuccessful in wet weather — and in fine. The players soon grew to hate the hours while, except where the state of play proved exceptionally exciting, the public went home for supper at half past six as they always had done. The summer was very hot and dry and many of the Counties were well below full strength. The authorities had in fact, done well to get the first class game going again at all. Of the great pre-War names, Hayward, Jessop and Tarrant were the best known of those who retired; Blythe, K. L. Hutchings and Major Booth had been killed in the War, many others who had survived had not yet returned from service — and everyone was five years older. The entry into the game of a whole generation had been delayed or indeed, written off.

Out of 124 championship matches, as many as 56 were drawn that year. Middlesex won only two and lost three out of 14, and Surrey drew ten games out of 20. A number of non-bowlers played an important part with the ball. Even Patsy Hendren bowled 100 overs for Middlesex whose leading wicket-taker was J. W. Hearne with 39 wickets at 31 each. The County championship was not played on a basis of equality. While Yorkshire played 26 matches (and won 12 to take the County championship) only Surrey and Sussex of the others played as many as 20 and Northants played only 12. Hampshire compromised at 16 championship fixtures. Five wins as against four losses gained them seventh place in the championship. They were fortunate in having Kennedy to bowl, but Jaques, as we have seen, had been a casualty of the War, and Newman and Remnant were still in the army.

On his pre-War form, Philip Mead was certain to benefit from the prevailing conditions and as far as batting was concerned, he soon picked up the threads. Hampshire's season did not start until 9th June, but the week before that, he had obtained match practice for M.C.C. against the Australian Imperial Forces touring side whose games extended, on their insistence, to three days. His scores of 36 and 71 marked a satisfactory return to first class cricket and a month later, 64 not out for the Players versus the Gentlemen at the Oval, maintained his reputation at a representative level. For Hampshire, his story was one of success all the way. The County's first game, at Lord's, produced a result in two days. Mark well the the scoring: Hampshire 347 and 187 (Mead 39 and 37) lost to Middlesex 608 for seven declared, by an innings and 74 runs. J. W. Hearne compiled an elegant innings of 218 not out and Hendren, a wonderfully prolific scorer for the best part of the next 20 years, hit up 201. Kennedy took seven wickets for 202 and the only other regular member of the pre-War attack, Brown, had one for 61 from eight overs. At The Oval, Hampshire then gave Surrey their only defeat of the season (Mead 72 and 25 not out, Kennedy five for 142 and seven for 47) before heading the Australians on first innings in a rain spoilt match — Hampshire's first post-War home game. Mead at number four, was the only batsman to exceed 20 for Hampshire and was left on 91 not out as Kennedy, S. Pothecary Snr., S. G. A. Maartensz and R. D. Busk, all failed, and if some of those names are unfamiliar, that typifies some of the sides put out by Hampshire that summer. Kennedy, whose professionalism was severely tried but not found wanting, captured six Australian wickets for 56 runs. After a draw with Gloucestershire which produced five centuries, and an innings of 98 by Mead, came a busy two days at Southampton when Hampshire, 315 and 289 (Mead 84 and seven) drew with Surrey whose score was 597 for four declared. Andrew Ducat 271, and Ernie Hayes, 153 not out, added 353 for the third wicket which remains a County record. Hampshire used eight bowlers of whom only Kennedy and Brown had any claim to be front-liners. Mead's contribution was six overs for 40 runs.

By July, Frank Ryan, the Canadian-born left-arm bowler who was discovered playing cricket professionally at Basingstoke, and afterwards played with such success for Glamorgan, was giving some help to Kennedy, but neither did much as Essex scored 331. It was left to Mead to have both Douglas and F. W. Gilligan caught and he then mopped up the tail to finish with figures of four for 57. This was not, however, the beginning of a new career with the ball for him as his total victims that season numbered only ten. Hampshire made a disastrous start, Brown and P. M. Hall of Hambledon both failing to score. This brought in Mead and over the next five hours, while G. N. Bignell (playing under the name of G. Newcombe), Tennyson, E. P. G. Causton another occasional player, T. O. Jameson and Kennedy, came, stayed and went, he drove hard and placed the ball cleverly on the leg side. He reached 200 without giving a chance before falling to Douglas for 207. This was no mean feat even on the easy paced Leyton wicket against the bowling of Douglas and the amateur, G. M. Louden, whose leg breaks bowled at medium pace were greatly respected among the cricketers of his time.

Centuries by Mead and Brown, and wonderful bowling by the indefatigable Kennedy (six for 55 and seven for 64) ensued a good walloping for Essex when the two sides met again at Bournemouth. Mead's 122 not out out of the first innings score of 278 was described by Wisden as 'even more cautious than usual'. This is the first such ominous reference which I have been able to trace. In the third, yes, third game of the Bournemouth week, Mead drove with great power, however, for his 79 in Hampshire's second innings when Somerset were beaten by 130 runs (Kennedy nine for 137 in the match). Hampshire finished their season at Southampton with a game against Yorkshire which was limited by rain to one day, but a day full of action for all that.

Yorkshire put out Hampshire for 201. Again, only Mead reached 20. He faced the attack, consisting of the England bowlers Waddington, E. R. Wilson and Rhodes, as well as Emmot Robinson, without playing a false stroke in his innings of 100 not out, combining fine all-round hitting with impregnable defence. Yorkshire had already passed Hampshire's score for the loss of only three wickets when rain overnight brought the game and the County's season to a close.

With his three centuries, as well as ten scores of 50 for Hampshire, Mead totalled 1,332 runs in 27 innings, averaging 60.54, but alas did not keep up this form in all the festival matches. For the Rest of England against the Champion County, Yorkshire, he made 13 in his only innings, and followed this with a duck for South of England against the Australians at Hastings. His second effort was a different matter when the South went in again with a first innings lead of 21. He played splendidly, hitting a six and eight fours, mainly drives and pulls and scoring 75 in 100 minutes from the Australian attack which included J. M. Gregory and H. L. Collins. The South won by 122 runs, but when a number of the team moved along the coast to Portsmouth to face the Australians again, they gave a feeble display against Gregory and the less distinguished C. S. Winning and were defeated by ten wickets. The fact that Mead's 21 was second highest score in the second innings indicates the poorness of their performance.

Before the season ended, although large crowds had watched the two-day games, the authorities decided to revert to the three-day pattern for the 1920 season. Conservatism and commonsense prevailed on the cricket field. About this time a whiff of industrial unrest entered into relations between the Hampshire professionals and the Committee. Mead, Brown and Kennedy had already negotiated themselves a rate of payment of £8 a match at the start of that season. In August 1919 Mead asked the Hampshire committee to grant him a benefit match in 1920. This was readily granted, and shortly afterwards, the Hampshire committee offered to pay Mead, Kennedy, Brown and Ryan, the only professionals to play regularly in 1919, what was described as a retaining fee of 25 shillings a week during the winter. This amounted to a payment of some £35 over 28 winter weeks. The professionals sent a letter to the committee asking that the figure be increased on the grounds that most counties were paying, not winter wages, but a bonus which, they said, varied between £40 and £60. The committee, chaired by Dr. Russell Bencraft, who though courteous and totally devoted to the County's cricket since the 1880s, was used to having his own way, thereupon interviewed Mead and as a result of his advocacy, agreed to the principle of the bonus payment at a figure of £70, payable by two instalments, one in October and the other January. In further discussions during the winter, they offered Mead and the others payment of match fees at £10 for an away match, £8 for home games together with reimbursements of one return railway fare as well as win and talent money. The system of talent money which ran until the captaincy of R. H. Moore in the 1930s, proved a very arbitrary means of rewarding important contributions, both in a general way and as between batsman and bowler. One point was awarded for 50 runs, two for 100 and three for 150, and one point went to the bowler who took five wickets. Forty-nine runs did not qualify at all, nor did a match-winning four wickets. However, an extra point was awarded to each member of a winning team. At the end of the season, the points were totted up and each equalled a pound for the player. The system was particularly hard on the wicketkeeper. Mead's figures we shall see, included one point in 1920 for taking five wickets in an innings!

During the season, Warner again expressed his opinion of Mead and a number of other professional cricketers in articles which were subsequently published in book form. He wrote under the heading 'A Fieldsman's Eleven': 'Woolley will be one of the slips and Mead the other. Mead is not a good outfield; he can neither run fast nor throw hard; but he is an extraordinarily fine slip and in this position I have seen him bring off some really great catches.' A little later, summarising the season of 1919, he noted 'Mead had a really fine season and is a terribly hard man to get out. His fielding also at slip was extremely good and he brought off many fine catches.'

Around this time, the family moved from Niton eastwards to a property in Portswood, 51a Westridge Road. This pleasant (now most of the traffic has been diverted) street consists largely of detached or semi-detached Victorian houses standing in fair-sized grounds. No. 51a was no doubt like the others, but is a disappointment to the pilgrim, for the present building dates only from the 1950s, the original, alone of the adjacent houses, having been the victim of a stray incendiary bomb during the Second World War. The original remained a Mead family home until 1928 and their third child, Phyllis, was born there.

It was a shock for Walter Toomer when he learned that Mead was going into business with a rival concern. The Philip Mead Bat Company was established in London in 1919 and was turned into a limited company in January 1920, with its registered office at 54 Great Eastern Street, London. The company grew rapidly, and was soon manufacturing its own equipment for cricket and tennis at fine premises in New North Road, Islington N1 which were described as the largest cricket bat factory in the world. Soon they were making bats for the firm of Mead and Toomer! The great novelty of their stock was a tennis racquet of which the tension of the strings could be altered by a turn of the handle.

The business grew and the share capital increased with it, and by January 1922, 11 individuals held 23,700 shares. In August, the company offered its shares to the general public, declaring assets of over £107,000 and a profit of nearly £10,000 on the year's trading. The public subscribed in large numbers, a tribute perhaps to the esteem in which Mead, or the company, was held by the public, or the stockbrokers respectively. The shareholders ultimately included widows, country clergy, clerks, commercial travellers and other small shareholders. They all lost their money. The company advertised extensively, its attempts to attract investors including a board game, akin to snakes and ladders, in which a youth progresses from junior to a place on the 'Board'.

In real life, a seat on the board became a dubious asset: the company's borrowing began to increase greatly during 1923 and in the following year, a receiver and manager was appointed. He advertised that the company was under new management and tried to retrieve the business. However, on 1st April 1924, the company was wound-up at the hands of Associated Newspapers.

Mead's association with this shallow-rooted growth can have done his name no good, but there is no point in going into further detail because Phil Mead was never a shareholder in the concern, let alone a director, and held no office in it. Indeed, how he was connected with the business, or what the financial arrangements were for him, remain shrouded in mystery. Happily for him, his connection with Toomer was not affected.

In 1920, cricketers' attention focused on another tour to Australia. In the face of the enthusiasm of the Australian authorities, M.C.C. reluctantly agreed to send over a side in the winter of 1920-21, although everyone with an understanding of the state of the game in England would have preferred to put off the trip for at least a year. Things might have turned out differently for Mead if that had happened. There was a genuine shortage of bowlers of quality; Foster had been permanently lamed as a result of a motorcycle accident, and Sydney Barnes was now aged 47. Nevertheless, he received an invitation, which he declined. Douglas, of the team which had bowled so well on the last tour, alone remained, but he was nearly 38 and none of the other fast bowlers still participating had achieved much at the highest level. There was a general feeling that Australian batsmen would have a grand time.

This was equally true of batsmen at home, as the high scoring in 1919 had demonstrated. There were some teams not worthy of the designation 'first class'; the counties at that time fell into three categories: the big six, Yorkshire, Lancashire, Middlesex, Surrey, Kent and Nottinghamshire, formed the top tier with Sussex at their best not all that much behind; the first five were likely to see off any of the remaining 12 without too much difficulty. Then came Gloucestershire, Essex and Somerset (thanks to the remarkable individual skills of Charles Parker, Douglas and J. C. White respectively) together with Warwickshire who were all, with descending degrees of probability, capable of extending each other, and any but the first five. There, first class quality in all but name, ended. Northamptonshire, Worcestershire and Derbyshire were so appallingly feeble that they were easy meat for almost anyone — except each other. This does a slight injustice to Northants who won three games and lost 16 out of 20 in 1920, Worcester who played 18 and lost 16 of them, while Derbyshire daring 18, actually lost 17. There was no play at all in the 18th.

Hampshire, with their strong nucleus of professionals, and their good pre-War record, entered the season with high hopes. Bowell, the opening batsman,

Livsey the wicketkeeper, and Jack Newman, were all available again, much was expected of Ryan while I. E. M. Barrett and J. G. Grieg, the pre-War military stars were expected to be available. Who could doubt that they would figure in the top group of counties?

In the event, they finished 11th in the Championship table between Somerset and Warwickshire suffering as many as 14 defeats offset by only seven victories. Kennedy enjoyed yet another successful time, relishing the support of Newman, but they missed the assistance which Jaques would have provided. The real problem lay in the batting. George Brown, aged 33, rose to the front rank, scoring 1,863 runs, but all the others proved woefully inconsistent. Anyone looking at Mead's figures year by year, for, say, the 20 years after 1911, sees a record of consistent success with only a slight hiccup in the mid-'20s, but his final figures for this season are as misleading an indicator of form as those of his last season, 1936. Until early August 1920, he faired very moderately and the end of July found him with little more than 1,000 runs. Early on, Hampshire's totals at Aylestone Road, Leicester, 77 and 91, were bettered by Mead on his own at the Oval where he scored 86 and 94, and he followed with a century at Worcester (and so he should have done as the hosts' only first class bowler was Fred Pearson aged 40 whose record for the year was 20 wickets average 47!). He followed up with 107 runs in his next seven innings. He may not have been entirely fit, as against Gloucestershire at Bristol in mid-June he batted at number seven scoring only three. However, this was a game in which Hampshire, who had only their victory over Worcester to set against defeat by Leicester, Surrey, Kent, Lancashire and Middlesex, showed what their supporters may have hoped was their true form. Brown 120, and Barrett 215, added 321 for the second wicket taking only two hours and 50 minutes to do so. Hampshire declared at 507 for seven, yet they still won the match in two days, after rain had washed out the first of the three. This success was due to Mead, the bowler. In the second innings of Gloucester, he dismissed their last five batsmen at a personal cost of 13 runs which included the capture of three wickets in four balls. This was his most successful performance with the ball since his famous achievement of seven wickets for 18 against Northamptonshire in 1907. Since 1909 he had hardly figured as a force in the Hampshire attack, but Tennyson showed every willingness to experiment, using both Mead and himself more than they had the right to expect (it was not long after this that Tennyson put himself onto bowl the last over of the day against Surrey from which Peach hit 22). Tennyson was also to ring the changes bewilderingly in the batting order, but this had less effect upon Mead than on the other professionals.

Mead enjoyed a long bowl too in the next game, the return against Middlesex. His one wicket for 58 from 18 overs compares quite favourably with the figures of

	Kennedy	37	4	121	2
	Newman	37	3	142	0
and	Ryan	27	3	90	2

59

as Middlesex accumulated 451 for five declared. His own scores of 54 and 85 did not prevent an overwhelming defeat. The second half of June began with a thoroughly satisfactory victory over Essex in the first match of an experimental cricket week at Colchester. It turned out disastrously for the home county as Hampshire began by amassing 415 for nine before declaring; the description of Philip Mead's batting at this stage of his career is illuminating: 'Mead gave a characteristic display. At times he hit quite brightly, scoring by a nice variety of strokes, but for the most part, he played in his usual stolid fashion, waiting for the loose ball to come along. At the wicket for five hours and 20 minutes he hit one six and 14 fours.' His score was 178 not out and the reference to the six is the first one which the writer has been able to discover. Only Bowell of the others got over 50. Mead also captured a couple of wickets as first Kennedy and Ryan and then Newman swept Essex aside for 87 and, with more effort, 266. Via Nottingham, where they were defeated again by two wickets, Hampshire travelled onto Headingley. Yorkshire's greatest days since the early 1900s, and their four consecutive championship titles, lay just around the corner but they were still in the top flight, boasting Waddington, one of the bowlers of the year, Wilfred Rhodes, Robinson and Roy Kilner. The match produced a genuine sensation for Hampshire, making best use of a perfect pitch, lost only two wickets before declaring. Bowell and Brown began by putting on 183 together before Claude Whiting, struggling for a place in the Yorkshire XI, had Bowell leg before wicket and quickly bowled Barrett. That was the extent of Yorkshire's success. The bowling cut no ice with Brown and Mead. Seldom had two English left-handed batsmen enjoyed such a triumph; this Saturday was Brown's day of days. Largely by enormously powerful drives he hit 29 fours in scoring 232 not out while Mead, playing second fiddle, progressed to 122 before the declaration made when the pair had put on 271 for the unbroken third wicket stand. The next round went to Kennedy after heavy rain on the Sunday night.

Sutcliffe, a bright young prospect, made 58 before falling as one of Kennedy's six victims at a cost of 61 runs but nobody else made more than 35. They did a little better when they followed-on 297 behind thanks to three hours of elegant defence by Percy Holmes (78) but a typical display by Rhodes who was ultimately run out only delayed the end. Yorkshire were renowned for nattering on the field of play and 26th, 28th and 29th June must have witnessed a great deal of that.

The fixture list allowed Hampshire three blank days for the crossing of the Pennines and beyond to Aigburth, Liverpool. This was also Kennedy's match as his analysis of 13.3 overs, six maidens, 33 runs, nine wickets in the Lancashire second innings testify.

Hampshire's attempt to make the 66 needed to win the game against bowlers handicapped after heavy rain met with an unbelievably miserable lack of success as the scoreboard crawled to 54 for five wickets. Against Dean, left-arm fast, and Cook, medium pace, the last five wickets subsided for only ten runs and Lancashire snatched victory by one run.

These eventful games formed an exciting lead-in to Mead's benefit match against Surrey on 7th, 8th and 9th July at Southampton. In those days, the benefit match was *the* fundraising event not only of the beneficiary's season — but often of his whole career. There were seldom the supporting events, dinners, raffles, golf matches which a modern professional enjoys. The disaster which befell Mead will be all the more appreciated. Alas, persistent rain prevented any play at all on the first two days and there was inevitably an air of unreality when play began on the third. It was, however, illumined by Jack Hobbs who, aided by three dropped catches, hit, in his inimitable way, 169, his highest score of the season. Mead returned the best bowling figures, two for 36 from 18 overs but as Hampshire got only half an hour's batting, he did not even get to the crease. Surrey were at the head of the championship table and Hampshire put out a really strong team including C. B. Fry, playing his first game since 1914, and the veteran A. J. L. Hill who had played in a 'Test match' against South Africa in 1895, so the event was all the more disappointing. Including the donations realised by a subscription list, the amount raised ultimately reached £817. In 1925 Roy Kilner received £4,016 from his benefit — but things were different in Yorkshire. However, Mead received the sum of £270 from insurance so the final sum exceeded £1,000.

Fry was sufficiently encouraged to play again ten days later in the game against Nottingham at Southampton when he top-scored in each innings with 137 (his 94th and last century in first class cricket) and 57. Mead's totals in that game were one and 13, and this, at the time when the England selectors were working up to completion of the side to tour Australia, was the beginning of a very lean period for him. He was selected for the Players in the set-piece match at Lord's where his scores of ten and 24 were not noticeably worse than those of Hearne eight and 37 not out, or Hendren one and 24 not out. Woolley scored nought but he had that second string to his bow and captured five wickets for 20 in the second innings. At this time, Mead scored only 121 runs in nine innings. The lowest point of all came against Gloucestershire at Clifton when he was

caught Smith, bowled Mills	0
caught F. G. Robinson, bowled Mills	0

and so for the first time in his career, completed a pair. Hampshire's two innings could muster only 36 and 55. The Australian touring side were selected at a meeting on 26th July. Hobbs received his invitation the following day. Mead was not selected. At this time he missed a couple of Hampshire's matches and was perhaps not entirely fit.

Too late, his form changed when the county moved on to Taunton and faced a side of nine amateurs (including J. C. W. MacBryan and J. C. White, both England players of the future) and two professionals, Len Braund and Ernest Robson whose combined service for the county was 45 years (their combined ages were 94). It was typical of Hampshire's in and out form that they beat Somerset by 191 runs — yet the Western County with their limited resources, finished above Hampshire in the championship table. The match marked a belated return to form by Mead. When Hampshire, dismissing Somerset for 88, batted a second time with a lead of 51, he played a remarkable innings; six Hampshire batsmen failed to reach double figures and only Newman and Kennedy of the others exceeded 20, but on the second day Mead, going in at number four, placed the result, a win for Hampshire, beyond doubt. At the wicket for four and a half hours, he hit 19 fours and combined fine hitting with his ever watchful defence. Newman and Kennedy both helped in century stands and he remained undefeated when the last wicket fell. This was the first 100 hit against the Somerset attack that season.

It seemed that Hampshire were recovering their form when in beautiful weather at Bournemouth they hit 492 against Essex. It was George Brown's turn to shine again (230 not out in six hours; Mead made 40) but Hampshire could not force a win and in the second match of the week, they were overwhelmed by the Somerset side they had just beaten so readily. Mead, with scores of 78 and 69, was the only Hampshire batsman to exceed 35 in either innings.

Nothing could illustrate more clearly the differing standards of the counties than Hampshire's fortunes in the Portsmouth cricket week. Warwickshire at least boasted Harry Howell, the fast bowler selected for the M.C.C. tour and Calthorpe who were to earn fame when they bowled out Hampshire for 15 in 1922, but on this occasion, they received a memorable hiding as Hampshire hammered their way to 616 for seven declared, a score which they were not to approach again until 1990. It was disconcerting for Warwickshire after Brown, 151, and Barrett, 148, had put on 280 for the second wicket and G. C. Harrison had been dismissed for 82 to find Phil Mead coming in at number seven with the total approaching 400. Tennyson did not declare that evening and in the morning, Mead carried his score to 102 in under two hours. Kennedy took 12 wickets and Hampshire won by an innings and 159 runs. Then came Yorkshire, thirsting for revenge for their defeat at Leeds in June, and greatly to the disappointment of the home crowd, they took it, winning by an innings and 235 runs. Percy Holmes played one of the most famous innings of the 1920s, batting for 7¼ hours. At the end of the first day, Yorkshire's score was 400 for the loss of Sutcliffe 131, who with his partner, put on 347 for the first wicket and when Burton, the Yorkshire captain declared on the second morning, the total was 585 for three — Holmes still not out at 302. The Yorkshire attack, strengthened by the presence of the Winchester College master, E. Rockley Wilson (a tantalisingly accurate slow bowler possessing just enough spin from leg to beat the bat and unexpectedly a member of the touring party to Australia) put out Hampshire very comfortably twice in the remaining day and a half (Mead ten and one).

It was little consolation to reach 447 for eight declared against Leicester at Southampton in a match spoiled by rain on the second day. Brown and Bowell put on 188 for the first wicket preparing the way for Mead who 'departed from his restrained methods and hit vigorously for 144'. Kennedy, nought for 110 against Yorkshire, prospered against Leicester: 28 overs, eight maidens, 62 runs, six wickets but there was not enough time for Hampshire to bowl them out.

So ended what Wisden described as an eventful but disappointing season for Hampshire. The same could be said for Mead. He headed the Hampshire averages but of his total of 1,773 runs, no fewer than 847 came from his six centuries, only two of which 122 not out versus Yorkshire, and 176 not out against Somerset, could really be said to have been made against quality bowling. Three of his six hundreds and 680 of his runs came after the Somerset match beginning on 7th August. His previous 29 innings produced only 1,093 runs.

These figures on their own probably account for the selectors passing him over for the tour to Australia. The side which went and received a tremendous beating in all five Tests from Warwick Armstrong's Australians, contained as its specialist batsmen, Hobbs, J. W. Hearne, Hendren, Woolley, Makepeace and Russell as well as Wilfred Rhodes who was still, at the age of 43, Hobbs' opening partner.

Picture of Newman.

63

Mead must have reflected that Hendren, who was two years his junior and had come to maturity only after the age of 30 with tremendously successful seasons in 1919 and 1920, and Russell his exact contemporary, who was regarded before the War only as a useful county bat, had overtaken him in the international stakes. The selection of Harry Makepeace of Lancashire strikes us now as odd, but at the time the only real criticism of the selectors' choice of batsmen involved the passing over of Percy Holmes.

It was Mead's misfortune that the least profitable of his succession of good seasons over 20 years, those of 1920 and 1924, both preceded English tours to Australia. Yet was form the only cause for his omission? It is in 1920 that the first complaints about the lack of speed in his run-getting occur, and only two years later Tom Webster published his famous cartoon showing grass growing over the ball as it trickled to the boundary with Mead in less than hot pursuit. The fact is that Mead had experienced a really bad war. Absence from the frontline, or any line, was not his fault, but contribution to the War Effort was the gauge by which men were measured after hostilities ceased and by that test, he was found wanting. The four years of inactivity in which he passed from the age of 27 to 31 did him no good. Omission from that touring team must have been a great blow to one whose ambition to emulate Clem Hill had been so widely publicised. How hard did one have to try?

The famous cartoonist Tom Webster in 1922.

Chapter Eleven
1921

None of the tourists, save Hobbs and perhaps Douglas and Strudwick, returned home in April 1921 with their reputations intact. By the end of that hot and crowded and disastrous English summer, only Woolley of the touring party had remedied his situation. Never, until 1993, have the Australians given English teams such a succession of hidings as they did during the Australian summer of 1920/1921. Beginning with 581 in the second innings of the first Test, they continued with 499 in the second, compiled 354 and 582 in the third, and 389 and 211 for two and 392 in the last two games, winning all five in the process. By the end, six batsmen had exceeded the century for Australia and this number did not include Bardsley, who was below his best, Taylor or Ryder who all scored heavily in other series against England. The two teams, stoat and rabbit, hunter and hunted, Australia and England, sailed to Europe in the same ship for the 1921 season. The public were prepared for Macartney and Bardsley, and for the depth of the Australian batting, and the pace of Gregory who had made a great impression here with the A.I.F. in 1919; they had not bargained for the performance of McDonald who did little in the winter tests (he had taken six wickets for 392 in the last three matches). To complete the picture, there were Armstrong who bowled phenomenally accurate deliveries which broke sometimes, a little from leg, and the prodigal Mailey whose leg breaks and googlies asked to be hit — or looked as if they did. All four bowlers captured more than 100 wickets during the 1921 season.

It was, however, Gregory and McDonald who captured the headlines. History regards McDonald, with what Neville Cardus has described as his sinuous run and beautifully smooth action, as the greater bowler, but Gregory, very tall and very long armed with a bounding approach to the wicket, was found to be more fearsome by timid opponents. By the end of the summer, that description could have been applied to most English players; only eight centuries were scored by the Australians' opponents, as against 37 hit up by the tourists.

It would not be entirely true to say that the Australians swept all before them. In May, affected by cold wet weather at Attleborough on the ground of their compatriot, Lionel Robinson, they were led on the first innings in a drawn game by a strong scratch side which included Hobbs (who made 85 before straining his thigh, thereby missing six weeks' cricket); still in May, an M.C.C. side containing only four players who played in that year's Test matches, obtained a first innings lead of 93 — but lost the match. There, the English success, such as it was, ended. The tourists swept aside Leicestershire, for whom only one player exceeded 50 in their two innings (McDonald taking 12 wickets in the match); Surrey who, of course, lacked Hobbs, Armstrong in turn taking the greatest credit and 12 wickets for 77 runs; the Army, through whose ranks Gregory burst with 11 wickets, and Essex, crushed by the eight wickets of Gregory and the seven of McDonald.

Then came the first Test match at Nottingham. It was limited to two days, not by the weather, but by the failures of the English batsmen, none of whom in the two innings could make more than 38. Gregory took six wickets for 58 in the first innings and McDonald five for 32 in the second. On the second afternoon, Australia won by ten wickets.

The second Test, at Lord's, was due to start on 11th June.

Meanwhile, Philip Mead was enjoying a good, quiet start to a season of success such as is given most of us only in dreams. Hampshire faced a truly formidable fixture list in May, meeting Middlesex, Kent, Lancashire and Yorkshire — twice. Mead's first outing brought him 76 against Oxford, and in the County Championship games which followed, against that strong opposition, he scored 465 runs in ten innings, in six of which he exceeded 50. These performances were not good enough to attract the attention of the selectors for Nottingham, although it soon became clear that they were looking to players who had not made the tour to Australia. The first three places in the batting order went to D. J. Knight, Percy Holmes, and Ernest Tyldesley who had not been implicated in the trip. When the England side for the second Test was announced, there were a number of surprises. First, 14 players were named: Tyldesley, Jupp, Rhodes, Howell and Richmond were dropped, the 49-year-old C. B. Fry, Hearne, Mead and Dipper of Gloucestershire, as well as A. J. Evans of Kent, were among the new batsmen named, while the attack was almost completely changed. Fry withdrew as he was not satisfied with his form with Hampshire (which had been by no means bad) and on the morning of the match, Lionel Tennyson, who had not even been mentioned as a prospect, was brought in. Hampshire hearts leapt, but on the day, Mead, to his intense disappointment, was omitted on the grounds of fitness. He had somehow damaged a finger, so the game does not really form part of the story. It was Woolley's match, his famous innings of 95 and 93 contrasting with the failures of his colleagues of whom only Tennyson, hitting a gallant and unbeaten 74 in the second innings, reached a higher score than 40. This time Australia won by eight wickets.

Mead was fit for Hampshire's next match, which happened to be against the Australians at Southampton. He may have been reminded of his debut, 16 years before, as Australia reached 569 for five by the end of the first day and added a further 139 on the second morning. To their total of 708, Bardsley contributed 209 before he was dismissed 'caught Fry, bowled Mead'. He and Macartney, who made 105, added 167 in 85 minutes, and J. M. Taylor also reached three figures. Tennyson rang the changes, using eight bowlers, in vain, but he at least had the satisfaction of obtaining the best bowling figures, two for 83. The Australians left themselves a little more than a day and a half in which to get Hampshire out twice. Gregory was not playing; McDonald was, but bowled only 14 overs for the wicket of George Brown. Fry, still regarded as a prospective captain in the Test matches instead of Douglas who had now lost seven games in a row, batted very well for 59 and Mead, joining him second wicket down, found the bowling of Ryder, Mailey and Hendry so much to his liking that, by the end of the second day, he had reached his 100. In the morning he was caught behind the wicket by Oldfield from the bowling of Hendry for 129. This was, up to that time, the highest score against the tourists, as indeed was Hampshire's total of 370, and the County comfortably saved the game. Some controversy surrounds this innings, as the Australians subsequently put it about that they had prompted Mead's success on the grounds that England would never win a Test match in three days with him in the side. Yet they were already two up in the series and a draw would ensure that they retained the Ashes. It is more likely that the tourists realised that the selectors were bound to call on Mead and decided to give their bowlers only limited exposure to him. Certainly, Armstrong undermined Mead's success by omitting Gregory and using McDonald so little, but immediately before the game, each had bowled over 40 overs in the second Test.

So the teams parted, the Australians to The Oval where, after something of a struggle, they beat Surrey, and from there to Leicester (wonderful; one side scored 621 and the other 69 and 68, it would be cruel to identify them); these were high days for this remarkable side as they travelled onto Trent Bridge where they defeated Nottinghamshire by an innings and 517 runs. That was the game in which, against an attack including four past or future England Test bowlers, Macartney dazzled the spectators, scoring 345 in less than four hours.

They were getting into peak form for the third Test at Leeds beginning on 2nd July.

Hampshire journeyed from Southampton to Colchester where they beat Essex by eight wickets. Mead contributed 87 and Kennedy an analysis of 23 overs, ten maidens, 37 runs, seven wickets in the Essex second innings. At this stage, Mead must have decided that something really out of the ordinary was needed to demonstrate his fitness and guarantee his selection for the third Test which was due to start at Leeds on 2nd July. Hampshire returned to Southampton on 22nd June to meet Nottinghamshire. Notts., who had yet to receive their softening up at the hands of the Australians (they went back from Southampton for that), led Hampshire by 222 runs when they reached 412 in their first innings. Mead's first effort totalled 45. In the second innings, Brown, Fry and Bowell soon fell. Mead and Hampshire's other veteran, the 50-year-old Greig, who scored 46, put on 100 runs together in 70 minutes, before Richmond's legbreaks caused something of a collapse. Mead went on to complete his own century in two hours, ten minutes, but Hampshire had scarcely cleared off the first innings deficit when the seventh wicket fell. Mead, again, monopolised the scoring in a stand of 88 for the eighth wicket with Newman who, defending stoutly, contributed only 17; Mead achieved his second hundred 75 minutes after reaching three figures and accompanied by Livsey, the wicketkeeper, took part in another long stand which eventually reached 157. By the end of the second day, Mead's score had reached 209 not out including one six and 24 fours, and Hampshire were 138 runs ahead at 360 for eight. On the third morning, Livesey, who was eventually caught for 69, and the last man, Remnant, continued the good work in support of Mead until Hampshire's score finally realised 507. Mead had put together a masterly innings of 280 not out which was, and remained, the highest score of his first class career. It was not a match-winning, or even a match-saving innings. To complete a remarkable three days, when Nottingham set about their task of scoring 286 to win in two hours 55 minutes, Newman dismissed the first five batsmen, only one of whom reached double figures, as the visitors plunged to 55 for six, but Whysall, 96 in the first innings, took part in long stands with Oates and Barrett, and as the bowling tired, Notts. scraped home by two wickets with 15 minutes to spare.

Hampshire that evening made the journey by train along the south coast and inland to Horsham where, against Sussex on 25th June, they won the toss and batted first. Mead contributed 113 to their moderate total of 260, but nobody else reached 40. Sussex, thanks to a whirlwind innings of 142 by Maurice Tate, led by 99 on the first innings. Hampshire's second innings resembled that against Nottingham. None of the first six batsmen could do better than the 18 of Bowell — except for Mead who went to the wicket fortified by the fact that he had scored 393 runs for once out in his last two innings. Supported by Kennedy and Newman, he batted on, impervious to the bowling of Arthur Gilligan, Albert Relf, Tate and Cox until he was bowled by Relf for 224.

This time the innings was a match-saving one — the game was drawn — but it is remarkable for more reasons than that: in making two 100s in a match for the third time, Mead joined a distinguished band. The feat of scoring 100 and a double 100 in the same match, had previously been achieved only by Armstrong during the previous winter and Hardinge of Kent earlier in the season. In three innings over four days, once not out, Mead had scored 617 runs. If it be argued that no victories resulted from this batting, then it should be noted that in the three Hampshire innings, only Fry and Livesey, the other Hampshire batsmen, had exceeded 50. Brown's scores, for example, were five, six and 13, and Bowell's three, 35 and 18.

Hampshire returned home to Bournemouth for the return game with Essex. Alas, on the first day, 29th June, they were involved in a series of mishaps. To begin with, Bowell, Kennedy and Livesey were held up by traffic and did not arrive, and it was fortunate that Colonel Greig, captain in the absence of Tennyson, who was playing for the Gentlemen against the Players at The Oval, won the toss. There, good luck, as well as goodwill, came to an end. Douglas bowled like a real champion and Hampshire, losing three wickets before scoring a run, proceeded to 21 for six, A. L. Hosie, Newman, Greig, A. S. McIntyre and Remnant all failing to get off the mark. At that stage, Mead, who had gone in second wicket down, sustained a cut over the eye which caused his retirement. Douglas allowed an interval for running repairs and the latecomers then arrived. Mead resuming, took his score to 45 but the others could muster only 26 between them. Essex, 360, led on the first innings by 289. Douglas followed his seven for 17 with a further seven wickets for 74 and Mead's top-score of 67 in the second innings, could only mitigate the extent of the defeat, by an innings and 55 runs.

We can be sure that Mead's leathery countenance remained just as expressionless (illuminated by the occasional grin) whether he was successfully defying Nottinghamshire or Sussex to his heart's content, or facing physical danger amid the debacle against Douglas.

What followed must have called for all his reserves of stoicism and calm. On 1st July the team for the third Test at Headingley was announced. Tennyson was now captain in the place of Douglas — and Mead was in the squad. Yet, when Hampshire began their next game against Surrey at The Oval, Mead was with them instead of playing against the Australians at Leeds. Sadly, following his injury in the Essex match, the selectors at the last minute left him out of the side. Going in for Hampshire at number six he made 52 against Surrey. Would he never have the opportunity of playing a constructive part in this Test series? He was now 34 and had not yet played in an international match at home.

The only thing to do was to keep bringing his name, form and fitness to the attention of the selectors, hard-pressed as they were following a third defeat in the series (and the eighth in a row won by Armstrong's Australians). England gave a greatly improved performance at Leeds, remarkable in circumstances in which Hobbs did not play after the first afternoon and could not bat because of appendicitis, Tennyson, the new captain, was handicapped by a split hand (but played two innings famous for his bravery), so Douglas resumed the captaincy before he in turn had to leave the field for his wife, too, developed appendicitis. Brown was also injured and had to bat in the second innings with a runner. It was hardly surprising that for all their improvement, England again slid to defeat.

Hampshire's next opponents were Sussex whom they beat by an innings and 100 runs. The Portsmouth pitch was tailor-made for Newman and Kennedy (it was prepared, according to Wisden, in a very unfortunate fashion, but Hampshire's supporters may not have agreed). Newman and Kennedy bowled unchanged, in the two innings, and only two players exceeding 27 in the match, Hosie who made 43 and Mead. In his display, described as masterly, he began by making 50 out of 53 in 35 minutes and increasing to 70 out of 93 and 100 out of 145 in 115 minutes, and by the end of the first day, batting for a little over three hours, he had reached 155 without a mistake. Next morning he added only a single when he was bowled by Tate. Sussex followed their first innings of 88 with 110 and were beaten early in the afternoon of the second day. Middlesex at Southampton proved a different proposition, obtaining a first innings lead of 89 and declaring in their second at 351 for nine to set Hampshire 441 to win. After the dismissal of Brown and Hosie for 25,

BROAD BACKS AND BATS
The Hon. Lionel (later Lord) Tennyson and Philip Mead
about to open the innings for Hampshire.

Kennedy helped Mead in a stand of 139 and the selectors must have been encouraged by the way Mead faced the fast bowling of Durston who took 12 wickets in the match. Mead in turn may have been encouraged by a collection on his behalf taken on the ground on the first day which brought him £41.11.0 (£41.55). Eventually he was bowled by Durston for 103, his seventh three figure innings of the summer in the course of which, on 12th July, he reached his 2,000 runs, the second 1,000 coming in his last ten innings. The scores: 280 not out, 113 and 224, 45 and 67, 52 and one, 156, and 12 and 103, resulting in figures of ten innings one not out 1,053 runs average 116.10, marvellous work over 20 days.

Selection for the Players against the Gentlemen at Lord's followed. By now the continuous sunshine of that summer was leading to drought conditions which produced a hard, fast pitch with a crumbled and dusty surface. First, Durston and Woolley bowled out the Gentlemen for 129. When the Players went in, Mead joined Hearne at 50 for two. Playing with every confidence, he was not out 58 overnight. Early next morning he was missed behind the wicket from the bowling of Fender and he rubbed salt into the wound by hitting the bowler for three fours in one over by means of a pulled drive, a straight drive and a hook. He added 50 to his overnight total at rather more than a run a minute before dragging a ball from Douglas onto his wicket. He scored 108 out of 228 for three. The Players, all out for 360, led on the first innings by 231 and the Gentlemen then collapsed to 109 for six. Fender entered on the scene and after the fall of two more wickets, actually added 89 in 35 minutes in the course of an unbroken stand with J. C. White. Next day the pair added a further 23 in two or three overs but nevertheless, the Players were left only 42 to win.

A quiet drawn game against Warwickshire at Birmingham followed, Mead contributing 52 to the 1,280 runs scored in the match, before Hampshire continued their little tour of the Midlands with a couple of two-day victories over Worcestershire and Leicester. Mead made 20 in the first game, but like Tennyson and Brown, was unavailable for the second game against Leicestershire which coincided with the fourth Test match at Manchester.

Mead was fit, he was in form, he was selected for England, he did play — and in that season of all seasons, the game was ruined by the weather. A persistent drizzle prevented any play on the Saturday, 23rd July. So the game was reduced to a two-day affair, something which Tennyson unhappily forgot when at ten to six on the Monday he went onto the field and declared the innings closed, an hour later than the rules for two-day matches allowed. His attempt to get the Australians to the wicket was foiled, for England, after a period of angry argument, had to return to the wicket and bat out the day. That in itself had appeared unlikely in the three earlier Tests, but on a soft, slow wicket, the efforts of Gregory and McDonald were nullified. This time Russell, who surely should have been considered before following reasonable success during the winter's Tests, and George Brown, opened with a stand of 65, and by lunch England were 143 for one wicket. Woolley then played delightfully for 41 before being caught by Pellew on the rails at wide long-on. Ernest Tyldesley was due to go in at number three, but gave way first to Woolley and then to Mead, through an inspiration on the part of Tennyson who decided that the continuing presence of a left-hander (Brown, Woolley and Mead in turn) was disconcerting to the Australian attack. At first Gregory and McDonald seemed to think that Mead would not like the fast bumper and they tried that method of attack three or four times an over against him, but only for a couple of overs. Gregory hit him on the shoulder, but Mead responded by twice hooking him off his eyebrows to the boundary; he turned to leg every ball which rose to a convenient height. Only twos or singles resulted, as Armstrong packed the leg-side field. When the Australian captain put himself on to bowl in place of McDonald, Mead showed what could be done by quick and daring footwork against the 'leg theory' bowling by moving to leg and forcing the ball away to the unguarded offside. He lost Russell bowled by Gregory for a valiant 100 at 240. Tyldesley was showing that he meant to get on with things when Mead was caught by Andrews at cover point from the medium paced Hendry. Fender and Tyldesley, who were told to get on and attack, added 98 in the hour following tea before Tennyson's misplaced declaration, and a further 21 runs after it. Wisden, however, said that Mead carried caution to an extreme and the period in which he occupied the crease was not the liveliest of England's 362 for four wickets at which, in the morning, Tennyson at once, lawfully, declared.

The Australian bowlers had been well and truly seen off. Gregory had one wicket for 79, McDonald nought for 112 and Brown's 31 was the lowest score for England. Yet there was little or no chance of a result with only one day remaining. Australia duly plodded to 175 from 116 overs. The figures of Parkin, Woolley and Charlie Parker would all have seemed impossible a few weeks before (Parkin took five for 38 from 29.4 overs, while Woolley bowled 39 overs for only 38 runs) but the game tailed off into a draw. English supporters began to feel, however, that England were putting together a team worthy of their opponents.

Opposite: On-driving during his innings of 182 not out, the fifth Test v. Australia, the Oval, 1921. W. A. Oldfield is the wicket-keeper.

Chapter Twelve
The new record by Mead

Next day at Southampton, Hampshire began the task of overwhelming Gloucestershire which took them two days. Mead contributed 63 to the County's 337 which was enough to give them victory by an innings and 83 runs. Tennyson quite often called upon Mead and himself as a little relief for Hampshire's overworked champion bowlers, but to no great effect, as that year they captured 28 victims at an average of close on 40 each between them. Newman and Kennedy needed little support, but the whole Hampshire team rallied for a wonderful finish to the season. Starting with the game against Worcester on 20th July, the team went on to win ten out of their last 11 matches.

The exception was in the game following the victory over Gloucestershire which was against Kent at Canterbury. Up to a point, the match followed a similar pattern to the one against Essex at Bournemouth. Several of the Hampshire side arrived late for the start on the Saturday before August Bank Holiday Monday, and Tennyson's decision — inevitable in the circumstances — to bat first, proved disastrous. There had been several hours rain on the Friday and Woolley and Freeman put out Hampshire in an hour and a half for 68. Mead, batting at seven, was caught off Freeman for a duck and contributed only 25 in the second innings.

He was back to form with 92 in the return with Gloucester at Clifton (another innings victory for Hampshire), and 54 at Weston Super Mare, when only J. C. W. MacBryan's 101 compelled Hampshire to bat a second time, and no-one else made more than 32 in the match. These two two-day victories earned for the team a very welcome rest, as did a third over Worcester at Bournemouth, which is memorable for the last wicket partnership of Bowell and Livsey. All seemed over when they came together at 118 for nine wickets (Mead 17). The limited Worcester attack had performed well above their rating (Pearson who, when over 40, became a fine all-round cricketer, took eight of the first nine wickets) but the last pair cut them down to size and actually put on 192 in under two hours.

The Australians too, were coasting — towards the fifth Test. They despatched Essex by an innings, then took the field against Glamorgan without Gregory or McDonald; this seemed misplaced when Riches and Bates put on 153 for the second wicket, but Glamorgan subsided against Armstrong and Macartney for 213. In both these games, the tourists made over 400 runs, but in early August the weather had temporarily broken and both the Glamorgan game and the following one against Lancashire were drawn. After disposing of Warwickshire by an innings, the tourists in turn encountered Kent in the game immediately preceding the Test. Armstrong, who insisted on short hours of play on the day preceding each international (which in those days began on a Saturday), earned widespread criticism by letting his team bat-on until late on the second afternoon while they amassed 676, and by going in again with a first innings lead of 438!

So, the Australians from Canterbury, and Mead from Bournemouth, after a welcome rest day, closed on The Oval for the fifth Test. England left out their fourth specialist left-hand bat, Hallows, and brought in Sandham, leaving out Parker for the fast bowler Hitch, which some thought strange as the weather had not recovered and the wicket was affected by it. Indeed, the start was delayed until 20 past 12 and play was interrupted for nearly three hours on that afternoon. In reality, a draw in this three-day match was already inevitable. Acute frustration spread among the crowd who became restive and barracked in large numbers in front of the pavilion. Tennyson won the toss and decided to bat. Amid the interruptions, Brown, Tyldesley and Woolley saw England to 129 for four wickets by the close of play. Mead, joined by Sandham, played defensively for the last hour or so. They faced a good or bad deal of short-pitched bowling from Gregory and McDonald. The *Times* corresponsdent, viewing the pitch early on the Monday, noted that the marks left on it by the ball as delivered by the fast bowlers actually overlapped. On the morning of Monday 15th August Mead and Sandham dispelled all fears of a collapse and took the score to 191. There was a nervous moment when Mead ran into drive Mailey and failing to reach the pitch of the ball was compelled into an ungainly half-cock stroke which, however, dropped the ball safely out of the reach of short leg; but generally he found no difficulty in placing his cuts and leg-side strokes; as so often when he was at his best, Mead's timing was so true that he hardly lifted the ball. Soon, Armstrong set a defensive field, which had the effect of reducing his scoring strokes to ones and twos. Then, with the score at 173 for two, Armstrong put himself on. He packed his leg-side field and bowled what were off-breaks to the left-hander, on or outside Mead's pads.

The departure of Sandham at 191 brought in Tennyson who immediately attacked the bowling. After watching Mead leave alone two deliveries outside his leg stump, Tennyson walked down and a brief conversation ensued. The effect was electrical: Mead thumped each of the next three to the leg boundary. While Tennyson drove powerfully, Mead continued to rely on cuts and strokes on the leg-side but continued to play with more than his usual vigour. Deep third man had a tiresome time as well placed cuts avoided him, whether he was placed square or fine. Mead gave a chance to Mailey when he had made 75, but the English pair demoralised the bowlers as they hurried their way to 121 in 90 minutes. Mead's share of these runs was 70 and he had passed his 100 when Tennyson was bowled by McDonald — the best of the Australian bowlers, who also had Fender caught for a duck, and bowled Hitch.

The score, 339 for eight, brought the sight, unwelcome to the Australians, of Douglas at number ten in the order; he allowed Mead most of the bowling and as he advanced his own score to 182, the England total rose to 403 for eight, when Tennyson declared.

Gregory bowled 38 overs for one wicket, but McDonald had nothing to be ashamed of in figures of 47 overs, nine maidens, 143 runs and five wickets.

Australia batted consistently until, early on the third afternoon, their last wicket fell at 389, only 14 runs behind England. Armstrong soon took off his opening bowlers when they made no impression on Russell and Brown in the home side's second innings, and he removed his 21 stone to the outfield, ringing the changes on Mailey and a variety of trundlers. As a newspaper blew across the Oval, Armstrong seized and read it 'to see who we were playing' but he was not likely to forget how Mead stood back and hooked him to leg or jumped out to drive or cut him to the off, nor would Gregory or McDonald.

Mead's total established a record for an England batsman in a home Test. It beat the 170 made by W.G. also at the Oval as long before as 1886. The highest score by an Australian in England at that time, and until the age of Bradman was 211 by Murdoch on the same ground in 1884. The highest score by an Englishman in a Test against Australia was R. E. Foster's 287 at Sydney in 1903. Mead's record for a home Test stood for 17 years until it was beaten three times in the 1938 series and exactly doubled by Len Hutton.

In 1921, English supporters rejoiced that the all conquering fast bowlers had been tamed, even if the wicket did not suit them. The series was already decided, and the match like its predecessor petered out into a draw.

Sydney Pardon, the editor of *Wisden*, wrote in the *Times*: 'It is sad to think that Mead should have played in only two of the five Test matches. Slight injuries, a bad finger and a blow in the head caused the selection committee to leave him out at Lord's and Leeds, but I believe that he was very anxious to play on both occasions and felt keenly disappointed . . . his good innings at the Oval may be regarded as the chief consolation of our disastrous season . . . against ground fielding less perfect than that of the Australians, he would have made considerably over 200. With all his good qualities, he is strictly utilitarian as a batsman. One admires his fine all-round hitting and his impregnable defence, but he plays so low that his style affords no joy to the eye. Woolley, when set and hitting, is as good to look at as THE MOST ATTRACTIVE RIGHT-HAND BATSMAN', the words in capitals should form the subject of a three volume treatise — by David Gower. Pardon ended his 1921 criticism 'our fielding was made to look worse than it was by the extraordinary brilliancy of the Australians . . . in order to get the solid batting that served us so well at Manchester and the Oval, we were obliged to play men who can only field near the wicket . . .'

Perhaps Tennyson should have the last word. 'When they bounced the ball at owd Mead's head, he just weaved inside it and hoisted it to the leg boundary . . . Good owd Mead . . .'

The combatants separated, each returning to the continuing round of what remained of the English season. Both Mead and the Australians had seen the best of it. Hampshire, on the other hand, continued their string of victories. In Mead's absence at the fourth Test, Kennedy carried his bat for 152 against Nottinghamshire, and while Mead was breaking records at the Oval, Newman in turn made the highest score of his career, 166 not out from the Glamorgan bowlers at Southampton, as well as taking nine wickets in the match and impelling Hampshire to their seventh success in eight games. Their season ended with three more, due largely to the bowling of Kennedy and Newman who shared 99 wickets in the heat of August.

The Australians lost to an amateur side raised by A. C. MacLaren at Eastbourne and even finished behind Sussex on the first innings, although recovering they beat them. The tourists were defeated again at Scarborough by a more conventionally composed England XI which included Mead, but they were by September very weary. They still had a further leg of their tour in South Africa to undergo that autumn and they were, perhaps collectively regrouping their resources. Mead, too, in the remaining three Championship matches on the Hampshire fixture list had only one further notable innings to play but that was remarkable enough. At Bournemouth, Hampshire dismissed Leicestershire for 71 to lead by 99 runs on the first innings. After three wickets had fallen in the second, Mead and Tennyson came together and proceeded to amass 254 runs in two hours. Tennyson, with fierce driving, took the eye but Mead scored run for run with his captain — their respective scores were Mead 154 and Tennyson 159. Hampshire completed their run of ten victories in 11 matches to finish sixth in the Championship table — which shows how poorly they had started!

Mead's scores against the tourists at Scarborough had been only five and 17, but he was more successful there for the Players, although in putting together his 86 against the Gentlemen, he was less than festive, being described by Wisden as carrying caution to the extreme. If he was weary in the legs, it is not surprising; his final figures for a great season were:

Innings	Not Out	Runs	Highest Score	Average
53	6	3179	280 not out	69.10

He easily topped the first class averages.

Mead exceeded the century ten times and, in addition, reached 50 in 16 other innings, made between 40 and 50 in five and achieved 30 in four more. Only six times was he dismissed for a single figure, including one score of nought.

Up to this time, there had been only seven instances of a batsman exceeding 3,000 runs in an English season; of these, only Tom Hayward in 1906 and his Surrey colleague, Bobby Abel, in 1901 made more runs than Mead.

Who would have believed that when he next figured in a match against Australia more than seven years would have elapsed? He was never again to play in a Test match in England.

Chapter Thirteen
Tate's Ball and another Tour

The physical strength which carried Mead through that strenuous season was put to the test during the winter. He returned home from golf or a walk feeling unwell, soon took to his bed and developed a high fever. The doctor diagnosed pneumonia, a cause of much anxiety in those days before the development of antibiotics. The onset was followed by a long crisis; he fell into a prolonged period of unconsciousness and was given up as beyond hope of recovery, although the doctors said so only after he had recovered — as he happily did.

When May arrived, it was hardly surprising that he found runs hard to get and by the end of the month he had only 272 runs to show for ten innings. The month of June, however, in spite of an oddly scanty fixture list, was a different matter. Over the years, Mead built up a formidable record against Kent — not always to the pleasure of Kent crowds — and he improved it at Southampton on 6th June as he followed 75 at the first attempt with 152, when Hampshire were set 444 to win in five and a half hours; with H. L. V. Day, making his debut, he added 219, yet the last five wickets fell for 38 to give Kent victory by 51 runs.

Worcester were still easy prey, but it was a remarkable feat by Mead to score 235 against them, following the early dismissal of Brown, Bowell and Kennedy and on a day when the next highest score was 22 by the last man, Boyes! Mead and Boyes added 127 in an hour for the last wicket before Mead's dismissal after batting over four and three-quarter hours for his 63rd century. Worcester's batsmen mustered only ten more than Mead in their two innings.

Leicester in turn were not ranked highly, but they boasted as bowlers Geary, Astill, Skelding and Alan Shipman, from whom Mead in three hours put together his third consecutive 100. That month, June, brought him 698 runs in nine innings. These figures included six not out and 24 against Warwickshire at Edgbaston. The six was quite a model innings against the attack of Harry Howell bowling at his fastest, and the Hon. Freddie Calthorpe who moved the ball both ways and came really quickly off the pitch. They were too good for the other Hampshire batsmen who totalled only five between them; of course, the Hampshire score was 15. When they followed-on 208 behind, they made a wonderful recovery after six of the side, Mead included, fell for 186. The unpredictable Brown rose to the occasion and with W. R. Shirley and then Livsey carried the score to 451. He proceeded to 172 while Livsey and Boyes added 70 for the last wicket and Livsey, too, reached a gallant century.

Howell's figures in the two innings were:

4.5	2	7	6
63	10	156	3

| and Calthorpe's | 4 | 3 | 4 | 4 |
| | 33 | 7 | 97 | 2 |

as Hampshire went on to win by 155 runs.

Tennyson, prevented by wiser heads from following Warwickshire to their next fixture, entertained the team royally on the train home and it was just as well that there was an interval before Hampshire's next match! Few remember the return match between the two teams but at Southampton at the end of July, Hampshire still had a point to make. They scored even more than at Edgbaston; 553 for seven declared of which 522 came on the second day as Mead drove and glanced his way to an unbeaten 211; after Day had reached a maiden 100, Mead and Tennyson added 150 in 75 minutes. Howell had none for 96, Calthorpe two for 109, and Hampshire won by an innings.

The County's season was full of incident, from the Surrey match in May when P. G. H. Fender, wearing glasses for the first time, celebrated with the highest score of his career, 185 in 130 minutes, actually scoring 52 from 14 consecutive deliveries, which was the principal factor in Hampshire's defeat by an innings. Tom Webster, the cartoonist, celebrated the feat with the drawing which also amusingly illustrated and perhaps added to Mead's reputation in the field to which reference has already been made in chapter ten.

Mead hit eight 100s that season and averaged 87 in June, 75 in July and 60 in August. After a warm and sunny start the weather deteriorated and never really picked up; he was less affected than most as the conditions gave more and more help to the bowlers; against Essex at Leyton in July, his contribution in five and a half hours was 179 not out from a total of 344. He went in at 41 for two, gave a chance at 20, and made no other mistake. The next most successful Hampshire player made 32. The runs he made in August were particularly hard earned — and important as another tour to South Africa was imminent. Travelling to Canterbury for the return with Kent, he played with irreproachable soundness in compiling 75 and 100 not out. There was rain about but the *Cricketer* magazine noted that he looked about the most difficult of batsmen to dislodge while grudgingly observing that 'for such a great run-getter, he is singularly unattractive . . . and almost clumsy in some of his strokes.' Was this an indication of the views of the Editor, the influential Warner? The writer continued 'perhaps no other batsman in the country is so well able to monopolise the run-getting for his side; he is not only a past master in securing the bowling but frequently seems to be the only player capable of making much headway. In this mood, the bowler seems to be at his mercy.'

That month, his scores against the very strong Lancashire bowling were 50 and 61 not out at Old Trafford and 131 at Bournemouth; he scored the 50 after Bowell and Kennedy had put on 70 for the first wicket — only Altham of the last nine, apart from Mead, made over three! The 61 not out was the

SCORE WARWICKSHIRE CARD
· COUNTY ·
CRICKET CLUB

Commence first day 12, other days 11.30   Lunch interval 1.30-2 10.   Stumps drawn 6.30

WARWICKSHIRE	1st Innings		2nd Innings	
1 Bates	c Shirley b Newman	3	c Mead b Kennedy	1
2 Smith	c Mead b Newman	21	c Shirley b Kennedy	41
3 Hn. F S.G Calthorpe Capt	c Boyes b Kennedy	70	b Newman	30
4 Quaife, W G	b Newman	1	not out	40
5 F R. Santall	c McIntyre b Boyes ..	84	b Newman	0
6 Rev E F Waddy	c Mead b Boyes	0	b Newman	0
7 B. W. Quaife	b Boyes	0	c & b Kennedy	7
8 Fox	b Kennedy	4	b Kennedy	0
9 Smart J.	b Newman	20	b Newman	3
10 Smart C.	c Mead b Boyes	14	c & b Boyes	15
11 Howell, H.	not out	1	c Kennedy b Newman ...	11
	Extras ...	2	...	10
	Total	**223**		**158**

1 wkt. for 3   2 36   3 44   4 166   5 177   6 184   7 184   8 200   9 219   10 223
1 wkt for 3   2 77   3 83   4 85   5 85   6 89   7 113   8 143   9 147   10 158

Bowling Analysis	O.	M.	R.	W.	Wd.	Nb.	O.	M.	R.	W.	Wd.	Nb.
Kennedy	24	7	74	2	—	—	...	...	...	...	...	...
Newman	12	3	70	4	...	—	...	...	...	...	...	...
Boyes	16	5	56	4	...	—	...	...	...	...	...	...
Shirley ...	3	...	21	...	...	...	...	...	...	...	...	...

HAMPSHIRE.	1st Innings		2nd Innings	
6 Kennedy	c Smith b Calthorpe	0	b Calthorpe	7
5 Bowell	b Howell	0	c Howell b Quaife W. G.	45
2 H. V L Day	b Calthorpe	0	c Bates b Quaife W. G.	15
7 Mead	not out	5	b Howell	24
1 Hon. L. H Tennyson ..	c Calthorpe b Howell ...	4	c Smart C. b Calthorpe	45
4 Brown	b Howell	0	b Smart C.	172
8 Newman	c Smart C. b Howell ..	0	c & b Quaife	12
10 W R Shirley	c Smart J. b Calthorpe ..	1	lbw b Fox	30
3 A. S. McIntyre	lbw b Calthorpe	0	lbw b Howell	5
9 Livsey	b Howell	0	not out	110
11 Boyes	lbw b Howell	0	b Howell	29
	Extras...	4		27
	Total	**15**		**521**

Scorers—G. Austin & L. Sprankling   Umpires—A. J. Atfield & B. Brown.

1 wkt. for 0   2 0   3 0   4 5   5 5   6 9   7 10   8 10   9 15   10 15
1 wkt. for 15   2 65   3 81   4 127   5 152   6 177   7 263   8 274   9 451   10 521

Bowling Analysis	O	M	R	W	Wd	Nb	O	M	R	W	Wd	Nb
Howell ...	4.5	2	7	6	—	—	63	10	156	3	—	1
Calthorpe ...	4	3	4	4	—	—	33	7	97	2	1	—
Quaife							49	8	154	3	—	—
Fox							7	...	30	1	—	—
Smart J ...							13	2	37	—	—	—
Santall ...							5	...	15	—	—	—
Smart C	..						1		5	1	—	—

The scorecard of Hampshire's famous
victory over Warwickshire in 1922.

only double-figure score in the second innings. At Bournemouth, he and Day added 157 in 175 minutes. This contributed largely to a stunning victory by an innings — Hampshire's first success over Lancashire since they rejoined the County Championship in 1895. Many said that Cecil Parkin, who shared the Lancashire bowling with Cook and Richard Tyldesley, was the most formidable bowler in the county game.

Mead's ability to leave alone — withdrawing the bat at the last moment — the delivery which, by a fraction, missed the off-stump became both proverbial and provoking. His sloping shoulders, long arms and blandly humorous aspect led a writer to compare him to a great brown bear.

This combination of technical skill and bland obduracy at Eastbourne on 26th July so frustrated Maurice Tate, the fairly well known bowler of slowish off-spinners, that he pitched in a quicker one. Tate himself wrote later that the ball nipped in from the off and clipped the top of the off-stump (it would have to be a rather wide ball to start with); Ralph Barker, depicted the ball seeming 'to put on a spurt as it pitched and to deviate right across the wicket. Mead had hardly begun to shuffle across before the ball hit the *leg* stump'. The consensus is that this wicket earned recognition for Tate's leg-cutter and was the beginning of his distinguished career as the great fast medium bowler, spearhead of England's attack for the best part of the next ten years. The metamorphosis was not as sudden as the story suggests but the delivery ranks as one of the most famous in cricketing annals. There is no doubt that Mead was taken by surprise. Years later, John Arlott asked him if he made any comment to the bowler. "Oh, no," replied Mead, "I never encouraged bowlers!"

He completed his 2,000 runs in the course of an innings of 103 against Somerset at Bournemouth in the match beginning on 19th August but could do no better than end the season with a succession of cameo performances against the background of a crumbling canvas provided by his colleagues. At Bournemouth, Hampshire trailed Yorkshire by 21 on the first innings; Mead (12) alone reached double figures as, on a drying wicket, Hampshire disintegrated to 44 in face of the bowling of Roy Kilner who took six wickets for 13 (ten for 90 in the match); to Mead he kept a perfect length on the line of the off-stump, turning the ball into the left-hander and making it jump knuckle high. For over after over, Mead battled on as wickets fell before hitting a return catch to Waddington, fast left-arm, and Hampshire were beaten by ten wickets. His 29 not out against Notts. at Trent Bridge was similarly heroic. Hampshire mustered only 73. It was in this game that the Newman incident occurred. Newman had a tendency to fiddle his fielders about, particularly if things were not going well, and the Nottingham crowd barracked. When Tennyson told him to get on, Newman suggested that his captain, in so many words, do the opposite, at which Tennyson ordered Newman to leave the field; as he went, Newman kicked down the stumps. He was seen to weep with frustration as he walked off. Fortunately, they were soon reconciled and the matter was not even referred to the Hampshire Committee.

Mead played in the major matches of the year: for the Players he exceeded 40 at both the Oval and Lord's; at Scarborough in September he scored a duck. His last appearance, on the same ground, was for the M.C.C. team for South Africa against C. I. Thornton's XI. His selection for the touring side came as Hampshire, thanks to his 131 and the bowling of Kennedy and Boyes, defeated Lancashire in two days.

Hobbs and Hearne decided that they needed the benefit of a winter at home. F. T. Mann, who as it turned out was to be one of the most popular captains ever to tour the Cape, was appointed to lead the side early in July; in addition to Mead, Brown, Kennedy and Livsey were all included. Mead's selection caused little surprise but there was consternation at the omission of Patsy Hendren and much grumbling from the north at the absence of Hallows and Ernest Tyldesley from Lancashire and of Sutcliffe and Percy Holmes.

It was, on the whole, a happy party which set sail. Woolley and Mead, who were the sole survivors of the 1913-14 tour (although Kennedy was already popular in the Dominion as a coach), were with Russell and A. W. Carr of Notts., the chief run-getters; in one respect the party resembled their predecessors. They were heartily confident of success.

They landed in Cape Town's dusty heat on 9th November 1922 and were on business there against Western Province the very next day. It was not surprising that facing a total of 145, they lost five wickets for 91 by the end of the day, but following the loss of Mann next morning, Mead and Fender regained their sea legs to add 143, mostly before lunch. Fender was bowled for 96 and Mead, too, after batting for three hours and 20 minutes was caught for 97. In the second innings he was bowled for one as M.C.C. struggled to 40 for four to win.

His scores of 73, 40 and 93 not out in the next three games were scored off bowling which was some way below first class as victory succeeded easy victory.

Livsey, terribly unlucky, soon dropped out in November after breaking a finger when the side had won seven matches out of eight. At the Old Wanderers Ground at Johannesburg they received their first check as they fought for runs against the Transvaal before a crowd of 14,000. Mead was lbw to Nupen for two, the hosts gained a substantial lead and he did not get the chance to bat again as Sandham and Russell played splendidly until a thunderstorm ended the match.

The wicket at the Old Wanderers was matting laid on hand-rolled sand. How would it respond to the rain which then fell only four days before the first Test was due to start? The immediate answer was that the pitch helped Alec Kennedy and Jupp who bowled out the South Africans, H. W. Taylor included, for 148; then Blackenberg and Francois in turn took advantage; at the drawing of stumps, eight England wickets were down for 132 — Mead

Mead, Alec Kennedy, George Brown and Walter Livsey about to embark for South Africa, 1922.

was bowled by Blankenberg for one. Only Kennedy, batting at number ten, exceeded 40 in the side's first innings. He collected another four wickets in the South Africans' second innings, but Taylor was not to be denied; in just over five hours he scored 176 and eight of the others reached double figures as the total reached 420, setting England 387 to win. Mead top-scored with 49 but the match was as good as lost at his dismissal — the eventual margin of defeat was 168 runs. England were handicapped by the inability of the injured Russell to play, but the result on 28th December came as a horrid shock to the team and its supporters at home.

The second Test at Newlands, Capetown (on a wicket composed of mat laid on grass) hardly brought much comfort as England struggled to victory by only a single run. Mead's scores were 21 and 31. It was disconcerting that for England in four complete test innings, no-one had done better than Mead's 49, and in the next game against Natal his 48 was topped only by Russell's score of 49; happily in the second innings, Russell and Sandham began getting their act together again with an opening stand of 130. Then Gilligan dismissed Taylor for a duck and Natal went down to defeat. There had been plenty of wins but little consistency among the English camp as with some trepidation they made the 800 mile train journey to Durban for the Third Test.

This was to be the first Test at the Kingsmead Ground — six months before, the site had been swampland; the hospitality was great and the humidity exhausting. There was rain there, too, which slowed up the outfield; any advantage which England gained from Mann winning the toss was dissipated when Russell, Sandham, Woolley and Carr were dismissed as the score reached 71. The temperature was 107 in the shade as Mead, second wicket down, replaced Woolley (who, like Sandham, had failed to score). Joined by Fender, he slowly improved the position but it was uphill work. Fender was unusually subdued. He batted for three hours for his score of 60 and hit only three fours while 154 runs accumulated — a record stand for the fifth wicket. At the end of the day, with Mann as his partner, Mead had scored 128 out of 256 for five wickets. Nights at Durban were, are, as humid as the day and not conducive to rest. First thing next morning he was dropped at slip, his only chance, and with Mann, whose innings of 84 included two sixes and 11 fours, he batted on into the afternoon to carry the total to 381. In all, Mead had batted for eight hours 20 minutes when he was caught by Dave Nourse from the bowling of Blankenberg. Wisden recorded that he scored with great skill on the leg-side and his defence was impregnable.

Alas, this gigantic effort proved to be nothing but the principal feature of an otherwise featureless draw, spoiled by the loss to rain of the third of the four days; that innings of 70 years ago is not entirely forgotten at Kingsmead. Between the stands grow fir trees planted by cricketers who performed memorably on the ground, their names and achievements recorded on plaques. Among them, Mead's 181, the first century at Kingsmead has an honoured place. Not far off is the racecourse where on that tour Mead's opportunities for backing losers were restricted by his success in batting.

Although he was given a rare rest in the match against Zululand at Eshowe (no Zulus unless Arbuthnot were one), he did not recover his full form, or perhaps his strength. In the drawn Fourth Test at Johannesburg, his 38 in a stand of 71 with A. W. Carr rescued the team from a poor start while back again at Kingsmead, following further phrenetic travel, in the final Test which it had been agreed should be played to a finish, he assisted Russell in a stand of 139 for the third wicket; here Mead's innings totalled 66 but the match was Russell's. He followed his 96 in the Fourth Test with scores of 140 and 111 at Kingsmead; only Taylor and Mead of the other batsmen exceeded 44 in this match which England were glad to win by 109 runs.

Russell was ill and should have been in bed rather than at the crease when he played his second innings, but his gallantry availed him nothing; a tree and a plaque stand there as a reminder that he was the first ever English batsman to exceed the century twice in a Test match — his last.

Mead's tour ended very quietly. Apart from his scores in the last two Tests (which were the ones which mattered), he achieved only 16 runs in his last six innings; so from the gratifying figures of 576 runs at an average of 52 by 6th March, he declined to 695 at 36 runs per innings by the end of the tour.

He and Russell were far and away the most successful batsmen in Tests:

Russell	436 runs	average 62.28
Mead	392 runs	average 43.55 with
Mann	281 runs	average 35.12 a gallant third

Woolley scored 115 in the Fourth Test but scored 71 runs in his eight other innings and Sandham fared no better. George Brown kept wicket in four of the Tests but averaged only nine with the bat. Kennedy excelled with 31 victims, average 19.32, against South Africa; he too, never gained selection again. The editor of Wisden declared that the prospect of beating Australia in the near future was remote and it was a thoughtful and rather disappointed party which steamed back to England to another Test-free season.

Chapter Fourteen
Success is not enough

But not tour free. Unheralded, the West Indies paid a visit in 1923. Five years were to pass before they were, prematurely, given test match status. They included George Challenor, the first top class batsman from the Caribbean, two great fast bowlers in Francis and John, and a youthful Learie Constantine. They surprised six first-class teams but Hampshire beat them easily enough by 144 runs at Southampton at the end of May. Mead contributed innings of 54 and 87 and Kennedy totalled 74 runs in addition to taking 11 wickets for 101; no other batsman on either side did half as well.

Mead no longer benefited from early season practice in matches for M.C.C. at Lord's; he had ceased to be a member of M.C.C.'s staff and the premier club no longer staged those useful practice games. He appeared in a number of representative matches: among them one for the Players at Lord's in mid-July in a match notorious for the blunders by the professionals in the field on the first day. One authority calculated that the number of missed catches approached double figures as the amateurs batted on until half an hour before lunch on the second day for 451 for nine. Amidst interruptions for rain and bad light, Mead compiled 35. He was not selected for the first Test trial in June (North v. South at Manchester in which Kennedy badly let himself down), but he did play for England against the Rest at Lord's two months later. England, led by Mann had the makings of the international side which was to do battle for England for the rest of the decade, containing Hobbs, Sutcliffe, Woolley, Hendren, Roy Kilner and Tate, as well as Mead. In fact, he played one of the worst, if not absolutely the worst, games of his life in this match. On the first morning, at backward short leg, he dropped Makepeace on 11 and lunch had not arrived when he perpetrated a horror, dropping J. C. W. MacBryan as the ball simply lobbed off his glove. The first mistake did not greatly matter but MacBryan went on to make the top score of 80. Torrential rain before lunch stopped play; on the resumption at 6 p.m., Mead at first slip lost no time in missing Makepeace again; so did Woolley. No doubt bad light and a wet ball contributed. England missed eight catches in all as the Rest lumbered to 205. After Hobbs and Sutcliffe had opened England's batting with a stand of 98, Mead succeeded Hobbs — but not for long; he was at once caught at slip. In the second innings when England were seeking 120 to win, he did no better before he was bowled by Geary. This may have been one of the occasions when, his usual calm shattered, he returned to the dressing room preceded by some seconds by his bat. The *Cricketer* observed ominously that the catching of England was deplorable and hoped that the fact would be borne in mind by the Selection Committee in 1924. Mead must have hoped that the Committee would then consist of men who had not seen the match. Yet that year he held 41 catches.

The course of the game was for Mead an ill omen. Five seasons after the end of the First World War, a new generation of cricketers was in contention for international selection. Altogether that season 33 players were selected for the two Test trials. Twenty-four of them played for England in the period up to 1930. The day of George Brown, Tennyson and Kennedy was already over. With Sutcliffe rising so readily to the top, the careers of other opening batsmen, Russell, Percy Holmes, Sandham, Makepeace and Hallows were inevitably clouded. For the moment, Hendren, Woolley, Hearne, Mead and Ernest Tyldesley were in contention for the middle ground, while Chapman, Leyland, Hammond, Jardine and Wyatt were making their reputations.

In the event, Hendren, by reason of his heavy scoring and fine outfielding, Hearne, for a time, and Woolley who still maintained a reputation as a front-line bowler, and as a batsman actually capable of winning a Test match limited to three days, were the regular choices.

Mead certainly did all he could by his form in county matches to justify his selection for representative games. The main treats in May were a century against Surrey at the Oval and that fine dual performance against the West Indians. In the course of an innings of 162 against Glamorgan, he took part with W. K. Pearce, a young Southampton solicitor, and a future chairman of the club (63), in a stand of 162 for the eighth wicket. In that match, the only other batsman to score over 38 was Stone, Hampshire's former wicket-keeper who, returning to county cricket for a solitary successful season for Glamorgan, hit up 37 and 81. His 162 was the start of another deeply purple patch for Mead; between 16th June and 23rd July his scores were: 162, 78 and 62 not out; 132, 222, 147 and 41 not out, 58 and 80 not out, 145 and 19 not out. In scoring his 132, against Worcestershire at Worcester in three and a quarter hours, he added with Newman (130) 177 for the fourth wicket in 140 minutes, and then Newman and C. P. Brutton followed with 120 for the sixth wicket in 70 minutes. Hampshire won that game and the following one against Warwickshire by an innings; Mead's contribution to the latter was a monumental innings of 222 which occupied five and three-quarter hours of pulling and driving and included 24 fours. With another young amateur, W. R. de la C. Shirley (64) he added 197 for the ninth wicket to help Hampshire on their way to 511. Apart from Tennyson's innings of 73, the next highest score in the whole game was 54 as Warwickshire made further atonement for Edgbaston — 1922.

If these two centuries were made against bowling which was not of the highest quality, the same could not be said of Mead's next innings which was against Sussex. Tate and Gilligan had risen to their brief and wonderful period of dominance of English batsmen; in the preceding few weeks the two had bowled out Essex for 115 and 110, Northants 154 and 73, the powerful Notts. side for 94 and 121, Glamorgan for 86 and 91, and Gloucester for 102 and 105 . . . Then to Brighton on 11th July came Mead. Tennyson sent in Sussex who tailed away from 94 for two at lunch to 160 all out. After the early loss of three Hampshire wickets, Mead, joined by Tennyson, added 105 in 70 minutes at the end of the first day. Next morning, Mead enlarged his score from 78 to 147, although his six colleagues who succeeded Tennyson made only 33 between them. Then at the end when Hampshire went in to get 64 to win, five wickets fell for 51 as Mead yet again held the remnants together, scoring 41 not out and steering Hampshire to victory without further loss. Yet again his performances stood out in contrast to those of the others of whom Tennyson alone in two innings made over 20.

In this way, Mead repeated his triumphs of the previous two seasons by scoring three 100s in succession and totalling 501 runs in the three innings. The distinction of the feat lay in the fact that Tate that year took 219 wickets at 18 runs each and Gilligan 163 at 17.50.

Mead was not done yet: as Hampshire defeated Notts. by four wickets, he contributed 58 and 80 not out; again, as Middlesex succumbed by eight wickets on 21st, 23rd and 24th July 1923, he played a masterly innings of 145 compiled in four and a half hours out of Hampshire's 443. Ten men reached double figures but only Kennedy reached 50. Over those five weeks his figures showed: 11 innings, three times not out, 1,146 runs, average 143.25. Against Yorkshire at Leeds he added a seventh century — it occupied six hours.

The rest of the season was an anti-climax, epitomised by a double failure, nought and 35, against Kent and 18 and 12 in another drawn game versus Lancashire. Perhaps after 18 months of almost continuous cricket, he and his legs were content to let the season fade away with two scores of 40 and a 50 in the cricket festival at Blackpool. Hampshire again finished sixth in the County Championship.

Only Hendren finished above Mead in the first class averages:

	No. of Innings	Not Out	Highest Score	Total runs	Average
Hendren	51	12	200	3010	77.17
Mead	52	8	222	2604	59.18
G. Challenor (W.I.)	35	5	155	1556	51.86
Makepeace	53	6	203	2310	49.14
Hearne J. W.	36	4	232	1519	47.46
Sandham	52	6	200	1894	41.17
Sutcliffe	60	6	139	2220	41.11
Woolley F. E.	56	5	270	2091	41.00

The Hampshire averages show all too clearly how much the county depended on Mead, Kennedy and Newman:

	No. of Innings	Not Out	Highest Score	Total runs	Average
Mead	43	8	222	2265	64.71
Kennedy	48	4	163	1146	26.04
Brown	40	1	120	941	24.12
Newman	43	3	130	947	23.67
Bowell	34	2	108	735	22.96

	O	M	R	W	Average
Kennedy	1201	328	3150	156	20.19
W. R. Shirley	199.4	21	733	31	23.64
Boyes	270.2	70	779	32	24.34
Brown	210.2	27	641	26	24.65
Newman	1114.4	207	3527	139	25.37
Mead	179	41	535	14	38.21

A. Kennedy

Chapter Fifteen
Need for Renaissance

Mead's two least satisfactory seasons between 1911 and 1930 were those of 1920 and 1924 and each preceded an English tour to Australia. In 1924 there was never really any chance that he would be selected. Wretched performances early in the season ensured that he was not chosen for the first Test match against South Africa and then Hobbs, Sutcliffe, Hendren and Woolley scored so readily against the tourists who brought with them the most impoverished attack (except that of the Pakistanis in 1962) ever to be butchered around the county circuit, scoring so many unmerciful runs that the selectors did not need to look any further. The outcome of the series was overwhelmingly comforting for English supporters and must have been intensely galling for Mead who in form would have inflicted as much damage on the visitors' bowling as anyone.

But he was not in form. In May, seven innings brought him only 108 runs, and while he found some sort of consistency in June, by the half-way stage of the season he had fewer than 500 runs to his credit without a single century and an average of 31.

When in the second half of July he at length ran into form, English cricket was changing gear; the selectors looking for supporters for Hobbs, Sutcliffe, Woolley and Hendren on the Australian tour, chose Sandham, Hearne and A. P. F. Chapman. That was reasonably predictable, but having other places to fill they called upon Whysall of Nottinghamshire and the Kent amateur, J. L. Bryan. Whysall was a very sound and well thought of opening bat but he was only seven months younger than Mead. No wonder that around this time Mead's aspect was sometimes that of a man with a grievance.

Not all was gloom and doom. The second half of the summer brought him 1,114 runs in 21 completed innings, including a period beginning in mid-July when he accumulated 884 runs in 12 innings, once not out, including three 100s. His final figures for the season: 45 innings; six not outs; 1,644 runs; average 42.15, indicate the paucity of his run-getting over the rest of the summer. It was admittedly one of the wettest seasons on record but that did not prevent Andy Sandham increasing his average from 41 to 59 or Hobbs rising from 37 to 58 or Woolley from 41 to 49, while the improvement in Sutcliffe's figures was much the same. Hendren's total fell from 3,010 runs at 77 an innings in 1923 to 2,100 but he still managed to average 56 for each visit he made to the wicket. They all went to Australia as did Whysall who now reached the top flight, having completed the season with 1,852 runs, average 46. This left Ernest Tyldesley and Mead like great fish snapping their jaws ineffectively in a pond. Whysall doubled as reserve wicket-keeper. He had a perfectly satisfactory tour; Bryan played a very minor part but that was true of most of the party. Hobbs, 573 runs, average 63, and Sutcliffe 734 at 81 runs an innings dominated the batting, scoring between them more runs than almost all their colleagues put together; Woolley scored 123 in the first Test but only 200 runs in his other eight innings, while Hendren, 74 in the first, 92 in the Third Test, and 65 in the Fourth, shone fitfully. Whysall twice scored over 70 in the Tests but the tour selectors still preferred Hearne when he was fit, although he and Woolley were displaced as top-line spinners by the rise of Roy Kilner of Yorkshire who was on that tour the only worthy supporter of Maurice Tate — as dominating in attack as were Hobbs and Sutcliffe with the bat. The Tests were all played to a finish — a series of situations to which Mead's skills were totally adapted.

As it was, England sank to four defeats out of five games, by 195 then 81 runs, diminishing to 11 runs in the third test before we won the fourth by an innings and 29. Hats were thrown in the air but then a new name, Grimmett, stepped in with figures of five for 45 and six for 37 and overwhelmed England on his debut in the fifth match.

Meanwhile, another team from England, led by Tennyson, was touring South Africa. It included five players who played for England against Australia and other Test players in Kennedy, MacBryan and Astill but not Mead. Why Tennyson did not take Mead with him remains a mystery. The Hampshire committee in an attempt to impose some discipline on their gifted but ageing professionals insisted that their leave be sought and obtained before a member of the staff made a tour overseas. The Club minutes contain no reference to Mead seeking permission — but there is no suggestion that Kennedy had permission either and he did make the trip (and was not much less successful than he had been with M.C.C. two years earlier).

Tennyson, like Mann before him, lost a great deal of money as a result of the trip. Perhaps Mead felt that the terms were not good enough or that he saw enough of his captain summer by summer or it may have been the other way round. Mead was happily at home for the birth of his only daughter, Phyllis, his 'little pet' in April 1925.

Hampshire's fortunes declined in the mid-'20s. From seventh in 1923, down to 12th in 1924; a rise to ninth in 1925 looks like an improvement until a glance at the Championship table shows Essex and Warwickshire above them, and such opponents as Gloucester and Northamptonshire, whose resources were much more limited, winning more matches. The professionals found it harder and harder to pull their acts together simultaneously. Brown did not have a decent season between 1921 and 1926; from 1924, Newman fell away. Boyes took years to fulfil the promise of 1922. These factors all threw greater responsibility on to Mead and Kennedy — and it showed.

For Mead, 1925 was like 1924 only more so; longer spells of success were interspersed with noticeable periods of failure.

The opening weeks of 1925 were fine and unusually hot but in July, with holidays imminent, the weather broke and the rest of the season was chilly and wet. In spite of the favourable conditions early on, Mead's only innings of note in May was 162 in a match with Gloucestershire, but his runs for the month were no more than 269. Then came an encouraging improvement as after scoring 58 against Northants at Portsmouth in the first week of June, he was not dismissed again for a single-figure score until 13th July when he reached his 1,000 runs; even so, he had still only the one 100 to his credit.

Then the second half of July brought him three more, against Surrey, Notts. and a prodigious double century against Worcestershire at Bournemouth (213) in the course of which he scored a 100 before lunch on the second day when he increased his score from 105 to 205. A steady accumulation of good innings in early August completed a spell of 981 runs in 13 completed innings which averaged out at 75. More than half his season's total came in that spell; his figures for the Championship were no better than: 44 innings, four not out, 1,854 runs, average 46.35.

Something was a little wrong in those two seasons; no more appearances for the Players at Lord's or the less important match at the Oval; no returns to Scarborough for the Festival. In 1925, his only game outside the County Championship (there was no touring side that year) was for Arthur Gilligan's XI against Tennyson's XI in the Folkestone Festival where his score (88) took his season's total to 1,942. Even his prowess in the slips declined for from as many as 41 catches in 1923 his record fell to 11 in 1924 and 19 in 1925. His approach to the game changed and this was noticed. At the end of the season of 1921, the Hampshire Committee had given the match-winners, Mead, Kennedy and Newman, each a present of 20 guineas (£21), and in the spring of 1923 they held a dinner for Mead and the other Hampshire players who had toured South Africa. At the end of that summer, the two sides of Hampshire's cricket industry met in less friendly circumstances at the request of the professionals. They wanted a minimum annual wage instead of the prevailing system of payment by the match and winter wages; the authorities presented their weightiest representatives to face Brown, Kennedy, Livsey, Mead and the spokesman, Newman. He began by putting forward the proposal for the minimum annual wage on the basis that if it were accepted, the professionals would not be penalised if they were ill or out of form.

Newman may have been the choice as representative but Mead interposed "we want £400 a year minimum, guaranteed." His intervention was ill-timed. Dr. Bencraft, still Chairman, was sure that the Committee would not agree; they might manage £200 and the Committee would expect valuable service for the wages paid. The professionals' match fees were £7 a match for a 28-match season (resulting in a maximum fee of £196) together with whatever talent money and winter pay the Committee awarded in their discretion, so Bencraft's proposition sounded unpromising. Their approach had backfired. Bencraft declared that new regulations would be drawn up for the professionals. To be fair, he added that he felt sure he could guarantee that a professional *playing in all the matches* would not be worse off under any new scheme than under the existing arrangements and that it might be possible to insure players against accident. Newman had the presence of mind to ask for a draft of the regulations as the Secretary, Colonel Greig, wryly observed.

Newman duly received his copy of the proposals while the Committee awarded winter wages to the old stagers at the current rate of £70.

On the morning before the next Committee meeting, Mead ran into Colonel Greig who asked him whether he preferred the old arrangements or the new draft; Mead replied that he did not like either, he wanted a guaranteed annual salary of £400. The Secretary, who had known and played cricket with Mead for the best part of 20 years, in the intervals between his dealings with all manner of men in the course of a long military career in India, replied that he had better come and lay his views before the Committee that afternoon and Mead gave him to understand that he would. When it came to the point, only Kennedy attended (he was in line for a benefit) and accepted the new regulations on his own behalf. The Committee resolved that Mead must abide by his existing contract — they did not allow him the luxury of unilateral alteration which they were giving themselves by their new regulations!

When the Committee adopted these new rules in January 1924, they rewarded the professionals for their rash approach by taking advantage of the fact that a number of benefits were in the offing: Kennedy, who had first played for Hampshire in 1907, and Brown (1908), were awaiting theirs; Bowell (1902) had received his long before as 1914 (it brought him £425); Newman's (debut 1906) was fixed for 1924. The new conditions gave the Committee complete discretion to give or withhold a benefit; payment by the match and separate winter pay were to continue. The increased rates of pay specified by the Committee (£8 for a home match and £10 for playing away), coupled with the new privilege of reimbursement for third class train fares for games away from Southampton, were to be the maximum rates. If a player was 'out of form due to lack of condition or effort', the payment could be reduced. Talent money, awarded by the Committee at the end of the season, would be granted only to a player who had signed his contract for the preceding season AND kept his County qualification during the ensuing winter; if he lost it, any bonus which he had received for services rendered would be clawed back as if it were only a loan, recoverable 'as a debt due at law'.

None of the professionals quit, but the master and man approach did not bring out the best in Mead or the others, as diminishing payments for talent money demonstrate:

	1923	1924	1925
Mead —	£43 + £10 bonus	£23	£27 + £10
Kennedy —	£39 + £10 bonus	£14	£17 + £10
Newman —	£25 + £8 bonus	£13	£11 + £10
Brown —	£17	£15	£16
Total for all professionals:			
	£157	£97	£123

93

In September 1925, the Committee awarded Kennedy a benefit — but only on condition that he signed a new seven-year contract — if they wanted him that long. The match selected was against Surrey early in July 1926 and it brought Kennedy £1,095. In the same year, Roy Kilner of Yorkshire received £4,016, a recordbreaking sum. Mead was no longer receiving his retainer from the Cricket Bat Company, which had died in 1925, or the fees for playing in the representative games. He had a young family to support and was living in comfortable fashion, having moved to his larger house in Westridge Road, Portswood, Southampton, where he maintained for a time two maids and a gardener, and he was the proud owner of a bullnose Morris car. His pay was by the standards of the time not to be despised, but he was living to the limit of it, even with the added support of his income from Mead and Toomer.

In January 1926, he encountered Sir Russell Bencraft (he had been knighted by King George V in the New Year's Honours' List for 1924 for public services) and took the opportunity to ask for a second benefit. Sir Russell, like Colonel Greig, was an experienced man-handler, schooled through years of administration of public health and the poor law, and of dispensing justice from the Bench. He no doubt made a non-committal reply. The riposte came loud and clear from the Committee via Colonel Greig; from it Mead learned exactly where he stood. The Secretary wrote:

'Private and Confidential   9th January 1926

Dear Mead,

I am directed by the Committee to inform you, in response to your verbal application to Sir Russell Bencraft, that having regard to your valuable services to the County, which they have always been most anxious to recognise, they are strongly in favour of granting you a second Benefit Match, without guarantee, in 1930.

'It must, however, be understood that the decision upon the subject must ultimately depend upon your continuing to play for the County in accordance with the Agreement of 17th October 1919 and upon their being satisfied that you have, to the utmost of your power, used your influence and example amongst the Players to maintain that spirit of loyalty to the Club and harmony amongst the Team that is essential to the wellbeing of Hampshire County Cricket.

'I am to add that they have noted with regret in the past that you have generally at times had the air of a man with a grievance, and trust that the proposed recognition of your unusual services will dispel that trait in the future, which obviously has not worked either for the good of or for the harmony of the side.

'Wishing you every success in the coming season.

Yours faithfully,

J. G. Greig, Lt.-Col.

Secretary H.C.C.'

94

The text says much about the way Mead had performed his duties over the preceding couple of seasons. The Committee, well aware of the strength of their position compared with that of a professional who was approaching his 40th year, offered a combination of carrot, at the end of a very long pole, and stick.

Mead's reaction can only be guessed at, yet he remained with Kennedy far and away the dominating force in the County's cricket. In 1925, the *Cricketer* noted 'Mead . . . proved himself about the most difficult batsman to dislodge when the ball is turning and the wicket not too fast'; only Tennyson joined him in scoring 1,000 runs for Hampshire and averaging over 30. Brown and Bowell reached totals of only 962 and 769 runs. They, and most of their colleagues, suffered at times from Tennyson's preference for frequent changes in the batting order, not only from match to match but sometimes innings by innings, and there was muttering in the professionals' dressing room about the captain's strategic and tactical ability. In the Committee room there was a definite sense that the professionals were not giving of their best.

A typically gingerish stroke early in an innings. 1924.

95

Chapter Sixteen
Out of the Rough

The choices available to Mead were to soldier on as before — a pretty satisfactory second best; he had still, after all, finished tenth and 11th in the first class averages in 1924 and 1925 and it was unlikely that the County would wish to do without him if he maintained something near that standard; or to accept the hint and consider whether some change in approach was preferable and work to secure the half-promised benefit; or to give up. This last was not really an option. In those days, no other county would have offered terms to a professional who left his county following a breach with his committee and no committee man would put himself out to help a professional in that situation find a job. He took some time to make up his mind to judge from the way he played his cricket.

Hampshire's fixture list for 1926 was oddly formed; the first four County games were all played away from home and there were only five games (two at home) in June. As this period of much travelling coincided with the General Strike in May, it must have been a tiresome period for strikers of the ball. When Hampshire visited Edgbaston, only eight players arrived, and urgent measures were taken — Mead opened the bowling and three players were despatched from Southampton, but they arrived in time only to endure two days of rain.

In May and June, Mead's form was similar to that of 1925; he reached 50 only once in his first eight innings in a spell which ended with scores of three and nought at Southampton when Hampshire were trounced by Kent to the tune of nine wickets towards the end of May.

Then everything changed. In the next game at Portsmouth against Somerset, Mead reached 87 when no-one else but Kennedy made over 30, and from then on he never looked back — for several years. An innings of 65 contributed to a ten-wicket defeat of Sussex at Southampton; fortified by this victory, Hampshire travelled to Gloucester and on to Knowle in Somerset. At Gloucester, Mead, missed when one, hit up 109 in two-and-a-half hours; at Knowle, which Wisden described as a well appointed ground in South Bristol, he played a much finer innings after the speedy dismissal of the opening pair. He was very cautious at first and took two-and-a-quarter hours to reach 50 but then ran into his best form. Bowell helped him in a stand of 82 for the third wicket and after Tennyson had knocked up 49 in 35 minutes, Kennedy (39) stayed with Mead while 93 runs were put on in an hour, and W. K. Pearce, who made only 16, saw another 68 added. Mead gave no chance until just before his dismissal for 161 and hit 26 fours, many of them beautifully timed drives. Rain then ruined the finish.

At Southend a week or so later, he varied 'plodding defence' with clever placing all round the wicket. He did not contribute much to poor Kennedy's benefit match — only the Saturday gave a full day's play; when Mead was settling down for a suitably memorable innings, Fender, the Surrey captain, artfully put on Bob Gregory, who was little known then as a bowler (he bowled leg-breaks which turned a little — sometimes, but did keep a length); Mead played for the non-existent break. Kennedy batting at number nine made the top score, 70 not out, towards Hampshire's total of 328 but when Surrey batted he missed Hobbs, who had then made only 22, and the great batsman proceeded to enliven the day by adding with Sandham 106 in only 70 minutes. This was only a curtain-raiser as Hobbs and Gregory put on in a little over two hours no fewer than 276. This made the day memorable for Kennedy whose bowling figures were one wicket for 92 for 24 overs; Newman's one for 102 from 21; Mead sent down two overs for 15 runs.

In the next game, he had Tiger Smith, still Warwickshire's wicket-keeper, caught by Livsey for one. His innings of 75 contributed to Hampshire's total of 465 and a victory by nine wickets. However, it is his bowling which comes to the fore for the time being. Against Notts. at Southampton he bowled six overs for seven runs. When Hampshire moved on to Hove, he alone withstood the bowling of Tate (bowled Bowley, 101) and Hampshire won by 82 runs. In the first innings of Sussex, the bowling figures included:

	Overs	Maidens	Runs	Wickets
Kennedy	14	6	21	0
Newman	23	6	79	7
Mead	1	0	10	0

While Hampshire were playing Yorkshire at Bournemouth, the Hampshire Committee met urgently there to discuss two complaints by Tennyson: that Mead had not tried his hardest when Tennyson told him to bowl at Brighton and that Kennedy had sulked when the skipper took him off. Called before the Committee, Mead explained that he had been fielding in soft shoes which were a handicap to him when bowling. Both players took the opportunity to complain about some of their captain's tactics. The President, Colonel Heseltine, observed that no captain was infallible and no professional indispensable, and there the matter rested. Mead's bowling figures against Yorkshire, two overs for ten runs were unremarkable but his batting, with that of Newman, easily saved the match.

The timing of that squabble was particularly unfortunate as up to that point Hampshire had been undergoing a resurgence and by the end of July, with a record of 20 matches played, ten won and only two lost, stood third in the Championship table; in August, Hampshire failed to win any of their last eight games, while Mead's fortunes soared — and how he flourished! Against the attack of Larwood, Barratt and Sam Staples, England bowlers all, at Trent Bridge he completed another splendid 100 in two-and-a-half hours; after one of the more tiresome journeys from Nottingham, Hampshire arrived at

Canterbury for their August Bank Holiday match with Kent. No-one could better Mead's 27 in a weary struggle to 144 (Freeman five wickets for 43) to which Kent replied with 412, to which Hardinge and Chapman contributed centuries.

Before tea on the second afternoon, Hampshire were batting a second time; 268 runs in arrears, they made the feeblest response, losing Brown, Newman, Kennedy, Tennyson, Judd and McBride for only 59. Mead was barely into double figures when he was joined by the young Portsmouth amateur, J. P. Parker; it was Parker's first season of county cricket and the crowd of 12,000 were, of course, hotly enthusiastic for Kent, but in the two hours after tea he and Mead added no fewer than 194 runs. Parker was a strong driver and puller who achieved great power off the 'wrong' foot. The climax of the partnership came on the third morning when he three times drove Freeman for six; 50 minutes batting brought them another 74 runs, taking the score to 329 and their partnership to 270 in something under three hours. Parker's score was 156 which he never bettered. Hampshire were still only 59 ahead but Livsey helped the tireless Mead in another century partnership. When the last wicket fell, Mead remained undefeated. His total, 175 not out, his seventh century of the season and the 91st of his career, was chanceless and, described as brilliant, extended over five-and-a-half hours. But there was no forgiveness for that first innings failure. Woolley and Chapman hit up 135 in only an hour to win the match for Kent. 'And there were giants in the land in those days . . .'.

Ten days later, Mead performed another rescue, adding 214 runs for the third wicket with H. L. V. Day at Bournemouth against Middlesex. The second match of the Bournemouth week against Lancashire brought some incredible cricket. When each side had completed an innings, only Mead, 94 not out, had succeeded in scraping together more than 26. His four-hour marathon ensured Hampshire a first innings lead of 125. In turn, Hallows (106) and P. T. Eckersley (99) were the only batsmen to make over 20 in Lancashire's second innings; no-one was up to it as Hampshire subsided for 49 to lose by 97 runs. When they played Lancashire again at Old Trafford, Mead's unbeaten 132 in the second innings (dropped first ball, he batted four-and-three-quarter hours) did not prevent defeat, but he had the satisfaction of having that dour defender, Harry Makepeace, caught.

On the other hand, a further memorable performance in a high-scoring game at Worcester nearly gained Hampshire a victory which had it come off would have ranked with their win over Gloucestershire at the end of the season of 1990; the home side led on the first innings by 200 runs, thanks to Fred Root's eight wickets for 46, and in the second declared at 307 for four, M. K. Foster scoring a century in each innings. So Hampshire were set 508 to win. Two wickets fell on the second evening but, as if the first two days had not been eventful enough, the third was even more remarkable; Livsey stayed until the score reached 92 and his was the only wicket to fall all day, for Bowell and

Mead stayed together for three hours and 50 minutes and in that time added 248. Bowell's 132 was his last century in first class cricket; Mead, 177 not out, reached his 94th. Hampshire earned an honourable draw.

The last match was also drawn after Mead (90) and Tennyson (111) had added 152 in only 90 minutes.

In spite of an August very deficient in victories, Hampshire still finished seventh in the Championship table, a position which they would not reach again for nearly 30 years, and they provided marvellous entertainment; of their total of 25 centuries, Mead hit ten (only two at home); Brown, at last recovering his good form of 1920, made six, and ten of that season's players reached at least one 100; others, Kennedy, Livsey and Boyes, achieved the feat in other seasons. Newman, who was now 43, although not many knew it (Wisden had him born in 1887) like Brown enjoyed a resuscitation in 1926 and captured 145 wickets in county games, in addition to scoring well over 1,000 runs. Boyes, too, captured over 100 wickets, but the pity was that Kennedy could muster only 79.

Nothing succeeds like a large total of runs and Mead had given reassurance to the Committee with a total of 2274 runs at an average of nearly 65 an innings.

A well-informed observer will recall that no mention has been made of the Australians. They were visitors here in 1926 but they hardly impinge on the story of Mead. He played against them only once, for the County in the middle of May, when his scores were six and 46. Gentlemen and Players, the festival games, and the Test matches all passed him by. His return to top form came too late for him to displace any of the, by now, established England batsmen — Hobbs, Sutcliffe, Hendren and Woolley. The Tests in 1926 were still limited to three days in spite of the obvious limitations of that arrangement in 1921. Mead's methods were not thought to be suited to such games at a time when it was necessary to place the emphasis on attack if England were to recover the Ashes won by Australia in 1920-21. If ever circumstances merited the inclusion of Frank Woolley, they were present in 1926 — and he was the man in possession.

England had to wait until the fifth and last game in August at the Oval before they could finally get to grips with Australia in a game which it was agreed should be played to a finish. In the first of the series, there was only 50 minutes play; the second produced high scoring from Hobbs (119), Sutcliffe (82), Woolley (87), Hendren (127 not out) and Chapman with an unbeaten half century, but like the third in which it was Australia's turn to score heavily, ended in a draw, as did the fourth, killed by rain which limited play on the first day to less than a couple of overs. Amid this frustration only Tyldesley, following an extraordinary feat of scoring, four 100s in succession, six in seven innings, seven in nine and nine in 12 between 26th June and 31st July, forced his way into the Test team for the fourth match of the rubber and scored

81 assisted by three dropped catches; he then gave way to Chapman who was appointed captain for that memorable fifth game which England won to reclaim the Ashes. Hobbs and Sutcliffe shone as openers, Hendren and Woolley followed, Chapman had the fifth place, save for Tyldesley's brief intervention, and G. T. S. Stevens and A. W. Carr, captain in the first four tests, held the amateur line. Roy Kilner (until he was replaced in the final game by his Yorkshire colleague, Test selector Wilfred Rhodes) and Maurice Tate were the all-rounders. There was no place for the 39-year-old Mead in spite of his return to his very best form, as the 39-year-old Woolley completed a run of 52 consecutive Test appearances.

If Mead felt frustrated at his non-selection in a season when he rose to be fifth in the first class averages behind Hobbs, Sutcliffe, Tyldesley and Hendren, no doubt Hearne, dropped after the first match in which he did not bat, and Carr, who batted only once in his four Tests that summer before he gave way to Chapman, shared his feelings.

At the end of the season, the *Cricketer*, still edited by Warner, commented 'on all types of wickets and against every sort of bowling, Mead is probably the most difficult batsman in the country to dislodge; his utter air of nonchalance, coupled with his backing up with his legs, makes him infuriating to bowlers. He was distinctly unfortunate in not being chosen for a representative game.' It had been in Warner's power to remedy that situation but that pat on the shoulder from the Chairman of selectors was all Mead had for his comfort in 1926.

Facing the bowler, about 1927. George Brown behind the stumps.

Chapter Seventeen
Success to Success

As Hampshire did not win a match in 1927 until 7th June and then had to wait over six weeks for the second, they were never likely to play a major part in the cricket scene. For the first time for 20 years they were out-gunned in game after game, their season was miserably wet, indeed except for 1958 or 1985, it would be hard to find one less encouraging to cricket, and their batting disintegrated; not really very surprising as it was so difficult to get going. In three out of four of the County's games at the end of 'flaming' June, not even one innings a side was completed. Six other games were completely spoiled.

All these acted as a spur to Mead who as never before stood alone. Collapses, damp uncovered pitches, long hours in the pavilion — and the opportunity for a substantial number of not outs — all combined to create conditions which seemed ideal for him. As so often, he started unremarkably, scoring 261 runs in eight innings while Hampshire were trounced in turn by Middlesex, Sussex and then Lancashire who at Liverpool lost only three wickets in winning by an innings. Newman was not fit to bowl in these matches and Kennedy had conceded over 100 runs in three consecutive innings, when on 26th May at Sheffield Mead went to the wicket in face of Yorkshire's total of 360 to begin another purple patch. He was undefeated with scores of 75 and 37 as Hampshire just saved the follow-on and achieved a fairly creditable draw. The next day at Southampton, two giants stood out above the pygmies; Walter Hammond completed his 1,000 runs during the month of May (he was the first batsman to achieve this since Grace in 1895) and went on to celebrate by completing in two hours 30 minutes an innings of 192. This was all the more remarkable as none of his colleagues reached 50 in a total of 320. Hampshire then gained a lead of 101. Mead's score was 187. He and Kennedy together put on 102 in 75 minutes and with Bowell at the other end, a further 100 was added in even time. Tennyson was one of three batsmen to reach a century on the last day when a draw became inevitable.

Four centuries dominated the game with Essex. The first two came substantially from the bowling of the overworked Kennedy, while Jack Russell (161) and H. M. Morris (162) shared in a brilliant partnership of 233 in under two-and-a-half hours. Mead broke the stand but Douglas did not declare the innings closed until 584 for nine. Although conditions were obviously entirely favourable to batsmen, Hampshire failed and Mead (49) alone reaching 20 then followed-on their innings. It looked as if they might need a third opportunity to make a game of it when Brown, Newman, Kennedy and Tennyson fell in nine overs to Nichols' bowling at a great pace. The first real help for Mead came from Parker who attacked the bowling in a stand of 126 for the fifth wicket which apart from the valuable runs occupied a precious 105 minutes; after his dismissal, the left-hander completely dominated a succession of useful partners, as the young pro Gibbons, W. E. N. Scott, an amateur trialist from the Isle of Wight, and F. A. Gross in turn kept up an end. Mead batted on and on without mistake for over five-and-a-half hours. His determination was never more noticeable than when he faced Nichols in a performance reminiscent of his assault on F. R. Foster 14 years before. He had just completed his second 100 and was undefeated when the last wicket fell. Hampshire's score was no more than 381; no-one save Parker, apart from Mead, had scraped over 30 and Hampshire lost by an innings and 26. This was Mead's 97th century. A week or so later came a repetition in a minor key at Chelmsford where his innings of 79 and 22 did not prevent an Essex victory, this time by 59 runs.

The only rest for Tennyson and company came on the journey to Portsmouth on the Southern Electric. Hampshire, a little frayed by their unrelenting schedule now faced Yorkshire who were smarting after a beating from Middlesex. Perhaps Brown and Mead thought it was time for Hampshire to show the aggressive but slightly off the boil opposition a thing or two. In the previous season, Mead had plodded to a century against Macaulay and Rhodes in six-and-a-half hours. If they had dared him to do his worst, he and Brown rose to the challenge. After Newman, opening with Brown, left at 76 to be followed at once by Kennedy, the two left-handers steadied themselves for a long haul. As to the rest of that day, Wisden reports: 'for such an exhibition of deliberation as that given by Brown and Mead it would be difficult to find a parallel. Settling down at once to a display of dogged resistance, these famous left-handers succeeded to such an extent that they defied the Yorkshire bowling for six-and-a-quarter hours' (the length of Mead's stay). 'Each man occupied four hours over his 100 but even with that object attained, neither player relaxed for a moment the great care and watchfulness that characterised his cricket.' More prosaically, Yorkshire bowled defensively to a defensive field. Wilfred Rhodes bowled with all the fieldsmen on the leg-side, save two, placed deep at extra cover and long off. By the end of the first day, they had carried the score to 297 for two and the next morning they increased this by a further 131 runs. By this time, Mead was finding small cracks and crevices and by skilful placing of the ball outscored Brown.

Finally, Mead was caught by Sutcliffe at short leg from the bowling of Rhodes (a short leg after the addition of 344 without the loss of a wicket!). The stand created a record for the third wicket, both for Hampshire against anyone and by any side against Yorkshire. Mead's score was 183 and Brown, at the wicket for eight-and-a-half hours, reached 204 before Sutcliffe threw down his wicket; whether Brown was attempting a quick single to short leg at the time is not clear. Hampshire's innings was declared closed on the second afternoon. The Hampshire captain did not complain at the slow progress of the first innings — the side was led by Mead in the absence on business of Tennyson. Sutcliffe and Holmes replied with an opening stand of 94 and a finish was never likely even before rain washed out the third day. It was Mead's 98th century and the 99th followed against Hampshire's visitors for the next match, Northants, in a display of on-driving which totalled 141 which took him three hours and 40 minutes. He and Newman (70) added 192 for the third wicket and Newman followed by taking ten wickets in the two Northants innings but their combined efforts were not enough to win the game.

His supporters waited with bated breath for him to join Grace, Hayward and Hobbs in taking his tally to 100 centuries. They had to wait; he made 81 at Nottingham but the home side hardly had time to start their first innings before rain came. The elements followed him to Birmingham where little more than an hour's play was possible over all three days. At the Oval for the Players he hit up 54 in 70 minutes — another 'failure' — and back at Southampton was unsuccessful like most of his colleagues as Hampshire sank to defeat against Lancashire by 10 wickets. He was caught from the bowling of Richard Tyldesley for 11 in the first innings and in the second was dismissed for a duck, oddly, hit-wicket in facing Macdonald, the Australian fast bowler in the first over of the third day. Macdonald's third ball lifted and hit him on the right arm. In drawing his arm away to lessen the impact, Mead hit the stumps and he departed ruefully rubbing his arm. Eastbourne brought no relief; Kennedy again conceded 100 runs and Newman fared little better against a Sussex accumulation of 435 for six. The rest of the match was a casualty to storms and Hampshire did not begin even one innings.

So it was with a sense of frustration that on 15th July 1927 they journeyed a little off the cricketing beaten track to Kettering in Northants. Some uninspiring cricket saw Hampshire to a first innings lead of eight. Mead's contribution in dull weather which threatened something worse was 34. On the third day came release. Tennyson contributed to Mead's success in a way for which he should have been forever grateful. First he hit the bowling, which including E. W. (Nobby) Clark and V. W. C. Jupp, both England bowlers, and the supernaturally accurate Taffy Thomas, was by no means lacking in variety and quality, all over that rustic field; his partnership with Mead yielded 195 in only 100 minutes — and he delayed his declaration until Mead reached the coveted three figures. Tennyson hit 19 fours and a six. Mead's caution was demonstrated by his hitting only 12 boundaries and he gave no chance in an effort which lasted for two-and-a-half hours. The stroke itself was a hit to leg from the fourth ball of an over from the occasional bowler, J. E. Timms. Tennyson then declared.

If his delay made a draw inevitable, as it did, and resulted in wails of complaint from the locals, which it did, no cricket lover in Hampshire cared.

A year before, Mead had described how, in a Test match, it felt to reach the century: "People talk as though batsmen should not think about the so-called nervous 90s but that the side and nothing but the side should be his only concern. Well, as long as human nature is what it is fellows will want to get a century (in a Test match); I certainly wanted to get one (in 1921) and though I had confidence enough that I should do it, I confess to many anxious moments . . . not the sort of thing a fellow with a weak heart ought to be asked to go through."

Now the moment had arrived, Mead could be forgiven for wishing that he had achieved the feat at Southampton or Bournemouth or on one of the Metropolitan grounds rather than before a fair but disinterested gathering by the railway at Kettering. But there was time for celebration on the train journey to St. Pancras and on to Bournemouth: for the next game against Surrey.

There were congratulations all the way. A large crowd collected to see Mead warmly congratulated by Sir Russell Bencraft before the start of the game. He also received a semi-official reception from the Mayor and Mayoress of Bournemouth, Alderman and Mrs. Thwaites, who found him surrounded by the Hampshire and Surrey players. He told the local press that he had 'received congratulations from all quarters'.

Tennyson was not available to lead the side and Mead captained Hampshire. There is no doubt that Tennyson felt affection for Mead, although he was capable once of sending a telegram to him at the wicket which said 'get on or get out'; it was a happy chance if not a generous gesture that his absence paid such a compliment to Mead who received a warm welcome from the crowd of 2,000 as he led his team into the field.

In the afternoon, the number had increased to four or five thousand spectators. who contributed to a collection on his behalf. On the second day, he celebrated with an innings of 61. All was now sweetness and light. Bencraft wrote a letter full of praise to the *Southern Daily Echo*. Mead had been 'the biggest asset as a batsman that the County has ever possessed. Many great cricketers have worn the colours of the club but none had surpassed or even approached Mead's brilliant record.' Sir Russell asked the *Echo* to start a shilling (5p) fund as a testimonial and the paper opened it with 1,000 shillings (£50) which the County Cricket Club doubled. Shilling funds had a long and honourable place in the history of sport testimonials, the intention being that even the most hard-up enthusiast could contribute. Bencraft himself and Tennyson each put in 100 shillings (£5). They were in the first list of subscribers which included laconically 'Captain A. W. Carter, one shilling'.

Other contributors were more generous and the total number of shillings reached 7,640. The position was a little difficult. Alec Bowell, whose career was coming to a close, had been refused a second benefit and as some recompense the County had awarded him a testimonial in 1927. The committee may have felt that a shilling fund would ensure a fair division of the public's generosity. If so, they succeeded. Bowell received £389 to reward his service since 1902; Mead received £382. He was presented with an engraved gold watch and chain and the balance in cash.

He achieved his century of centuries in 892 innings which makes him the 12th most speedy accumulator of 100s; the feat took Sir Donald Bradman only

295 visits to the crease, Dennis Compton 552 and Sir Leonard Hutton 619. At the other end of the scale, Frank Woolley needed 1,031 innings, Colin Cowdrey 1,035 and W. G. Grace, 20th and last in the list, 1,113. Mead, the first left-hand bat to score 100 centuries, had taken little over a year to advance from 90 to 100 such scores in 40 innings.

In that year, soggy for most but golden for him, his good form continued to the end. In the second match of the Bournemouth Week, he contributed an undefeated 95 to a drawn game with Middlesex, and at Canterbury his score of 128 in the second innings saved Hampshire from worse humiliation as they were defeated by Kent. He batted for over four hours in an attempt to save the match. With one over to go, the last man in and Tich Freeman bowling, Mead played five balls in the middle of the bat. Freeman's last ball was a googly from which he was caught by Frank Woolley at slip. Everyone commiserated but he asked what they meant and maintained that he was not out. Having defied the bowling all that time and almost saved the match, his reaction was to disbelieve that he had got out to the last ball.

Hampshire bucked up a little in August, winning three of their last seven games, thanks to a late recovery of form by Kennedy and Newman who benfited from the many opportunities for rest provided by the weather. After Mead had contributed another characteristic century (142) to victory by an innings over Worcestershire, Kennedy struck, bowling out Warwickshire for only 36 at Portsmouth; his figures were ten overs, seven maidens, eight runs, seven wickets. He had already captured all ten wickets at a cost of 36 runs for the Players at the Oval.

Five victories as against nine defeats gave Hampshire a humble 13th place in the Championship table but they could not really expect much better as they were virtually a six man team — Mead, Brown, Kennedy, Newman, Tennyson and Livsey. At the end of the season, Bowell left the County. He had never been as prominent as his slightly younger colleagues but his departure was a strong indication that time was passing. By virtue of that single game against Darling's Australians in 1905, Mead was at last in length of service as well as reputation the County's senior professional.

1928 Hampshire Team: Back row, A. S. Kennedy, G. S. Boyes, G. Brown, L. Harfield, W. H. Livsey, J. Bailey. Front row, C. P. Mead, A. L. Hosie, Hon. L. H. Tennyson, A. K. Judd, J. Newman.

107

Chapter Eighteen
1928

In the autumn of 1927, Mead's association with Walter Toomer came to an end. For several reasons, Mead could not set up as a competitor in Southampton. The major manufacturers limited their commercial agencies in each town to one or two selected firms and were not likely to supply a rival in addition to, let alone instead of, Toomers; and there may also have been some restriction against competition in the Mead and Toomer partnership agreement.

Mead solved the problem by opening a sports shop at Bourne Avenue in Bournemouth and moved house as well to Verwood near Ringwood, ten miles inland. The chronology is not entirely clear but by the spring of 1928, Toomer was advertising under his own name as 'formerly Mead and Toomer'.

It was not the best of times to start a new business. The financial collapse of 1929 was just round the corner and for most of 1928, Mead was not available to run his new shop.

Tennyson, accurately described by the writer, R. C. Robertson-Glasgow, as an inveterate tourist, had first visited the West Indies in 1925-26 with the M.C.C. and took his own side to Jamaica early in 1927. Huge crowds watched the matches and the fixtures with 'All Jamaica' were regarded in the island as Test matches. Ernest Tyldesley and Fender as well as Tennyson were the most famous of the visitors. When Tennyson accepted an invitation from the Jamaican authorities to repeat the visit in 1928, Philip Mead was among the party which on 23rd January embarked from Avonmouth in Elders and Fyffes' S.S. *Changuinola*. The Sussex committee did not allow Maurice Tate to make the trip but Tennyson took with him Maurice Allom, the enormously tall Surrey and Cambridge fast bowler, and Nobby Clark, the Northants fast left-armer. Two other professionals, G. M, Lee of Derbyshire, and Sullivan, deputy to Strudwick as Surrey wicket-keeper, with Mead completed the professional contingent. Apart from Allom, most of the amateurs were useful rather than distinguished. Storms and heavy rain which caused serious flooding in London and the south-east accompanied the side for the early stages of the journey and the delights of a voyage south across the Atlantic in a banana boat were not unmixed.

On arrival at the Port of Kingston early on the morning of 7th February, the first hurdle was breakfast on board with a reporter from the *Gleaner* newspaper which had for weeks been recording the preparations for the tour in Jamaica, the selections for the visiting team and of the West Indian side for their tour in England later in the year. Mead, interviewed over breakfast, said only that they had had a very pleasant voyage, and asked if he was confident about the tour gave little away — 'a glorious game, cricket'. He had accurately gauged the weakness of the side. The *Gleaner*'s own comment was just as cryptic:

'Although there is no outstanding run-getter like Tyldesley, there is a much more formidable wicket to be got in Philip Mead; heartbreaking to bowlers, he will take the edge off the bowling for the hitters.' It did not work out quite like that.

The side were immediately faced with two problems. The first was the accommodation which was rather less luxurious than on the previous tour. Because of a shortage of funds, the English tourists were put up not in a hotel but in camp by the Argyle and Sutherland Highlanders, the amateurs in the officers' mess, the professionals with the sergeants. The second concerned the fixture list which the Jamaican authorities seem to have reserved as a surprise for Tennyson to discover on arrival. The first match was to start on their second full day and it was no trial or colts' match but was to last five days against the full might of Jamaica.

They were formally greeted at a civic lunch within a few hours of arrival. Sir William Morrison, lawyer, grandee and chairman of the local Cricket Board, told Mead in his speech of welcome: "We are very glad to have you here — your name is a household word," while Tennyson, in reply, declared that he would bet ten sovereigns that Mead would make the highest score ever seen in Jamaica (G. J. V. Weigall of Kent, one of the amateurs in the side aged 57 and a devoted supporter of Frank Woolley, thereupon wagered the same amount that he wouldn't).

Constant hospitality, the honorary membership of clubs, invitations to dances, shows, the races, could not conceal the fact that they had a demanding programme of cricket, comprising three five-day games against All Jamaica and two two-day games over their 23-day visit.

Undeterred, some of the team spent their first day playing golf (Mead was described as having a handicap of 18) before the real business started in conditions of heat, light and atmosphere to which they were unaccustomed, with the first 'Test' at Sabina Park. The home side were led by R. K. Nunes, already selected to lead the full West Indies team to England in their first Test series, and included four other future Test players: George Headley (then 18 years old), O. C. Scott, L. G. Hylton and F. R. Martin, as well as J. J. Cameron who had toured England in 1906, and J. K. Holt, the grand old man of Jamaican cricket. They all made runs in their first match, but the lesser known C. M. Morales outshone them all with 143 as they amassed 429 which, as it happened, was the lowest score for which Tennyson's side dismissed them on the tour. In the course of the innings, both opening bowlers, Clark and Allom, victims of the heat and lack of practice, broke down, and when the Englishmen batted, it was like Hampshire all over again. They subsided for 227 and only Mead made over 40; going in at number four, he was undefeated at the end with 103. He made only three as they succumbed by 209 — his only failure on the tour. The relief of a game against a Middlesex County XV was greatly reduced as Tennyson had to open the bowling, but Mead contributed another century. More valuable was his 117 in the first innings of the second Test.

Up to this stage, he alone had reached 50 for the touring side. In the second innings, G. M. Lee and F. J. Seabrook led off with a century stand, but only Mead, a comparative failure with 44 provided any support as they collapsed to defeat by an innings and 98. Jamaica had scored 609 — Headley 209, Holt 100 and Morales 84.

Mead was then given a little rest, receiving only one ball as Tennyson (125) led his team to a nine-wicket victory in a second two-day game, but then he developed a fever and was unfit to play when the third representative game began. Mead sick was worth more to Tennyson than most of the others were, fit, and was included in the side. He did not field or bat — the scores, Jamaica 438, Tennyson's XI 327. Eventually they were set 450 to win.

Lee, the other professional stalwart, fell cheaply; three wickets were down for 69. Mead crawled in to bat and as the large crowd, swelled by the small boys in the trees, showed their appreciation and the sun beat down, he faced the varied bowling with his usual calm. P. T. Eckersley, the future captain of Lancashire, helped to put on 87, but he, Tennyson and Arnott left in quick succession — 176 for six. Rain which caused a break handicapped the bowlers; after the wicket-keeper had missed a chance of stumping, Mead reached his hundred and began to score more freely, while Kemp-Welch held the other end. They added 89 before, a draw almost certain, Mead played a weary shot and was bowled for 151. He had batted for five-and-a-half hours, earned cheers and another speech from Tennyson, and the prospect of a restful voyage back to the English spring.

The sun had done him a power of good; he returned a fitter and more active cricketer. He recovered his wristy throw — little seen since 1914 and found it relatively easy to chase around in the field — although in a side composed largely of youngsters, he did not have to demonstrate these skills too often.

In some ways, 1928 was a repetition of 1921. Runs flowed from his bat from the start — 50 and 97 against Surrey at the Oval followed by 157 out of 540 from the Middlesex bowling at Southampton, and 129 mainly from Root and Tarbox of Worcester. All these games were drawn. His score of 50 not out against Gloucestershire at Southampton formed almost half of Hampshire's total in their first innings which the visitors exceeded by 167, and his 110 in the second did not save Hampshire from a seven-wicket defeat. It was Hammond's match: scores of 64 and 65 not out accompanying his nine wickets. Mead was one of his victims — almost uniquely for him, stumped.

In a week's cricket against Yorkshire — three days at Southampton followed by a game at Bradford — he shared in a stand of 240 at home with A. L. Hosie for the third wicket but scored only 28 and 21 in the north. Of some interest is his bowling in these games. At Southampton he broke a tiresome eighth-wicket partnership and then dismissed numbers ten and 11 to finish with three wickets for 24 and earned Hampshire a first innings lead. At Bradford, he broke the opening stand having Percy Holmes caught and later dismissed Arthur Wood, the wicket-keeper, at a cost of 23 runs — five for 47 in the week! Both matches were drawn like the following ones at Nottingham (Mead 89 not out and 41 not out as Hampshire narrowly avoided an innings defeat) and at Horsham (Mead 28 and 75); so by the last week in June they did not have a single victory to their credit. The reasons are not hard to find because only Hosie, apart from Mead, was making runs with any regularity and Newman and Kennedy, in that bakingly hot season, could not get the opponents out. On 26th June they beat Middlesex at Portsmouth but followed this with a caning by 128 runs from Kent. Mead's scores were eight versus Middlesex and 40 and 30 at Dover.

From the end of June, it is easier to pick out the matches in which Mead failed: in mid-July 11 run out at Lord's for the Players; on to 11th August and another 11 versus Somerset at Weston, and 11 again in the game with West Indies at Southampton ten days later; a very short list. In the latter match, Brown was bowled for a duck by Learie Constantine at the start of the Hampshire innings, and after a brief disagreement with him as to the merit of the great West Indian's bowling, Mead in turn fell cheaply, leg before wicket. His return to the dressing room was preceded some seconds by his bat and not a word was said as Tennyson and Newman set-to to remedy the situation and eventually put on 311 in something over four hours.

Mead's eight in the following match against Northants also looks like failure but the wicket at Northampton was ruined following a temporary break in the weather. Newman and Kennedy between them dismissed all the home side's batsmen, of whom only one scored over 20 in their two totals of 101 and 71. Tennyson put himself in first to hit the bowlers off their length. After the early dismissal of Kennedy and Hosie, Mead in at two for two held up an end when runs were as gold dust as his captain with 57 scattered the field. Newman completed a fine all-round performance with 50 and Hampshire won by an innings.

Much more enjoyable to recall his string of successes: 130 and 60 against Surrey and 156 from the Essex bowling represented one week's work at the turn of June/July, followed by 63 in the Lancashire game and 130 against Kent at Southampton in the next. He was so exhausted by his last innings that at his own request he did not travel north to Old Trafford (however successful he was the committee were reluctant to pay his match fee for this non-appearance and eventually compromised at half). The disappointment at being run-out for 11 against the Gentlemen and loss of half that match money disappeared as he put together a leviathan of an innings of 180 which led to a handsome victory by eight wickets over Warwickshire in a high-scoring match which formed for him the first part of a phenomenal week's cricket at Bournemouth. He shared the honours with R. P. H. Utley, a young officer from the Royal Air Force, who later became a monk; Utley's figures: were 12 wickets for 140 runs as Warwickshire, batting first, scored 277 and 351. In between, Kennedy and Hosie hit up 134 in 80 minutes; with five wickets down, Mead and Newman added 251. Mead reached his eighth 100 of the season and with help from T. O. Jameson progressed in three-and-a-half hours to 180. Hampshire totalled 536 but R. E. S. Wyatt earned reward for his 38 overs of toil by capturing seven wickets for 145; his side were defeated by eight wickets as Mead added a further 20 not out. In the second game, Hampshire would have been on the receiving end of it if there had not been rain on the last day; this time it was Notts. who scored 500, leading Hampshire on the first innings by no fewer than 306. Larwood was not playing but Hampshire lost wickets regularly at the second attempt but only at one end. Mead who had scored an unbeaten 59 in the first innings battled for four hours for his 138, and when rain brought the match to a premature finish, Hampshire were 78 ahead with three wickets standing.

He followed this with 79 as Hampshire beat Essex by an innings and his tenth 100 of the season easily saved the game when they were faced with the task of scoring 426 in the last innings at Bristol and a match-saving 148 against Leicestershire . . . but enough is enough. It had indeed been 1921 all over again in terms of the continuous baking sunshine and the pile of runs. His figures in County Championship games were 2,843, run at an average of 81.22. This overtook the previous record of 2,814 held by Tom Hayward since his triumphant season of 1906 (Woolley's figures of 1928 (2,586) remain the fifth greatest). Only four batsmen have exceeded his total of 13 centuries in an English season. His total of runs remains the highest aggregate in a Championship season; so does Mead's combined tally for the seasons 1927 and 1928 — 5,174 runs, average 78.39. (His totals for 1921-22 and 1926-27 are not very far down the list.)

There was one overriding difference. In 1928, all his runs up to September, save that 11 for the Players at Lord's, were made for Hampshire. He did not figure in the Test trial in June nor in any of the three Tests against West Indies. The extra matches which he did play — Players v. Gentlemen and South v. North — were at Bournemouth under the aegis of Hampshire in a revived festival — shades of W.G. The first three innings took him beyond the 3,000 mark so his final figures were 50, ten, 3,027, 180, 75.67.

He had finally broken the jinx, that of performing at less than his best in the season preceding a tour to Australia. He had risen to the front rank in such a season, 1911; that was 17 years before, and the very improbability of selection for the imminent tour to Australia may have enabled him to enjoy batting in 1928 in fairly relaxed fashion.

Of those who were chosen in the Test trial, four from the Rest and eight from the England XI, were eventually selected for Australia, but one object of the selectors was to raise teams to face the West Indies; 17 players figured in those Tests, all of which were won overwhelmingly by England.

As the season burned on, the selection committee began to take notice of Mead's rare continuity of form in conditions as near to Australian ones as England could show. For the first time, the M.C.C. Committee delegated to a sub-committee the task of selecting the players for an overseas tour; those responsible were Lord Harris, Douglas, Warner, Arthur Gilligan, F. T. Mann and H. D. G. Leveson-Gower, with Jack Hobbs co-opted for their last meeting.

Their first act was to name Chapman as captain and they announced the other members of the party at the end of July. Some were readily predictable — Hobbs, Sutcliffe, Hendren, Tate, Duckworth, Larwood, Hammond, while the names of Jardine, Tyldesley and Leyland were not unexpected, but the inclusion of J. C. White, and as vice-captain too, was a surprise as was the absence of at least one all-rounder in addition to Tate; this was nothing to the general astonishment at the exclusion of Frank Woolley. His sequence of Tests, begun in 1909, had at last been broken in the West Indian series in 1928. That omission mattered very little, but that he should not go to Australia after a summer in which he had scored 3,352 runs was unbelieveable. It has been said that Kent almost seceded from the United Kingdom in protest; specifically, Mead's former fellow tourist, G. J. V. Weigall, complained bitterly at the choice of left-handers, describing Mead as a leaden-footed carthorse and Leyland as a cross-batted village greener. The Yorkshireman at once justified his selection when given the opportunity at the end of the tour.

The omission of Holmes, again, Hallows and R. E. S. Wyatt was also criticised. Mead, at 41, and Tyldesley, 39, were the lucky ones, so it is not simply a case of balancing the choice of Mead against the omission of Woolley, but had the choice to be between them, it is not difficult to justify the selection of the former; the period of three-day Test matches between England and Australia in which 80 runs in an hour by Woolley could change the course of events were over. The Tests of 1928-29 were to be played to a finish and that would exactly suit Mead's methods and, moreover, Woolley's bowling was no longer a factor at the highest level; again, Mead's dominance throughout 1928 made him very hard to overlook, while Woolley the man in possession had performed only moderately on his three tours of Australia.

Criticism was fairly polite. The *Daily Mirror* commented: 'The biggest surprise probably concerns the call to Hants for the veteran Phil Mead who has apparently been included to play the Australians at their own marathon game . . .' The well-known critic of the day, H. J. Henley, wrote that Mead's selection was justified but added: 'It is depressing to find that so few youngsters are capable of cutting out the veterans.' The selection is well summed up by Leslie Ames, a great friend and colleague of Woolley, in his book 'Close of Play': 'It was an indication of the strength of the party and the abundance of talent that Frank Woolley was not selected. He was extremely unfortunate but . . . it would have been grossly unfair had any one of the players selected been forced to stand down . . .'

Chapter Nineteen
Australian Autumn

The side is widely regarded as one of the strongest ever sent to Australia, but the selectors created a number of hostages to fortune. The absence of an all-rounder has already been noted; Larwood's fitness was doubtful and Geary whose selection came later than the others was prevented from bowling for most of 1928 by elbow trouble and underwent an operation. The form, in both a cricket and a physical sense, of Chapman himself also bothered the selectors who tried to insure against all contingencies by including as many as 17 players — a strategem which did not last long as one of the party, Sam Staples, was unable to play at all because of a rheumatic condition and returned home after a few weeks.

The team left England in two stages: a sort of advance party which included Mead sailed in the S.S. *Otranto* on 18th September. The main body comprising the players who formed the Rest against the champion county, Lancashire, crossed the Channel from Folkestone and entrained through France to pick up the boat at Toulon. They benefited from a wonderful send-off at Victoria and avoided a violent and fearsome storm which affected Mead and his colleagues as they sailed down the Channel.

From Toulon they luxuriated through seas as calm as mill ponds and with a break at Naples reached Port Said on 26th September and steamed on to Colombo. The ports of call, the usual match at Sri Lanka (Ceylon) and the tremendous heat were all reminders to Mead of that journey he had made as a 24-year-old in company with Hobbs, the only other survivor of it in the 1928 team. Mead did not play in 1928.

The side arrived in Freemantle only two days before their first fixture at Perth against Western Australia which began on 18th October. The selectors' policies were soon put to the test. Tate strained his arm and missed the first two games; Geary struck on the nose by a rising ball in the dying moments of the Perth match was hospitalised and did not play again for nearly a month; Staples, as we have already seen, was sick and did not play at all; Freeman's affliction was a stiff neck. However, 'all the more for us' might have been the motto of those who *were* fit and Mead played in five matches out of six before the first Test match.

He did not start well, scoring one and one not out at Perth but did better in a high-scoring match against South Australia at Adelaide. In the first innings he was overshadowed by Hammond and Chapman — 145 apiece, and in the second by Leyland with 109, but 58 and 58 not out against an attack including J. D. Scott, Tim Wall and Grimmett showed that he was soon adapting to the conditions. By this time Jardine had a century to his credit and Tyldesley, Hendren, Hobbs and Sutcliffe had all made scores of over 60. The heavy run getting continued against Victoria when Jardine and Hendren scored centuries and Chapman and Larwood both exceeded 70. Mead (37) added 71 for the second wicket with Jardine. The M.C.C. score of 486 paled before their effort at Sydney which mounted to 734; Hammond's contribution was 225, Hendren made 167 and Jardine in tremendous form hit up 140. Mead missed this game which like the others was drawn but he contributed another 58 as they defeated an Australian XI at Sydney. The prospective Test attack, Larwood, Tate, Geary (now fit again) and White asserted itself for the first time at Brisbane. There Mead was run out by Hobbs for a single when Queensland were demolished by an innings in the last game before the First Test which was to be played there too. By this time, Hobbs, Sutcliffe, Hammond, Hendren, Chapman and Jardine had all batted with such success as to make their places secure. Larwood, Tate and a wicket-keeper were also certain of selection (Duckworth took the place behind the stumps); that made nine. Much interest centred on the choice of the remaining members of the attack including, it was assumed, a slow bowler. Both Freeman and White had put in good performances and one of them, if not both, would gain selection. If only one were included, one place would be left to fill. An independent observer might have concluded that Leyland, Mead and Tyldesley were in contention for the other batting position — if there was one. The tour selectors decided to take a risk, leaving the attack to Larwood, Tate and White, with support from Hammond and to include an extra batsman.

Tyldesley, who was a member of the tour selection committee, had hit two 50s but had failed four times; Leyland on the other hand had hit two 100s but at 28 he was a youngster by English standards and the choice fell upon Mead but only after many hours deliberation. The balance of the team caused what Wisden described as perturbation.

No-one anticipated the outcome, an overwhelming victory for England by the huge margin of 675 runs. Nine members of the side reached double figures in the England total of 521. Hendren, last out led the list with 169, Larwood (70) and Chapman (50) also shone — and Mead made eight. He may have been disconcerted by the running-out of Hobbs when he was his partner in the course of an unwise third run; unwise because the batsmen's combined ages were 87 and the fielder was Bradman. Mead was then leg before to Grimmett.

England led on the first innings by 399 but Chapman did not enforce the follow-on. Australia had lost not one but both opening bowlers by this stage — J. M. Gregory limping from the scene forever with an injured knee, and Kelleway who was sick. Grimmett and Ironmonger bowled heroically as England determined to rub Australian noses in the dirt. Mead again went in first wicket down, when Grimmett dismissed Hobbs, with the score of 25. From the start of this innings there were storms on the horizon and although the match would be played to a finish, England needed to get a move on.

Sutcliffe and Mead carried the score to 69 when five minutes before tea Sutcliffe, attempting a drive, was caught. With Hammond in, play was held up by bad light and a shower so at 5.40 stumps were drawn with the score at 103 for two wickets. After a little overnight rain, conditions were not much better the next morning. Chapman did not declare although England were 504 runs ahead. Grimmett and Ironmonger bowled practically unchanged, both turning the ball and making it rise at varying heights. At 117, Hammond was brilliantly caught from the bowling of Ironmonger which brought in Jardine. Strange that Chapman did not yet send in one of his hitters — Jardine had a reputation for pawkiness and he and Mead batted quietly against the accurate slow bowling supported by defensive field placings.

Mead's batting had not impressed the locals overnight. The *Brisbane Daily Mail* reported: 'Mead came in and played forward and back, straight and across but seldom for runs.' He was a little more pleasing the next morning. A straight drive brought him to 50 in 161 minutes. 'He moved out to the bowling better and spectators cheered the drives in hope of better things to come.' By lunch he had accumulated 68 out of 161 for three wickets; the dour Jardine was on 20. In the first over after lunch, when they had put on 48, Mead missed a straight one from Grimmett and 'as his legs were in their usual position, he had to go leg before' (as Fender put it) for 73.

As others see us — the *Brisbane Daily Mail*: 'Mead's innings will be remembered for all time. A stubborn, practically graceless exhibition of defiance by an ungainly batsman . . . that he can make strokes was shown now and again as he drove and square cut Grimmett; his sense of the pitch of the ball was uncanny — he put the bat in front of the pads with consistent accuracy!' Wisden felt that in his innings of three-and-a-half hours he was never really at home.

During the afternoon, with the wicket easier, runs came readily. Hendren, Chapman, Tate and Larwood all hit fiercely while Jardine carried out the role intended for Mead and kept one end impregnably secure — 'like an old maid defending her honour'. Just before 5 o'clock, Chapman made what is believed to be the first ever declaration in a test match in Australia at 342 for eight.

Australia were set to win the overwhelming target of 742; they were duly overwhelmed. They lost their great white hope, Ponsford, that evening and after overnight rain were bowled out next morning in hot sunshine for 66. Larwood followed six for 32 with two more victims, Tate had five wickets in the match for 76 and White, who was not wanted in the first innings, gave the *coup de grâce* mopping up four Australians for only seven runs. England looked like a side of giants; with Hendren (169) leading the way, eight scored over 35 in their first innings while all nine, save Jack Hobbs, exceeded 20 in the second. The fourth bowler, Hammond, conceded only 38 runs from his 15 overs in the Australians' first innings.

There were good arguments for retaining the winning team. Mead top scorer in the second innings had played his part; his fielding at third man or fine leg had been adequate though barely tested in two innings in which none of the opponents had achieved a higher score than 33.

England's Team

Left to right – Front row: E. Tyldesley, J. C. White, A. P. F. Chapman (Capt.), D. R. Jardine, Jack Hobbs. Middle row: M. Leyland, S. J. Staples, W. Hammond, Sir F. C. Toone (Manager), H. Sutcliffe, H. Larwood, A. P. Freeman. Back row: G. Duckworth, L. Ames, C. P. Mead, M. W. Tate, E. Hendren.

But the selectors knew that they had had all the luck. They were unlikely to bowl out Australia twice another time with only three specialist bowlers. When they chose the side for the Second Test, they brought in Geary and left Mead out. Geary returned figures of five for 35 and two for 55, Larwood and Tate had four wickets each; the attack was complete and the die was cast.

Mead did not play in the last four Test matches as Hammond thus early reached the height of his career. The same names happily recurred — Hammond, Sutcliffe, Hendren, Hammond, White, Hammond as England won the Second, Third and Fourth Tests by diminishing margins. New names established themselves in the Australian side — Bradman and Jackson, although there was only a hint of the success which Bradman was to enjoy in England in 1930.

England fielded an unchanged XI for the Third and Fourth Tests; in the Fifth when Sutcliffe was prevented from playing by an injured arm and Chapman decided to stand down, Jardine opened the innings with Hobbs, unsuccessfully; White led the side and Ernest Tyldesley and Leyland were given a chance to share in the spoils. Australia won; Tyldesley's scores were 31 and 21 but Leyland made a big impact on his first appearance with totals of 137 and 53 not out.

The members of the team who were not actively involved in the big games were left with the 1920's equivalent of today's one-day internationals — games against local up-country teams composed of 11, 12 or 13 opponents. Mead was unlikely to shine in such company where there was no real challenge and made a succession of small scores. In spite of a rough crossing, at Launceston against stronger opposition, he batted with relaxed freedom and shared in a partnership of 224 in a little over two hours with Jardine. He hit 13 fours in the only century he ever scored in Australia. He wound up with 41 against an Australian XI at Perth as the tourists edged wearily towards the liner for the journey home beginning 25th March 1929.

Four weeks of relaxation followed on the S.S. *Ormonde* but the festivities were hardly begun. From Toulon on 20th April they took the Channel ferry and on the following day, heavily overcoated against the cold, arrived at Dover to be greeted by Lord Harris and a civic reception; even this was only a prelude to the tumultuous welcome which they received at Victoria. Later, their fame was prolonged well into the English season which began almost at once. On 1st July, following the second day of the Gentlemen v. Players match, the team were entertained at a banquet by the cricketing Lord Mayor, Sir Kynaston Studd, at the Mansion House.

So again, Mead was associated with a hugely successful touring side, although his own share in its success was marginal. If he had begun the tour knowing that good judges, the selectors, ranked him among the leading nine batsmen in England worthy for the task of retaining the Ashes, he returned aware that he was not in the first six. Had Woolley made the trip, he would inevitably have suffered the same fate.

If Mead's achievements in Australia were not immortal, he was the subject of one story that is. At a civic reception at Brisbane, the Lord Mayor referred to the pleasure it gave Australians to greet again the heroes of former tours and named Chapman, Hobbs, Tate, Sutcliffe, Hendren and Freeman. Chapman remedied the omission: "You appear to have overlooked one of the members of the side, my Lord Mayor in the shape, no pardon me, in the form of Phil Mead." When the laughter had subsided, Chapman continued that in Sydney an enthusiast had sought out Mead, shaken him by the hand and remarked "I knew your father when he was out here in 1911."

An offside dab.

Chapter Twenty
When Winter Comes

It was a bad time to be starting in business. Mead had some time to look to his shop during the summer of 1928 when Hampshire were playing at home, but he was away with Tennyson from mid-January to the second week in March and soon after the end of the English season he left for Australia. In many ways 1928 formed a second high point in his career; during the calendar year the results of his labours in the cricket field were:

	Innings	Not Out	Total Runs	Average
Jamaica	5	1	418	104.50
England	50	10	3027	75.67
Australia (to the end of December)	10	3	300	42.85

but Mead inevitably depended heavily on the shop manager. He was found wanting. As Phyllis Mead says, the manager took the profit and the family didn't. The recession of 1929 may have been an additional factor.

However, at that time of disappointment, she was only four years old and details are, happily, lacking but the business does not appear to have existed after 1929. In the absence of comment from his bank manager, we may assume that Mead was not much worse off for income after this failure than he had been before he took the shop; for the present, the income no longer received from Toomer's was made up by the payment for the tour in Australia (£400) and a special award of £300 from M.C.C. when the team returned home (which the Club could well afford — the profit on the Tour was £17,968). The £700 would have purchased rather more than a handsome detached house in 1929; moreover, for over six months, Mead had lived with all expenses paid. As Ric Sissons points out in 'The Players', the touring professional had to cover only his drinks, cigarettes, parties, betting and what may be broadly described as his own entertaining. At the end of 1928, Mead was awarded £56 talent money and a special bonus of £20 by Hampshire. He also received winter pay of £70. There was the prospect of his second benefit in 1930. As, by 1938, only one in eight of the working population earned more than £250 a year, things were not so bad for Mead and his family; he was, however, totally reliant on retention of his batting skill.

His form at the start of the 1929 season was particularly depressing. Whether from reaction from the activity of the winter tour, business worries or the cold of May, he made as bad a start as could be imagined with scores of six; five and eight; two and nought. Then in the course of an attempt to stave off collapse against Somerset at Taunton on 18th May when he had made 23, he was hit on the left hand by a delivery from George Hunt, a not particularly dangerous medium pacer, and had to retire. His thumb was dislocated. He accepted the disappointment and the discomfort cheerfully enough, as he was to treat other disasters, and helped in a collection for the young Somerset batsman, Frank Lee, who hit his maiden 100 in the game but Mead could not play again for almost six weeks.

The cricket field is a romantic concept but the county circuit is a shop floor for those who work on it — fatiguing, humorous, sometimes rewarding and often profane. It is essentially competitive, not only as between the rival teams but also among the players who make up the teams. Except in times of redundancy, there may not be much competition between, say, ten machinists on the shop floor but a cricket team contains only one wicket-keeper, one pair of opening batsmen, not more than four specialist bowlers (probably all medium pacers nowadays) and the struggle for places may be intense. So in 1922, Stuart Boyes saw off the incumbent slow left-arm bowler, Remnant. That was the only major change in the professional constitution of the Hampshire side between the displacement of Stone by Livsey in 1914 and Livsey's own retirement following a breakdown in health at the end of 1929.

Mead and Newman, and Bowell, Kennedy and Brown, with Livsey and Boyes and led by Tennyson, were thrown together, frequently to the exclusion of their wives and families, from April to early September. They travelled by train (some amateurs used cars) in a routine involving hasty departures from one venue to another, long waits at railway junctions like Reading or Crewe and tedious Sundays away from home. The Hampshire professionals did not emulate P. R. Johnson, the Somerset amateur, who is reported to have spent his day of rest in bed reading Jane Austen, but among other pursuits they passed their journeys and rainy days playing bridge at which they mustered two schools. Mead formed one, latterly with Arnold, Herman and R. H. Moore. They were competitive at that, too, and journeys were often prolonged to the last minute and trains delayed as they struggled to finish a hand.

Mead and Newman shared with Tennyson an interest in the horses, but although there are reports of Tennyson celebrating big wins with champagne and feasting, there were no reports of big wins by Mead. It would be a mistake to imagine that these flesh and blood characters worked together like a well oiled machine. Well oiled they may have been from time to time in the company of their captain, but to use the words of a younger member of the side, for the most part they tolerated each other. Kennedy, very strong, hard working and totally professional, did not find tolerance easy; his resemblance to George Robey, the comedian, was only a facial one. While he and Jack Newman shared a famous partnership for almost 20 years, Kennedy invariably had the choice of ends; their relationship, based truly enough on mutual respect, did not extend beyond the field of play. Newman, kindly, gentle, edgy, was in some ways like the thoroughbreds he fancied. Unmarried, unlike the others, he found greater consolation than they did in his success in his profession and took occasional failure more to heart. George Brown was large, unpredictable, unavoidable and some would say unbalanced. Because of his great strength, he was alleged to be able to tear in half a pack of cards — or was it the phone book? Among other unprofitable activities, he carried an early version of the whoopee cushion: 'Will you sit down for a word, my Lord?' . . . 'Oh, weally, Brown . . .' and on long train journeys played by the hour with a yo-yo. He also travelled to home matches on a huge motor cycle and on occasions rare before 1930, when Livsey was not playing, kept wicket in his motor cycling gauntlets. Selected as wicket-keeper for the crucial Oval test against Australia in 1926, he kept wicket for Hampshire to get match practice beforehand and thus unprotected broke a finger and missed the Test.

Kennedy's assurance of his own status did not make him altogether popular with his younger colleagues (he was always critical of any young bowler he was asked to look at for the Club, suspecting a rival; he derided at least one who afterwards served the Club with distinction for nearly 20 years). Once, at least, his younger colleagues made him an apple-pie bed; they put fly-papers up the arms and legs of his pyjamas, and Kennedy who was extremely hairy had great trouble in removing them.

Incidents like these never attached to Mead. Usually good humoured, he got on equally well at a distance with the young amateurs who made a welcome addition to the batting strength in the 1920s and their largely professional successors in the '30s. He was always prepared to offer advice to younger players like Dick Moore, who took it to heart, and Ronald Aird who preferred to go his own way. On the pitch, Mead had been compared to a jovial dancing bear, an image to which his long arms, bulky figure and long-peaked cap contributed, but the joviality was to a great extent in the eye of the beholder. He shared fully in the backchat between the players on the field; to successive generations of bowlers he was a great irritant. As already noted "I wish I was carrying you about in my bag" he said to Cecil Parkin, the outstanding Lancashire bowler in the 1920s. Parkin retorted that his bat ought to be shaved. He would always hit the bad ball, but even when the attack was accurate and testing, he found ways to work ball after unlikely ball round to leg almost as if fulfilling a dare without appearing to take any trace of risk. His judgment in leaving alone balls outside the off-stump was by this time legendary. Early in his career, Bill Bowes was unwise enough to mention this in Mead's hearing; he gave a demonstration, leaving ball after ball alone. Bowes, as quoted by Partrick Murphy, says: "I was throwing up my arms as the ball missed his off-stump by a couple of inches. I couldn't believe it. I wish I had never said a word." In his autobiography, 'Express Deliveries', Bowes elaborates: 'Hobbs, Mead, Sutcliffe and Hammond rendered the off-theory (persistent bowling outside the off-stump) a waste of time. They made a back foot movement a fraction of a second before the bowler's delivery. This brought the leg and body directly in front of the stumps. From that position they made their strokes.'

Mead's team mates had equally to be on the lookout. It takes two to run these well chosen quick singles which he could take 'off almost every ball'. Even batting partners less than half his age, such as Cecil Paris and Dick Moore found themselves diving for safety with a murmured 'good luck' echoing in their ears. His economy of effort extended to his own running between the wickets: Gerald Brodribb quotes Ian Peebles, the Middlesex and England bowler and writer who, on the field, saw Mead notice that the umpire at the bowler's end was intent on watching the ball and fielder and take the risk of running three yards short of the crease — and get away with it. By his judgment in running, Mead could seize the lion's share of the bowling but in later years he sometimes used it to the opposite effect. He told Hedley Verity 'they've got to face it sometime' as he took the proferred single early in an over (but he did not accept easy ones offered by Tich Freeman — he could never get enough of Tich). Arthur Holt tells of the evening at Leicester on his debut when going in at something like 65 for seven he seemed to be on the receiving end of all the bowling. Note that as many as one in three of Mead's centuries were undefeated.

Away from the field of play, he was quiet and 'backward in coming forward' and had a gently quizzical sense of humour which seldom told the whole truth: he often reminisced about his meeting with the Prince of Wales at the Oval in 1921; it was the Prince who told him, he said, that his innings of 182 not out had broken the record; this was a proud moment for him but to friends his story was that the Prince was tipsy and had to be held up by his aides! Totally unassuming, he had many friends, both male and female. He got maximum pleasure from a party when, a half-filled glass in his hand, he would savour the company from a corner. He was a welcome visitor for a hand of bridge. He played golf and badminton and displayed unexpected skills; Cecil Paris, inviting him out at Chelmsford around 1935, found himself spending the evening with Mead — roller skating. After a rainy day at Worcester, C. V. Tarbox, a hospitable opponent, offered to row Mead and friends on the Severn. From the stern, Mead encouraged him to greater efforts, admiring his style and lamenting that he could not emulate it: progress was slow and the Worcester player was so blistered and stiff by the end that the next day his play was affected. Only then did it come to light that Mead had won prizes for rowing, a skill which he had picked up at the *Mercury*, and thought little of his host's performance.

The question remains: why his qualities of humour and good temper did not communicate themselves more readily to the spectators? Because they did not. The best of Mead was mostly savoured close at hand by other players. Patrick Murphy, in the Centurions, rightly concludes that he never caught the public imagination. It is improbable that he greatly cared; his attitude may be compared to that of a steeplejack or fireman, professionally carrying out a difficult and arduous task in a way which incidentally excites public interest, but cricket is first and foremost a public spectacle; there is no end product apart from the effect upon the spectators. This aspect of the game seems to have passed him by.

The explanation may be that the way which from 1919 onwards suited Mead also suited Hampshire and once he realised that he did not have an automatic right to a place in the England XI, he was content to accumulate runs in a quite unspectacular fashion, season by season. His sense of playing to suit himself is reflected in two anecdotes, one certainly fiction the other not. The first begins on a chilly morning: two Hampshire wickets soon fall; Mead rolls to the wicket clad in a heavy polo necked sweater; at 35 he removes this revealing a V-neck with long sleeves which shed at 50 shows a third short sleeved woollen garment; working up a lather in the sunshine half an hour before lunch, he removes that, too, unveiling a black waistcoat complete with watch and chain; the reality is almost as good for when Hampshire started the 1936 season at Worcester on a cold and blustery day, Mead *did* don pullovers and flannels on top of his ordinary clothes before he went to take the field at slip.

History is silent as to whether he used his unwelcome leisure in 1929 to try to save his business or to wind it up. During his absence, Hampshire did not fare too badly, winning four and losing four of the ten matches in what turned out to be a bowler's season. The rain glistened; Hampshire's batsmen did not shine; Mead's own poor start has already been indicated. Only two innings over 50 were played by Hampshire batsmen in the four matches before his injury. Only two more occurred, almost incidentally, in five additional completed innings up to the end of May. Brown, who started the season just as badly as Mead, first reached that figure as late as 10th June. Lord Tennyson who had succeeded to the title during the winter was conspicuous by his absence until that match, but neither he nor any of the others followed Brown's example at Leicester or in two innings at Lord's. The batting did not pull itself together until the following Glamorgan match in which seven players scored over 25, and Tennyson won the game with the first Hampshire 100 of the season on 21st June. Mead was back in the side for the Essex match a week later.

Hampshire's successes over that part of the season resulted from the greatly improved performance of the bowlers (a feature of the side's operations over the next five or six seasons was that batsmen and bowlers tended to meet with success in alternate years). Kennedy had nine for 46 and 13 wickets in the match against Derbyshire and 14 Glamorgan wickets at Swansea, and six wickets in an innings on two other occasions while Creese, working his way into the team, Newman and Boyes all returned match-winning performances.

It was business as usual straight away when Mead resumed his place in the side against Essex at Leyton and followed 36 with a perfect and match-saving innings of 166 not out; in between, the home side had put together 505 for seven. Hampshire finished 11 ahead with five men out in the second innings. In July, he hit two 100s: 129 against Leicestershire at Southampton, and an undefeated 120 in the next, the return game with Essex, both match-winning innings; against Essex, he and Brown added 193 inside two-and-a-half hours. A week later at Bournemouth against the old enemy, Kent, he excelled twice following calamitous starts in a drawn match; in the first innings he played admirably for 82 out of a total of 189. Facing a deficit of 110, Hampshire lost two wickets for six runs; Harfield helped Mead raise the score to 90 before Tennyson and Mead put on 118 and remained together when the game ended with Hampshire 208 for three, 98 ahead with seven wickets to fall. These efforts which showed that he retained in full his ability to out-stay bowlers under all conditions were followed by five 50s in a row (two against the visiting South Africans) and a couple of 80s represented a good end to an interrupted season's work.

In championship matches, he reached an average of 51 for 1,436 runs, but his season was entirely domestic; the selectors tried numeous experiments in the Test matches. He did not play for the Players against the Gentlemen at Lord's although he was a guest at the celebratory dinner to the winter tourists given at the Mansion House by the Lord Mayor, Sir Kynaston Studd, during the match: Domestic, yes, until September when he had a major share in another celebration of the success of Chapman's team. At long last, he returned to Scarborough where 11 of the touring side faced Lord Hawke's XI which was a kind of England second team, opening with Whysall, Sandham, Duleepsinjhi and Wyatt and more to the point, benefiting from the bowling of G. O. Allen, Rhodes, Haig, Jupp and Alan Peach of Surrey. Chapman, winning the toss, saw Hobbs and Sutcliffe rapidly dismissed. Mead was then joined by the joyous Hendren who speedily ran into his best form; on this occasion, Mead matched him in brilliance. Hendren hit a six and 21 fours, his usual variety of strokes contributing to a masterpiece of 156 in little over two-and-a-half hours. His last 55 runs came in 20 minutes before he was caught when 272 had been added. By that time, Mead, too, had reached three figures but this was hardly more than the prelude for him — he pressed on with further huge stands in company with Tate and Leyland. Tate, with five sixes and nine fours, hit 81 in an hour. The climax of Mead's stand with Leyland came on the second morning when the two left-handers sent the bowling to all quarters in adding 94 in the space of 35 minutes. Mead reached his second century in five hours, taking 11 in an over from Jupp — a typical shot to square leg for four, another to fine leg for two and a third to square leg again which brought him another four. He was at last caught behind the wicket from the bowling of Allen when he had hit a five and 30 fours. The total, 553 for five wickets declared, and Mead's 233 were reminiscent of his memorable earlier performance at the Marine Parade Ground, the score of 223 which had preceded the tour of 1911-1912.

The performance in 1929 came as a revelation to the vast crowd at Scarborough and to the managing figures of the game, including Lord Hawke, who had the good fortune to be present.

Hawke's side just saved the game; the bulk of the tourists wearily made their way from Scarborough to another 'festival' at Folkestone for the season's and their own swansong. The side was cracking up as a result of the players' exertions; only ten of them made the start of the match (the side was completed by P. G. T. Kingsley, the Oxford Blue) and only eight of these lasted to the end — even two of the survivors, Ames and Freeman batted with the services of a runner. Mead, who formed one of the able-bodied six, scored 62 in the

first innings. In the second he was bowled by Nichols for two; the Rest had pillaged 543 runs and won by an innings and 103 runs.

It was an anti-climatical end to Mead's career as a representative cricketer. He finished fourth in the first class averages, below Hobbs, Hammond and Woolley with figures of: 38 innings, seven not outs, 1,733 runs and an average of 55.90.

He came nowhere near to such figures again as the 1930s came in and ran on towards the middle of their course.

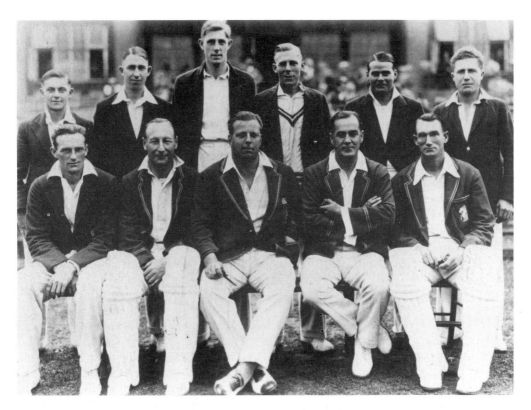

Hampshire 1932

(Back) N. McCorkell, W. L. Creese, O. W. Harman, A. E. Pothecary, J. Bailey, J. Arnold. (Front) G. S. Boyes, C. P. Mead, Lord Tennyson, A. S. Kennedy, G. Brown.

Chapter Twenty-One
Age can Wither

The Hampshire Committee were as good as their word and granted Mead as his second benefit the game with Gloucestershire at Southampton beginning 14th June 1930. The local press gave plenty of advance publicity and the match itself, in spite of the absence of Hammond playing in the First Test match against Australia, and Parker, injured, was a splendid one played in perfect weather. Hampshire, who included Giles Baring, the amateur fast bowler, for the first time, won the toss. The beneficiary received a telegram from the England team at Trent Bridge which read 'Mead outside left, County Cricket Ground, Southampton. Best wishes. Kick with the wind. Dickpatsygeorgewally. The onion kings Suttate.' Mead explained that he had played at outside left in a football game in Australia, the long compound word represented the names of Dick Tyldesley, Patsy Hendren, George Duckworth and Wally Hammond. Sutcliffe and Tate, with Mead, were known as the onion kings on tour: fortified by this, Mead went in to bat at 95 for two. A glance to leg and an off-drive brought two fours in his first over and he followed with a succession of beautiful square cuts and drives, reaching 50 in 55 minutes in front of a crowd of 2,000 who gave him a standing ovation in which the fielding side joined.

Hampshire led by only 13 on the first innings but went on to win by 28 runs. Mead with scores of 59 and 44 played in something like his best form, but that cannot be said of much of his play in 1930 and his benefit produced no more than £681. Money was still tight. This represented a last opportunity to accrue some capital and he must have been very disappointed. He was supplementing his income in a minor way with some coaching at a cricket school in Bournemouth run by the very youthful Charles Brockway, but began to find the cost of travel from Verwood even to Southampton an expensive nuisance — in 1930, only four Hampshire matches were 'at home' at Bournemouth: the railways did not always profit by his presence as a passenger.

He followed the success against Gloucester with 90 against Glamorgan; a fortnight later he played a truly magnificent innings of 143 against Nottinghamshire (who lacked Larwood) at Trent Bridge. Facing an inhospitable 511 and following the early loss of Brown, John Arnold, Kennedy and Newman, Mead with Tennyson (97) added 195 in 150 minutes — it was the same old story, no-one else contributed more than 31 to Hampshire's 383. Whysall hit two 100s in the drawn game. Alas, that 143 stood alone as Mead approached mid-August with much the same lack of success as had followed him through May into mid-June; between 23rd July and 12th August, he played nine innings which produced only 87 runs; he rallied a little towards the finish with 330 runs in eight innings, but playing 18 innings overall, in which he did not reach double figures, including a pair against the Australians, he scored only 1,305 runs at an average which fell from 55 in 1929 to 29 in 1930 — the worst season he had experienced since the earliest days of his career.

This was surely for Mead in his 44th year the beginning of the end. For the first time since 1906, another professional headed the Hampshire batting averages — it was Johnny Arnold who had qualified for the County at the beginning of June who beat him to it.

At this low state in his fortunes, Mead had the good fortune to receive an offer which would bring the family both a livelihood and a home. The Ellis Brewery had built a fine new house, the Bear Cross Inn, on the rural edge of Winton, Bournemouth, and they installed Mead there as licensee in 1931. Established in this base he could feel secure. He was admirably suited to play mine host when he was available and there was plenty of accommodation for the family and extensive land behind the house on which geese and chickens were kept: in summertime, good numbers of customers came out from Bournemouth to enjoy an evening drink.

At the same time, he fulfilled an ambition which had been brewing for some time when his second son, the 18-year-old Frankie, was taken on the Hampshire staff as a batsman. Whether or not his poor form in 1930 was due to money worries, from his new base he batted much more convincingly in 1931. He met with early disappointment: needing only one more 100 to equal W. G. Grace's total of 126, he had reached 99 when he was dismissed by the New Zealanders. If he did not show his frustration then, he did for a different reason in the next game against Surrey at the Oval. Kennedy bowled them out for 245. Arnold and Jim Bailey then settled down to an opening partnership which had reached an undefeated 127 when the Hampshire captain, Stephen Fry, declared, to what purpose no-one could say. According to Richard Streeton in his biography of Fender, Mead sitting in the professionals' dressing room and suspecting the Surrey captain of subterfuge, rocked to and fro crying 'it's that Fender'. In the end, Hampshire set 222 to win were struggling at 125 for five, Mead 56 not out.

He had to wait until mid-June for the century which equalled W.G.'s record, an innings of 106 not out in two hours at Northampton, and he surpassed it with another undefeated 106 when Hampshire beat Sussex at Portsmouth — there was only one other innings over 50 in the two Hampshire innings. His other century of the season, 169 against Surrey at Bournemouth three weeks later, witnessed some remarkable play under the genuine influence of Fender. Hampshire led by 53 on the first innings but then lost five wickets for 84. Pothecary and Creese, both left-handers, stayed while Mead brought Hampshire to a stage where a declaration might be anticipated, but Baring, captain in the absence of Tennyson, delayed the closure. Boyes who batted right-handed, coming in seventh wicket down, held up an end while Mead placed the ball with freedom. Fender responded to what he regarded as stalling. He directed his fielders to change over to their identical positions for right and left-hander as Mead and Boyes changed ends; cover, third man, mid-off and mid-on all moved across when the batsmen scored a single or a three. Sandham who ran was crisply told to walk. In one over there were six singles — it took 11 minutes.

The crowd did not know who to blame for the impasse. Baring at last declared and the game petered out.

Much of Hampshire's play was mediocre — in August, Parker and Goddard found them easy meat. At Southampton, sunshine followed rain and Hampshire facing a Gloucester total of 253 lost nine wickets for 90. Baring stayed while Mead (72 not out) played admirably and they almost doubled the score. In the second innings, they collapsed again and no-one but Mead exceeded Baring's first innings score of 32. It was much the same against Kent; only Brown with 82 passing 30 in the two innings, and no-one at all could reach that total against Essex (Hampshire 91 and 54) while only Mead (65) did so when Leicester were beaten by nine wickets. Mead comfortably headed the Hampshire averages:

Mead	43	9	1463	169*	43.02
Arnold	45	6	1363	128*	34.94

The next year their positions were reversed:

Arnold	46	1	1506	227	33.46
Mead	44	5	1189	121	30.48

It was back to 1930 again for Mead and his inconsistency is shown as a third of these runs came from his three centuries; he had an oddly poor record against Derbyshire: his career figures against them were about half his average overall. The century which he contributed to a thrilling win over them at Southampton was his first; he had now completed a three-figure innings against each of Hampshire's 16 county opponents. He also hit 100s against Kent at Dover and Lancashire at Portsmouth. His record must be judged against the background of one of the wettest summers of the century — but the previous year had not been much better: the conditions did not prevent Herbert Sutcliffe of Yorkshire from averaging 96 in 1931 and 74 in 1932.

There was a prodigious amount of low scoring in 1932. Hampshire's first six innings totalled 70 and 71 v. Middlesex (who scored 76 and 18 for no wicket in a drawn game); 135 and 77 against Somerset who won by ten wickets, and crowning unglory, 57 and 30 against Voce and Sam Staples of Notts. whose own second contribution amounted to no more than 42, Jim Bailey collecting seven wickets for seven runs from seven overs; Notts. were nevertheless successful by 161 runs. Still in May, it was All India's turn — Kennedy and Bailey bowled them out for 51 and 119 and Hampshire beat the tourists by an innings. The absurdly small scoring continued well into June — as Mead contributed only 133 in his first 14 innings, it is a tribute to his recuperative power that his final figures were not worse. On 3rd August, he was injured while batting and missed that and the following two matches. Returning, he immediately hit a splendid 121 and 67 not out against Kent.

Hampshire enjoyed their most successful season since 1926, rising to eighth position in the championship. If the batting failed in the miserable conditions,

Hampshire had the bowlers to make the most of them in the eternally running Kennedy (134 wickets), Boyes 85, Herman 94 and Bailey 69, all with average runs per wicket ranging from 18 to 23. After three mediocre years, the County, now represented by an almost entirely professional XI, had a most interesting season. Neil McCorkell, who had only just joined the side, Creese and Pothecary all received their county caps, while Herman was working up to replacing Jack Newman. Livsey and Newman had both faded out; Livsey was ill during the winter of 1929-30: the Committee paid his salary during the following summer but he was not well enough to play and his association with the County came to an end. Newman had a pretty fair season in 1930 with 77 wickets, but he too became unwell and heart trouble was diagnosed. The Committee paid his salary during the 1931 season but he did not play. Almost all the amateur talent of the 1920s had evaporated; it is difficult to think of Tennyson in such evanescent terms but after succeeding to the peerage in the autumn of 1928, he never played as regularly as he had done over the previous ten seasons and the absence of the captain was a considerable handicap to the side: as latterly was the wicket-keeping of George Brown who at 42 took over the duties from Livsey and was succeeded in turn by McCorkell. In 1932, the basic Hampshire team was, in general batting order, Brown, Bailey, Arnold, Mead, Pothecary, Tennyson, Creese, Kennedy, Boyes, McCorkell and Herman (including five left-handers), with such young cricketers as Gerald Hill, R. H. (Dick) Moore and Ted Drake as reserves. This team was the successor to that of the '20s: it included nine batsmen who reached 1,000 runs in a season at one time or another, ten who hit 100s and four men who captured 100 wickets in a season. A pity that only rarely did they all make good together! It seemed that Johnny Arnold and Kennedy were the leading personalities of this side, whose peak years were 1932-36, with Mead a useful elder statesman whose best years were already some time back.

Not a bit of it.

131

Chapter Twenty-Two
West Indian Summer

Mead and Brown, too, were bound to be prominent personalities in any team which would have them because of their mannerisms as well as their success. They and Arnold were the only moderately successful Hampshire batsmen in the wet summer of 1932. At the start of the next season, which turned out to be a memorably flaming one, George Brown played one of the finest innings of his career. After Sandham had batted all the way through Surrey's innings for 169 not out, Brown set out to emulate him, beginning with restraint but later pulling and driving in great style. No-one else bettered Arnold's 27 as Brown, in turn, carried out his bat when the last Hampshire wicket fell. His score of 150 not out was the last great performance of his brilliant but erratic career. Mead did nothing out of the ordinary until the return game with Surrey, the fourth in Hampshire's programme later in May. It was Tom Barling's turn to dominate the Surrey batting with a massive 269 out of 506. In spite of a maiden century by Pothecary, Hampshire followed on 201 in arrears but they were never in real danger as Mead, first with Arnold and then Kennedy, saw off a not very formidable attack. His log contained only four fours yet Hampshire scored at nearer three runs an over than two — an awful lot of singles. His 80 against Martindale and Griffith, the West Indian fast bowlers, was brighter but did not prevent the tourists gaining their fourth successive victory.

And so to the hot Whitsun of 1933. Kennedy (who had just returned figures of four for nine in 17 overs against Derbyshire) kept one end closed and Herman bowled valiantly to dismiss six Kent batsmen for 131; yet Hampshire faced a total of 299. On the Whit Monday, Mead replied with an exhibition which displayed all his qualities to the full. His first real assistant was Bailey, the fourth left-hander in the top six, who helped him put on 98 before Creese, another one, hit up 67 out of 103, and at number ten Boyes (28) stayed while a further 98 were accumulated. Mead batted almost all day without mistake, his chief scoring strokes a five and 23 fours. His enjoyment of the bowling of Freeman, who finished with three wickets for 141 from 46 overs was there for all to see as Hampshire's score climbed to 468 and Mead's to 198. Then wonderful to relate, Herman and Boyes bowled out Kent for 178 and Hampshire won by ten wickets.

KENT

W. H. Ashdown lbw, b. Kennedy	11	— b. Herman	7
C. Fairservice c. Boyes b. Herman	4	— c. McCorkell b. Herman	15
L. J. Todd c. McCorkell b. Kennedy	28	— c. McCorkell b. Herman	9
L. E. G. Ames retired hurt	69	— b. Boyes	38
Mr. B. H. Valentine c. Boyes b. Herman	65	— c. McCorkell b. Boyes	9

Mr. A. P. F. Chapman c. McCorkell b. Herman	16	—	c. Pothecary b. Boyes	20
H. T. W. Hardinge not out	38	—	c. McCorkell b. Herman	51
Mr. W. H. V. Levett c. Boyes b. Herman	3	—	absent hurt	0
E. J. Sheffield c. Kennedy b. Herman	14	—	lbw, b. Kennedy	15
A. E. Watt c. Kennedy b. Herman	23	—	not out	10
A. P. Freeman b. Kennedy	25	—	b. Kennedy	0
B 2, l-b 1	3		B	4
	299			178

HAMPSHIRE

G. Brown b. Watt	25			
J. Arnold c. Levett b. Sheffield	22			
A. E. Pothecary b. Watt	17			
C. P. Mead c. Chapman b. Watt	198			
A. Kennedy c. Chapman b. Watt	12			
J. Bailey c. Chapman b. Watt	44			
Mr. A. K. Judd b. Freeman	2			
W. L. Creese c. Ames b. Ashdown	67			
N. McCorkell c. Ashdown, b. Freeman	8	—	not out	6
G. S. Boyes st Ames, b. Freeman	28			
O. W. Herman not out	11	—	not out	3
B 13, l-b 20, n-b 1	34		B	2
	468			11

HAMPSHIRE BOWLING

	Overs	Mdns.	Runs	Wkts.	Overs	Mdns.	Runs	Wkts.
Kennedy	37.2	14	78	3	23.3	13	46	2
Herman	27	3	131	6	23	2	68	4
Boyes	19	5	36	0	17	4	48	3
Creese	4	0	24	0				
Bailey	5	0	27	0	5	1	12	0

KENT BOWLING

	Overs	Mdns.	Runs	Wkts.
Watt	40	6	123	5
Sheffield	25	1	96	1
Freeman	46	4	141	3
Ashdown	12	1	34	1
Todd	12	3	38	0
Valentine	2	0	2	0
Chapman	0.4	0	9	0

Umpires: F. Chester and J. Hardstaff

Success was rare for the team after that. There followed three defeats away from home before the County beat Middlesex by an innings at Portsmouth on 20th June (Mead run out 25). By the end of that month, their record showed: P13, W2, L7, D4 and they did not win another game that season. That row of defeats resulted from poor batting but from then on it was the bowlers' turn to toil as the batsmen benefited from the conditions during the longest, hottest summer of the 1930s. A succession of drawn matches was the result — four on the trot in July and after defeat from Lancashire came a further seven in succession.

No-one benefited more than Mead from the conditions and the need to build up high scores to match, or anticipate, the high totals made by opponents. Up to the end of June, he had performed solidly in a middle-aged sort of way and just reached his 1,000 runs, with six half-centuries to back up the 198, his sole century.

From 1st July when he hit 150 out of 275 against Leicestershire, the years fell away: both in the runs he compiled and the way he made them, he was right back to his best — the confident and prolific form of the years from 1911 onwards. Hampshire crowds marvelled as he harvested large scores in match after match up to a slightly premature end of his cricket for the season. Between 1st July and 26th August, his performances in 21 innings included eight scores of over 100, three over 50, and only three in single figures — 1,571 runs at an average of 92.41 per innings. Amid this plenty, he cannot have been all that pleased to return scores of 50 and eight and 27 and 12 not out in two drawn games against Yorkshire, especially as in the first match at Bournemouth, the visitors were without Bowes, Verity and Macauley, and Brian Sellers, to the respectful amusement of his team mates, had to bowl 11 overs in the two innings. The novelty was not without effect. He dismissed George Brown each time.

August saw the most remarkable run or runs of all. Mead had taken the greatest possible fancy to the bowling of Freeman as the score card shows:

HAMPSHIRE

G. Brown b Watt	7	—	c. Ashdown b. Freeman	29
J. Arnold c. Ashdown b. Freeman	25	—	b. Watt	15
N. McCorkell c. Ashdown b. Freeman	43	—	b. Freeman	18
C. P. Mead c. Woolley b. Ashdown	87	—	b. Hardinge	135
A. E. Pothecary c. Chapman b. Freeman	24	—	c. Chapman b. Watt	95
A. Kennedy b. Watt	17			
W. L. Creese c. Todd b. Ashdown	39	—	c. Todd b. Knott	22
J. Bailey lbw, b. Valentine	49	—	not out	13
G. S. Boyes not out	32	—	c. Chapman b. Knott	21
Mr. A. E. G. Baring lbw, b. Freeman	5			

134

Mr. R. H. Palmer lbw, b. Freeman   0
B 9, l-b 6, n-b 1   16   B 6, l-b 5   11
                                  344   *359
*Innings declared closed.

KENT

W. H. Ashdown b. Boyes	106	— not out	52
Mr. C. S. Marriott c. Boyes b. Baring	2		
A. P. Freeman c. Mead b. Baring	2		
L. J. Todd c. Kennedy b. Baring	0	— not out	28
F. E. Woolley c. Boyes b. Kennedy	14		
L. E. G. Ames c. Brown b. Boyes	79		
Mr. B. H. Valentine c. Brown b. Boyes	78		
Mr. C. H. Knott c. Palmer b. Brown	51		
Mr. A. P. F. Chapman c. Mead b. Boyes	15		
H. T. W. Hardinge not out	13		
A. E. Watt run out	16		
B 7, l-b 6	13	B	5
	389		85

KENT BOWLING

	Overs	Mdns.	Runs	Wkts.	Overs	Mdns.	Runs	Wkts.
Watt	20	5	58	2	15	3	52	2
Ashdown	19	2	56	2	6	1	17	0
Freeman	42	7	120	5	35	8	102	2
Marriott	27	5	67	0	21	6	63	0
Hardinge	10	3	22	0	6	0	20	1
Valentine	3	1	5	1	6	0	46	0

2nd Inns. — Todd, 2-2-0-0; Woolley, 3-0-30-0; Knott, 6-0-18-2

HAMPSHIRE BOWLING

Kennedy	22	4	75	1	Creese	11	1	18	0
Baring	25	1	101	3	Bailey	4	0	17	0
Palmer	16	0	70	0	Arnold	11	0	28	0
Boyes	27.1	5	94	4	Pothecary	3	0	17	0
Brown	8	1	36	1					

Umpires: A. E. Street and F. Walden

In the second innings, going in at 63 for two, only 18 ahead, he played so freely that he scored 135 out of 260 in two hours 35 minutes. He drove more than usual, often going out to the pitch of the ball, hit 16 fours and with Pothecary put on 206 in just over two hours. Baring, captaining Hampshire, delayed the declaration and a draw was inevitable; yet who can blame him for his caution against a side containing Woolley, Ames, Knott, Chapman, Valentine, Todd and Watt, in which Hardinge, opening bat for so many years, was now batting at number eight, nine or ten?

Returning to Southampton, Hampshire took part in one of the matches which gave cricket in the 1930s a bad name; even allowing for the fact that storms prevented any play after lunch on the third day, it was a dire reflection on the approach of the captains that not even an innings a side had been completed by then. This was not altogether the fault of Mead who played the attack (minus Larwood who following his injury during the bodyline tour hardly bowled in 1933) with masterly ease. He reached the 100 in two-and-a-half hours but took a further two hours to add 52 more. With Pothecary also reaching three figures, Hampshire had reached 379 for five by the end of the first day. Baring did not declare and when Notts at last went in, they occupied the rest of the time available in reaching 396 for seven.

As it happened, there was no amateur available to captain the County for the rest of the season, and the Committee had no alternative but to get Mead to lead the team. He had already led them in the games with Essex at Leyton and Nottingham at Trent Bridge, both of which were lost. From the game with Somerset at Bath in mid-July he captained in all the matches, save those in which Baring was able to play, until he himself had to drop out. This period included the seven successive drawn matches in the course of which he hit three 100s in four innings. The weather remained hot, the Hampshire attack was simply not strong enough in the conditions to dismiss opposing sides, and it was logical in the circumstances to pile up runs as the best form of self-defence.

When the weather became unsettled as it did when they played Lancashire at Manchester, the batsmen were not able to fulfil their role and it was left to Mead to save the side from an inglorious display by batting for four-and-a-half hours for 113 and remaining undefeated when the last man, Herman, was run out with Hampshire on 271, only 26 behind Lancashire.

That innings, following his 87 and 135 against Kent and his 152 from the Nottinghamshire attack, made three 100s in a row, the third time he had achieved the feat. After breaking the sequence by scoring only 44 at Leicester, he took his side to Ilkeston and there set the seal on his season. He and Gerald Hill were responsible for an imposing performance against the by now formidable Midland side. First he won the toss, then after the early dismissal of Brown and McCorkell, raced to three figures in only two hours. Up to that point, his hitting was brilliant but afterwards he seemed to tire but batted on and on for another three-and-a-quarter hours while Kennedy and Bailey assisted in long stands, increasing his score to 227. This was his highest score since that memorable performance at Scarborough almost four years before. Even after his own dismissal on the second (Monday) morning, he did not declare the innings closed. A draw seemed inevitable but Derbyshire were out faced by Hampshire's total of 478: Hill dismissed Alderman, Denis Smith and Worthington in his first two overs without conceding a run. The home side did not recover and Mead made them follow on 291 runs behind. This time it was Kennedy's turn to take early wickets and only a stubborn innings by Garnett Lee, playing in his last home match, narrowly prevented a Hampshire victory. Had Hampshire — Mead — ended their innings earlier a win might have resulted, but this is the only occasion that year when under Mead's captaincy Hampshire lost a chance of victory by batting on too long.

Speculation as to how Mead would have fared as captain of a well balanced side is fruitless. He was leader in 1933 only because no amateur of any maturity was available and when the Committee decided that Tennyson's time was up, they of course looked for another amateur. They were following the custom of the time; between 1890 and 1946, the only professional formally appointed to lead his County side was W. E. Astill of Leicestershire in 1935. His county rose from 12th to sixth in the County Championship that season but as soon as his Committee could find an amateur able to play with some regularity, they ditched Astill for the 1936 season: under his successor C. S. Dempster, the great New Zealand Test batsman, they dropped back to 15th position. Hampshire were not likely to be revolutionary in this respect.

By the end of the Derby game, Mead had scored over 800 runs in August alone and still had the prospect of six more innings in the month, all at Bournemouth. He scored 39 as Hampshire facing a Worcester total of 100 failed to overtake it by one run, when brilliant sunshine followed heavy rain. After his dismissal, the last five wickets fell for ten runs. The wicket recovering, so did the batting. C. F. Walters and Maurice Nichol together added 256, setting Hampshire 427 to win with five hours left. Arnold, who had a poor season, and McCorkell fell for seven; it was of course Mead, with his fifth 100 in six matches, who ensured that they comfortably saved the game. Pothecary and Creese were his chief assistants in carrying the Hampshire total to 295 for four wickets. Mead's total of 131 not out took his runs for August to 967, but his season's cricket came to an abrupt halt. He contributed 20 to a pretty feeble Hampshire innings of 221 against Gloucestershire who piled up 403 even if Hammond failed before Hampshire succumbed to Tom Goddard a second time.

Mead did not bat in that innings. After so much endurance at the wicket, something had to go. It was the varicose veins. Dick Moore says that they burst — and that was the end of Mead's cricket for the season. Moore, who had played in a dozen or so matches since 1931 and was still only 19 years old, was summoned to replace him for the last game of the season against Essex at Bournemouth and made the most of his opportunity with an aggressive innings of 159 in a high-scoring draw. Either Brown or Kennedy led the team. At least Mead did not have to stand at slip as Essex amassed 564 for eight wickets while everyone except the wicket-keeper bowled. Another draw resulted.

His total of 987 runs in August brought Mead's total to 2,576 runs for the season and his average of 67.78 runs an innings placed him a close second to Hammond in the first class averages. Wisden commented that 'these figures did not approach those of some years back' which was in a way true and was yet an unnecessarily disparaging comment. Only in the years of 1921 and 1928 did he achieve more runs at a higher average in spite of his missing these last five days' cricket.

Such a recovery of top class form at the age of 46 is without parallel among professional batsmen. Only W.G. himself, a quasi-amateur, who aged 47 scored 1,000 runs in May 1895 and went on to an aggregate of 2,346 runs (average 51) after averaging 19 in 1891 and 29 in 1894, showed a similar ability to recapture his best form when nearer 50 than 40. Now, nobody plays first class cricket regularly so far into middle age.

However, in spite of the continued success of that generation, with middle aged batsmen continuing to score prolifically well into the 1930s as did Ernest Tyldesley (who hit his 100th century in 1934 followed by Sandham in the following year), Sutcliffe and others, a new generation — another new generation were pressing behind those veterans of nearly 30 years' service. 1934 saw the entry of Leonard Hutton at 18, 29 years younger than Mead and 34 years junior to Jack Hobbs whose last season it was. Other youngsters like Cyril Washbrook and Joe Hardstaff were also establishing themselves.

George Brown, a few months younger than Mead, dropped out of the Hampshire side at the end of 1933 after a dispute over terms. Tennyson's time was drawing to a close, too. In 1933 there was a constant need to find a replacement. Enjoying himself in America, he did not return to cricket until towards the end of June. In his fourth match, he was taken ill and played no more that season. Mead led the team most frequently. A. K. Judd was captain in the first seven matches; G. L. O. Jessop, son of the great hitter, played only three times for Hampshire, aged 22 — and acted as leader in two of them, Baring in four and in all, seven individuals took their turn.

The Committee deliberated and were prepared to hope for better things, but when their veteran leader — back in the U.S.A. — telegraphed that in 1934 he was to write about the Test matches for the *News of the World*, so making himself unavailable for five summer Saturdays, the Committee gave the *coup de grâce* and appointed as captain W. G. L. F. Lowndes, an Oxford Blue in 1921, who had only very limited experience of Championship cricket. Tennyson had indicated that he would play under any elected captain and he did play with and in substitution for his successor over the next two seasons.

138

One of the results of his success in 1933 was to remind Mead of his value to Hampshire. In 1931, when the Government cut the salaries of judges, civil servants and school teachers, retrenchment was in the air — and in the Club's minutes. The Committee reduced the players' basic pay for the following year. The secretary, too, suffered. None of them objected to signing their contracts and when a year later the Club reduced match money as well, no complaints were recorded.

It was different when in the autumn of 1933 the question of wages came up again. Mead refused to sign his contract and sought an interview with the Committee. It took place in October. Mead 'stated his case and retired'. The Committee, lacking Sir Russell Bencraft who was not in the chair for this meeting, offered Mead a sweetener of £20 in recognition of his services in 1933, provided that he signed. When he told them that he would not have it, they raised the spectre of Sir Russell, deciding that he should be invited to interview Mead and offer him £25. The threat sufficed, Mead accepted that sum and did not have to meet the Chairman.

Fortunately for his relations with the Committee, he fared just as well for most of 1934 as he had done in 1933. A big score early on, 179 not out against Middlesex, reminded the pundits at Lord's of his continuing ability to pile up the runs, and he followed with 50 against Gloucestershire in preparation for the imminent match against the Australians.

No other game of Hampshire's during the 1930s caused as much interest or is as well remembered as that one played at Southampton in glorious May weather. The tourists, led by Woodfull, arrived with four victories in six matches behind them. They had a powerful array of batsmen headed by Don Bradman and Ponsford, Woodfull himself, Bill Brown, McCabe, Kippax and Chipperfield, but their attack looks strange to modern eyes consisting as it did of Grimmett (who did not play in this match) and O'Reilly, leg-break bowlers, and the commandingly named Fleetwood-Smith, unorthodox slow left-arm. Old men remember how large crowds were queuing for entry to the County Ground many hours before the start, by which time the attendance already numbered 7,000. Lowndes won the toss for innings with Woodfull but batting first even on a perfect wicket seemed a doubtful advantage when Hampshire were soon 19 for two. Mead joined Arnold and they quietly carried the total to 34 when O'Reilly came on to bowl with his bounding run to the wicket and aggressive approach to the batsman. Mead at once glided him to the leg boundary for four and treated Fleetwood-Smith in the same manner; then Arnold drove O'Reilly for an enormous six. They added 60 in only 35 minutes when Arnold, attempting a second six, was well caught by Bradman running in from the deep. Joined by Lowndes, Mead seemed unsettled for a time; dropped by Bromley at short leg, he hit the next delivery hard to him again but along the ground. Bromley's smart stop found Mead out of his crease and in regaining it he slipped and measured his length to the amused relief of the spectators. After lunch, with the score at 93 for three and in front of more than 10,000 spectators,

139

there were no more uncertainties: Mead and Lowndes took only 55 minutes to double the score, Lowndes rivalling his senior professional in the certainty and timing of his cuts and drives. Only when he reached the 90s did Mead play warily. The pace slackened and the crowd waited with some anxiety until with a push to leg and a sharp single he reached three figures; his goal attained in under two-and-a-half hours. The crowd cheered as if at a cup final. Lowndes also reached his century. The partnership continued until it had added 247 runs in under three hours. Tennyson contributing 56, Hampshire's total reached 420.

There were more sensations to come; the early Australian batsmen found Giles Baring unplayable: if Woodfull was called 'the unbowlable', Baring caught and bowled him, then had Brown, the other opener, taken behind by Neil McCorkell: Bradman followed but to the joy of the onlookers, Baring at once dismissed him, too: a thick edge flew straight to Mead's stomach: a cry of 'catch it' went up and he gratefully hugged the ball: Bradman caught Mead bowled Baring, nought: six for three wickets but the next pair, McCabe and Darling added 174 and Chipperfield at number eight hit an unbeaten century to give the Australians a lead of 13. O'Reilly and Fleetwood-Smith asserted themselves in the second innings and only Arnold, who reached three figures, enabled Lowndes to declare with a draw assured.

Almost anything would be an anti-climax after that but Mead's batting in the Australian match was the prelude to another long-running spell of success which did not end until he was dismissed for a single in the Surrey match at Bournemouth on 22nd July. In the seven intervening weeks, he contributed 138 to a victory over Derbyshire at Portsmouth, 125 not out which did not prevent defeat by Worcester, and 198 again in a draw with Kent at Folkestone; virtually a single innings a side match as Hampshire batted well into the second morning for 528. Mead's innings took only four hours and ten minutes and during long stands with Paris, Pothecary and Kennedy, he cut, drove and placed his on-side strokes as well as ever. He and Kennedy added 149 in 90 minutes; nevertheless, Mead was booed by the Kent crowd, not for his batting but for his failure to declare. The next day, Kennedy completed a chanceless century; so did Woolley when Kent replied with 400.

HAMPSHIRE

J. Arnold c. Fagg b. Lewis	54	— c. Ashdown b. Freeman	27
Mr. R. H. Moore lbw, b. Watt	0	— c. Todd b. Freeman	67
Mr. C. G. A. Paris c. Chapman b. Ashdown	47	— run out	0
C. P. Mead c. and b. Ashdown	198		
A. E. Pothecary lbw, b. Watt	33	— c. Fagg b. Lewis	13
A. Kennedy lbw, b. Lewis	130		
N. McCorkell c. Levett b. Watt	2	— c. Lewis b. Freeman	3
W. L. Creese c. Chapman b. Ashdown	19	— not out	58

140

E. J. Drake c. Todd b. Ashdown	5	— c. sub b. Freeman	13
G. Hill not out	15	— not out	27
O. W. Herman b. Valentine	10		
B 9, l-b 6	15	B 2, l-b 2	4
	528	(Six wkts.)	212

KENT

W. H. Ashdown c. McCorkell b. Kennedy	8
A. Fagg c. Paris b. Kennedy	27
F. E. Woolley c. Drake b. Creese	122
Mr. B. H. Valentine c. Hill b. Kennedy	30
L. J. Todd c. Creese b. Herman	78
Mr. I. Akers-Douglas b. Herman	44
Mr. A. P. F. Chapman b. Herman	3
Mr. W. H. V. Levett c. Hill b. Kennedy	32
A. E. Watt c. Arnold b. Herman	18
C. Lewis not out	16
A. P. Freeman b. Herman	5
B 6, l-b 11	17
	400

KENT BOWLING

	Overs	Mdns.	Runs	Wkts.	Overs	Mdns.	Runs	Wkts.
Watt	37	7	106	3	6	0	20	0
Ashdown	36	11	110	4	3	0	28	0
Freeman	28	6	98	0	20	3	58	4
Lewis	36	12	103	2	20	3	64	1
Fagg	9	0	43	0				
Valentine	7.3	0	34	1				
Woolley	5	3	2	0	3	0	19	0
Akers-Douglas	4	0	15	0				
Todd					6	1	19	0

HAMPSHIRE BOWLING

	Overs	Mdns.	Runs	Wkts.
Kennedy	42	9	113	4
Herman	39.2	7	97	5
Creese	23	3	88	1
Hill	18	4	50	0
Drake	4	1	25	0
Pothecary	1	0	10	0

Umpires: J. W. Hitch and A. E. Street

141

Stuart Boyes, Mead, Len Creese and Neil McCorkell take the field against the Australians, Southampton, 1934.

As July burned into August, he had one or two lean patches, especially at Bournemouth where he scored only one and 15 in the first week and 14, one and nought a month later, when the fortunate supporters at Dean Park enjoyed nine sunny days of cricket. Mead contributed another remarkable performance against Yorkshire when facing a total of 346, Hampshire collapsed but this did not deter him from driving hard and placing the ball skilfully on the leg side. Soon after Tennyson was sixth out, Mead received a blow on the elbow from a delivery by Bowes and had to retire. To the relief of Hampshire supporters, on the fall of the ninth wicket, he came out to join Gerald Hill, completed his century and was undefeated on 120 when Hill was caught. Only Pothecary (40) of the others scored more than 17. Mead finished the season by helping in yet another recovery, scoring 57 in a rain-spoiled game with Worcestershire.

He and Arnold headed the batting averages:

	Innings	Not Out	Runs	Highest Score	Average
Mead	46	8	2011	198	52.92
Arnold	52	5	2261	160	48.10

Lowndes and the hugely promising Dick Moore were well ahead of the others but Pothecary, Creese and the perennial Kennedy all batted well: Kennedy finished with totals of 990 runs and 91 wickets but his legs were not everlasting and he accepted the post of coach at Cheltenham College at the end of the season. He and Boyes each conceded little more than two runs an over (against Notts., Boyes bowled 80 overs in one innings for only 138 runs) but wickets were hard to get. Lowndes proved a strong personality as captain and made plenty of runs but did not play in August. As John Arlott has put it 'he preferred fishing'.

That did not matter much in 1934 when the County put the same side into the field for most of the season and Tennyson was available to captain when Lowndes was not, but things were very different in 1935.

That year, Mead and Arnold again figured at the top of the batting:

| Mead | 55 | 12 | 1650 | 151 not out | 38.37 |
| Arnold | 58 | 3 | 1713 | 142 not out | 31.14 |

The reader may ask, where did Mead go in that year to remain not out so often? The answer is number four as usual, save on one notable occasion, and the number of his undefeated innings is an indication of what little support he and Arnold received. As Hampshire had batsmen capable of excelling in a dry season and bowlers capable of turning a wet one to advantage, you might suppose that the least they would achieve under average conditions, given reasonable fortune, would be a respectable mediocrity. But not in 1935. Instead of 18 players in the previous year, 27 participated; defeats increased from 11 to 16. Their final position in the championship table, 15, was only one position lower than before, and victories increased from three to five but much of their play was wretched. They greatly missed Kennedy's expertise until he returned during the summer holidays when he took 32 wickets in seven games.

Few sides can have been so stricken by illness and injuries; Moore, afflicted by scarlet fever during the match at Nottingham, did not play after the end of May and he was greatly missed; Creese and Pothecary were both injured during that match and Pothecary never ran into his best form; Boyes, too, was unfit to play in some games as was Herman; Lowndes took part in only half the matches and after an early century against Kent, achieved little as batsman or bowler; Hosie, Paris and Tennyson all shared the captaincy with him. The side never got their act together and both batting and bowling deteriorated in spite of the improvement of Hill (93 wickets and 549 runs). Although they lost the first two matches comfortably, Hampshire looked to be capable of normal progress when against Northamptonshire they hit up 401 for six wickets before declaring, to which Mead's contribution was an immaculate innings of 151 not out — his 149th century. Next, they fell victim to the South Africans (Mead 27 and 31), Worcestershire and Nottingham; then to Derby and Yorkshire, too. After two drawn games, relief came in the form of victory over Gloucestershire.

One of Mead's colleagues said of him that "of course, he played for himself in those last seasons"; one is tempted to ask who else was there to play for in 1935? The Nottingham game was, if not the lowest of the low, the beginning of the worst patch. During that game, Moore was taken ill and as Creese and Pothecary were both injured during the match, only eight men batted in each innings. Already in that team was S. Fenley, a leg-break bowler, whose career with Surrey had reached its end in 1929, so hard pressed were Hampshire to raise a side: facing the home team's score of 499 for nine declared, Hampshire's tail began with Boyes at number four. Mead, leading the rump, chose to go in first with Arnold, who was bowled by Voce for five, and was himself missed when he had scored a single. After McCorkell was run out, Boyes stayed in with Mead for two-and-a-quarter hours while 123 were added. Apart from the one mistake, Mead batted without fault for nearly four-and-a-half hours and when Fenley was seventh and last out, was left undefeated and so carried his bat through the innings for the third time in his career — and the first since 1911, 24 years earlier. When they followed on, he was caught off the bowling of Voce for one and all resistance ended. Dismissed for only 37 by Larwood and Voce, Hampshire lost by an innings and 241 runs. Even with a full complement of fit cricketers they showed little improvement for weeks: restored to the number four position, he was again undefeated for 50 in an innings defeat by Derby and unconquered twice for totals of 25 and 18 in completed innings against Yorkshire at Hull (Hampshire's scores were 63 and 117).

In the game at Hull, Boyes, while bowling, broke down and a succession of unfamiliar Hampshire sides took the field before, supported by the return of A. K. Judd and Tennyson, they beat Gloucestershire by six wickets at Portsmouth. Set 305 to win, they owed almost everything to Arnold who batted splendidly for 142 not out and Mead (75) who helped him add 173 in two-and-a-quarter hours. At Leicester, it was Hull all over again. Facing the Midland team's first innings score of only 157 in thoroughly miserable conditions, Hampshire on the first evening collapsed. Mead was still there as Arthur Holt, on his first appearance, entered onto the stage at 57 for eight. Mead was in complete control — he took a single from the *first* ball of each over. Holt was proud to survive to fight another day but by the end of it, in the second innings, Mead was again in occupation with the last man, Herman, in and they saw the game into the third day — and another defeat. Mead's scores were 20 not out and 47 not out: Hampshire's XI were completed by Alastair Macleod, shortly to take over as secretary. Early in August, Mead was again the survivor at the end of the completed innings — this time against Somerset at Southampton. The press hinted that with a little more effort he might have completed his 150th century, but J. C. White, also well into middle-age, bowled with all his renowned accuracy, conceding only 61 runs in 35 overs; he then excelled with a score of 142 and Somerset led by 101. Hampshire wiped out the deficit for the loss of McCorkell. It must have occurred to Mead, after a careful start, that he was again in with a chance — perhaps there was a financial incentive — and he began scoring so readily that just before the end he duly completed his century in two hours ten minutes. He never missed an opportunity of scoring but there was a degree of contrivance: Ingle, the Somerset captain, had completed a century from a Hampshire attack weakened by injury to Herman, to which Pothecary, Paris and Arnold contributed 19 overs (for 82 runs), and many of Mead's runs in turn came from change bowling; he eagerly spent only 25 minutes over his second 50. He was the third batsman to reach the total of 150 centuries after Hobbs (197 by the time he retired after the 1934 season) and Patsy Hendren, who by the end of 1935 had brought his total to 156.

Mead reached a fourth century that season against Surrey at the Oval and went on to finish the season quietly with 29 not out, again, towards a total of 99 against Yorkshire at Portsmouth — and a duck out of 94 in the second. Most Hampshire players must have felt glad that the season was over but as Wisden commented, his defence remained 'as solid as a rock'.

A wet day? Bridge with (clockwise from left) Gerald Hill, Ted Drake, Lofty Herman, Neil McCorkell and Johnny Arnold.

Chapter Twenty-Three
Not with a bang . . .

Hampshire were under new management in 1936. Sir Russell, approaching the age of 80, had finally, and against the wishes of his colleagues, retired from the post of Chairman and A. J. L. Hill took over. George Muir, regarded by many as Bencraft's right-hand man, was succeeded as secretary by Alastair Macleod, who, like Hill, had played for the County with Mead before the 1914-18 war (and, unlike Hill, had in the interim married Lou King-Hall, the writer of girls' stories): Lowndes departed and R. H. Moore took over as captain at the age of 22, with Cecil Paris, two years older, as vice-captain.

There were problems with the management, or lack of it, at the Bear Cross Inn. For some season, money was getting short again but the trouble was not yet coming to a head.

Macleod led the side in pre-season training and his enthusiasm paid off. Only 18 players were called on by the County during the season and for three months the side performed with admirable consistency. By the end of July, five batsmen had reached their 1,000 runs and Paris, who missed a few games, was not far short. Herman captured over 100 wickets; Boyes, in spite of yet more injury, had over 90, as did Creese who, showing considerable development of his medium paced left-arm spin, missed the double of 1,000 runs and 100 wickets by only five victims. By then, the County stood third in the championship table and if they beat Kent they would gain another place.

By that time, Mead was the one batsman who had not reached four figures; indeed, he stood oddly low in the list of averages. At the start, he picked up his bat where he had left off and by the end of May had 419 runs to show at 38 runs an innings. At the end of the month, he took yet another 100 from the Kent bowling at Southampton when Hampshire faced a Kent total of 502, more than half of them from the bat of Arthur Fagg (257) and a large proportion of the remainder from Frank Woolley. Mead and Creese put on 115 in even time and Hampshire finished only 33 behind.

Then for most of June and July, he underwent a long and barren period which contained only two scores over 50, both in June. In July, his figures ran: three and two; 18 and ten; one and one; two; 44 not out and eight; 12 and 32. It must have come almost as a relief when following an injury to his thigh, he had to stand down from five matches. It was at this time that he was seventh in the Hampshire averages with only 769 runs from 33 innings.

On 29th July, while he was resting, the Committee met. Tennyson had not been asked to play at all that year: indeed, Hampshire's side hardly varied except when one of the regulars was injured, and it was clear that his County career was over. The Committee decided to make presentations to him in appreciation of 'all he had done for Hampshire cricket in the past', and to the retiring Honorary Treasurer and Secretary. They then moved to discussion of re-engagement of the staff for 1937. The Hampshire Committee minutes never recorded the discussion but only the resolutions which resulted. The relevant one read: 'All to be re-engaged with the exception of P. Mead and G. Heath. Terms to be discussed later'. The new Honorary Treasurer, E. C. Redman, then proposed that 100 guineas (£105) be paid on account to Mead and that a 'public subscription be organised next season for this professional'.

This decision was not made known to the public and subsequently the Committee changed their minds about George Heath who made his first appearance as an opening bowler with great success for Hampshire in 1937. The decision about Mead was not rescinded but he returned to the side early in August for the match against Essex at Southend. The home side made a pretty challenging start to the tune of 503, but this gave him the opportunity to play himself back into form, which he accepted, batting for over four hours against Kenneth Farnes, Nichols and Peter Smith, all England bowlers. His 104 was his 153rd and last 100 in first class cricket. He retained his good form to the end of the season, never scoring less than 25, and averaging over 70 in his nine innings in August. The last four games were all played at home. In the first, against Gloucestershire at Portsmouth, in the course of his innings of 51 he passed W. G. Grace's total number of runs in first class cricket, 54,896. The match with All-India at Bournemouth produced a crowd of 8,000 on the first day. Kennedy, returning to the side, and H. M. Lawson bowled out India for 192. In reply, Paris, batting particularly well for 74, and Mead added 97, but Mead was hit by a ball from Jahangir Khan and had to retire. He returned but was left high and dry on 53 not out as the last five wickets fell for 50. Nevertheless, Hampshire's lead was 46 and they looked set for victory when the Indians lost nine wickets for 99. Perhaps Hampshire took things too easily as Moore rang the changes on the bowlers and the last pair hit up 100 runs in 50 minutes, but Hampshire still needed only 154 to win. Before the close on the second day, they lost Moore, Paris and J. E. Manners for 43; on the last morning, Creese, McCorkell and Pothecary hit while Mead, held back to number seven, displayed his usual soundness, but when Lawson, the last man, came in, nine runs were still needed. He hit a couple of lusty blows but was caught with Hampshire still three away from victory. This time, Mead, again undefeated for 53, had batted two hours and 40 minutes in vain.

He contributed 25 to a high-scoring draw with Surrey before the last match of the season, also at Bournemouth. Match? Hampshire were out-matched from the start. Moore won the toss on a good wicket and in beautiful weather, but they made very heavy going against the Yorkshire attack. Mead was top scorer with 43; McCorkell batted for one-and-three-quarter hours to score nine not out. Yorkshire found batting easy and took their score to 378 for eight, a lead of 204. On the second evening, Hampshire lost Arnold for four. In the circumstances, Mead's reaction next day was surprising; he scored with freedom in a lost cause, hitting 52 out of 77 in 80 minutes. Paris stayed for three-and-three-quarter hours but Yorkshire needed only 25 to win.

So his career ended on a reasonably high note as his young colleagues just faded away to such an extent that by the end of the season the County lay not second or third in the championship table but as low as tenth. His form in August, when all about him were losing theirs, took him yet again to the head of the averages, but there was no reprieve. His name was top of the agenda when the Committee met on 22nd September. They granted him a weekly payment of £4 as an interim measure until the next Committee meeting. Presumably, Mead was aware that these payments were not simply part of the usual arrangement for winter pay. When they met again, the Committee had before them a proper retirement package — in 1937 terms at any rate. The original resolution of 29th July was rescinded. This did not result in his re-engagement but they granted him a gratuity in recognition of his long and valuable services to the Club of £4 a week for 12 months from 1st September 1936 and opened a public subscription for him during the season of 1937.

Dick Moore and Cecil Paris were not consulted about the decision which ended his first class career and both subsequently had reason to regret the absence of his sound and reliable batting. They had, however, noticed early on in the season that in Mead's case bending had, in John Arlott's words, 'moved from anathema to impossibility'. The side seemed almost one fielder short: it was John Arnold who pointed out that Mead at slip had taken to standing more and more directly behind the wicket-keeper. Indeed, the number of his catches had diminished from 25 in 1934 to eight in 1935. In 1936, the total was only three. The captain and vice-captain decided to remove him from the position he had occupied for so long and put themselves in the slips. He was exiled to mid-on and third man; not an efficient use of fielder power.

The move served to focus attention on Mead's lack of mobility in comparison with his team mates; only Stuart Boyes, greatly respected on the county circuit for his fine fielding at short leg, was within 12 years of his age; he in turn was seven years older than Sam Pothecary, the next most senior member of the side. Johnnie Arnold, Creese and Herman were all 29, McCorkell was 24 and Gerald Hill, 23, as was Moore himself. The retirement of Kennedy and the departure of Tennyson had left Mead isolated. His lack of speed between the wickets deprived not only him but his batting partners of runs. Patrick Murphy, whose description of Mead differs in most respects from the one given by this book, writes that in 1936 it was common knowledge that his colleagues vied among themselves to try and run him out; if so, not one of them succeeded.

Then his batting had gone through that lean patch in June and July. Just as important to the Committee was that their 'new' Hampshire side had played so consistently together while he was achieving so little. He would be 50 years of age before the start of the next season AND there was yet another and highly promising left-hander waiting in the wings in Donald Walker who would be qualified to play in 1937.

All these matters contributed to the Committee's decision. As it happened, the year 1936 saw the best of that generation of Hampshire players; they never rose to such heights as a team again as the County's positions in the championship of 14, 15 and 16 in the remaining years before the war testify.

The really sad thing was that as his departure did not become generally known until Christmas 1936, there was no chance for the public to show their appreciation for what he had done over 30 years. When in 1938 Frank Woolley decided that the time had come for him to retire, his decision was announced at the beginning of the season which then consisted of a succession of triumphant farewell performances. However, the manner of Woolley's departure was not typical. Mead, like Maurice Tate and Andrew Sandham in the following year, just disappeared.

The local papers described his life in cricket at great length and in the manner of the day, without comment on his achievements or the manner of his departure, C. L. R. James, writing in April 1937 in the *Glasgow Herald* under the headline 'Exciting Cricket Depends upon Exciting Personalities' grieved 'Mead is to go this year. It is complained that he is too slow. Mead in 1936 made 1,000 runs at an average of 30 and two centuries. He is still, as figures go, one of the best batsmen in the side. But they say, he was not exciting enough. Well, I part company from all critics of Mead, even long past his prime. How I loved to see the man: his stance, his pulling at his cap, his sound foundation, his pawkiness, his deep enjoyment of every minute. In the field he rolled from short slip like a sailor on deck. Of course he was slow. But for me it didn't matter . . . I devoutly hope that the last word has not been said on Mead's retirement. As a run-getter, he is still worth his place and I am thinking that perhaps Hampshire may find it necessary to call on him again . . . how is one to legislate for people who find so grand and weather-beaten an old character as Mead dull and unexciting?' An anonymous writer in Wisden observed 'always a personality on the field, noted for his mannerisms at the crease, he presented to bowlers one of the biggest problems of the last decade: Mead was hardly an attractive batsman but his rock-like defence and clever placing of strokes enabled him to put together many large scores . . . his position will be hard to fill'.

Wisden spoke more truly than it knew. It was over 20 years before Roy Marshall, quite unlike Mead in every possible way, brought world class batsmanship back to Hampshire.

The Committee had taken particular care to provide him with an income for the year up to September 1937; this was certainly necessary as another disaster befell the family. Signs of financial embarrassment again appeared — late arrival for the train and departure from the platform at Waterloo surrounded by a phalanx of his colleagues to avoid formalities with the ticket collector were the most common signs; more positively, one morning as he left for cricket, the bailiffs were observed removing furniture; the brewery were alerted and an acrimonious correspondence came to a head when they gave him notice

149

to quit at Michaelmas 1936. The pub had prospered in the summer months but the local trade was not sufficient to sustain the host and his family during the long watches of the autumn and winter — the surrounding area was not as yet developed, although it was soon to become a populous suburb of Bournemouth. So another business venture ground to a disastrous halt and as Mead was the only member of the family in gainful employment, the situation again looked dire.

If Mead had any hard feelings about the termination of his career, he kept them to himself. In January 1937, over 200 guests gathered at the South Western Hotel, Southampton, to honour Sir Russell Bencraft's 60 years of service to the County's cricket. The President of M.C.C., Sir Stanley Jackson, P. F. Warner, H. D. G. Leveson-Gower and Sir Francis Lacey, for nearly 30 years secretary to M.C.C., were among the company. There was a long toast list but after Jackson had proposed Sir Russell's health, an additional speaker was called upon to add his own tribute. Philip Mead said: "My brother professionals, past and present, would never forgive me if I let this opportunity pass without saying how very grateful we are to Sir Russell Bencraft for the many kindnesses and help we have received from him. Any of us who went along to see him went to him not only as a boss but as a friend. We hope you will be able to go to the County Ground and see the greatest game of all for many years to come."

On this friendly note, Mead's formal connection with Hampshire County Cricket came to an end.

Seasoned campaigner.

Chapter Twenty-Four
Suffolk Punch

Mead rehoused his family, first in temporary accommodation and then at the address which has remained their home ever since; he was guaranteed an income until September 1937. He had for years pursued some retailing during the winter and this he continued. He did some travelling for Spillers, the agricultural merchants, and also sold light bulbs upon which there was an extraordinarily high mark-up. Then he was offered a summer job. How or why it came about that he became cricket coach at Framlingham College in Suffolk remains a mystery. He was there for the summer of 1937, living in a hotel in Framlingham which is a small town with a magnificent parish church, a castle and a lake situated about 12 miles north-east of Ipswich.

It soon became clear that the arrangement suited both sides. The college was a well-established public school founded in 1864. Until 1929, the headmaster was F. W. Stocks who had made a reputation as a cricketer at the turn of the century by gaining a blue at Oxford and representing Leicestershire and the Gentlemen. J. D. F. Larter of Northamptonshire was a later well-known cricketing product.

The boys were proud to have such a famous batsman as Mead as their first professional coach; they found him great fun and a genuine enthusiast.

If there was irony in the fact that he who had never set much store by practice now spent two hours each afternoon, four days a week bowling and coaching in the nets, his enjoyment and concentration on the job in hand well genuine and unselfconscious. The boy who received his attentions was left with the impression that no-one and nothing else mattered than that he should address the bowling in the correct manner. One of Mead's great strengths was that he could bowl all the afternoon. His understanding of the technique of batting ensured that he knew exactly what he was trying to do and he could put ball after ball on the spot appropriate to the practice of a particular shot. He soon made redundant the wooden bowling contraption previously in use at the college, but it was some time before the progress of the First XI could be assessed as because of an outbreak of mumps, they played only club sides that first year.

Inevitably, he was drawn into games for scratch sides which played against the boys and local club sides. As word of his presence circulated in the county, he was called on to play in matches against a wider variety of opposition. Freddie Houldsworth of the Hampshire Cricket Society has described such an occasion: "In the summer of 1937 I was in Ipswich. Phil Mead in his first season out of county cricket was coach at Framlingham College.

"We had both been invited to play at Campsea Ash Park, the home of a former Speaker of the House of Commons, against a Cambridge University XI; it could have been the second team.

"Our side was quite strong with a number of Suffolk County players. I remember it was a very hot day and at lunch we were about 120 for one. It was suggested as number five it would be doubtful if I would be required to bat, so I enjoyed my lunch.

"So much for my leisurely post-lunch period; we lost two wickets inside two overs and I found myself out in the middle with the Great Man who made it quite clear there would be no quick singles! I have never seen a bat apparently so wide and which could be used to stroke the sixth ball of each over into the open spaces, so the required single could be taken at leisure.

"We? No! Phil put on 77 for the fourth wicket of which I managed five. The education continued in the field, keeping wicket to Phil bowling something under medium pace and moving the ball sharply off the pitch at a rate I had not encountered before.

"I cannot recall the result, but I can remember the day when I discovered how little I knew about cricket."

That season Mead hit at least one century but at club level he was equally formidable with the ball. His engagement was renewed for 1938: the school won five but lost six of their 15 matches. That year the Suffolk County authorities realised that they had a valuable asset in their midst. The county club had returned to play in the Minor Counties' Championship in 1933 after a lengthy absence. They were anxious to build up their strength and extended an invitation to him which he was free to accept once the school term was over. His family had now moved to their permanent home in Bournemouth; they were reasonably comfortable and he joined the Suffolk side at the end of July.

His first game, by an interesting turn of fate, was against Surrey — the second XI at Ipswich. The visitors hit up 374 at a rate of four runs an over: called on to bowl during a troublesome second wicket stand, Mead broke it by dismissing Arthur McIntyre. He also had the top scorer, McMurray, caught for 110. His other victims were Pierpoint, the opening bowler, and Alec Bedser and Stuart Surridge — famous names well into the 1950s. His final figures were 26 overs, seven maidens, 69 runs, five wickets. Before Suffolk went in, he visited the Surrey dressing room where as they prepared for a period in the field, which as professionals playing a largely amateur side, Surrey hoped would be as short as possible, he announced to the young professionals (who also included Eric Bedser and Bernard Constable from the Surrey side which won the County Championship eight years in succession in the 1950s) that he was going to get 100. In fact, his total was 125. However, shades of Hampshire, no-one else could get more than 37.

But still an active player with Suffolk CCC. Back row: C. Perkins, J. V. Daley, B. H. Belle, Murray Sangster, Ted Forrest, E. W. Lovegrove. Front row: G. W. Hockey, Dr. H. Porter, P. Waugh, C. P. Mead, A. G. Powell, R. Durham (scorer).

If only Mead had been allowed to play against W. G. Grace in 1904, he would have created an awesome record of longevity and continuity.

He made 54 in a high-scoring draw against Hertfordshire at Felixstowe before still in the first week of August they moved on to Fenners, Cambridge, where he had made 140 for Hampshire against the University as long before as 1912. With the Cambridgeshire number eight, Covill, reaching three figures, they put the Suffolk bowling to the sword for 418; Mead with two wickets for 62 had the best bowling figures: yet Suffolk passed that total without difficulty. Porter, their opening bat, was the first to his 100. Mead at number four displayed all his old skill in driving, cutting and placing the ball on the leg side as he batted on without mistake; at this level of cricket he remained virtually invincible as he reached 147, while Adam Powell who had played first class cricket for Cambridge University and Essex was third to reach three figures.

In the return game at Lowestoft later in August, Mead was the only bowler to keep the runs down as Cambridgeshire again approached 400: his figures were 32, 13, 56, nought. Not surprisingly, he sought a rest. At number seven, he top-scored with 40, and 18 in the second innings was his contribution to an innings defeat. In five innings that season, he scored 384 runs at an average of 76 runs an innings.

In 1939, he played in all the County's matches, except the first. In nine innings he hit two centuries versus Lincolnshire at Grantham and Bedfordshire at Felixstowe, as well as 90 against them in an earlier game at Luton and two other scores over 50. His only disappointment was that when they played Berkshire at Reading — the nearest he came to home — Robert Relf, the old Sussex player and former Hampshire coach, four years his senior at 56, dismissed him cheaply.

On 31st August, having made 69 in his only innings against Cambridgeshire at Lowestoft, he walked off a county cricket pitch for the last time. That season his record showed 499 runs and his average runs per innings again exceeded 70, although his bowling was hardly used. He had greatly relished his play in East Anglia: indeed, the continuous cricket, the presence of his young team mates and the movement from hotel to hotel had most of the characteristics of a tour.

By 1940, he was very much part of the Framlingham scene and with his engagement renewed for the fourth year, the family contemplated making their future in Suffolk while he began looking for a house. For a time the war hardly affected his activities but at mid-summer the college was under the threat of air raids and temporarily evacuated to Repton in Derbyshire. Mead did not accompany them and when the state of affairs permitted their return and the next summer came round, he was no longer that welcome presence. By then, Philip Mead was in danger of losing his sight.

Chapter Twenty-Five
Unseen Bournemouth

During the early part of 1941, Mead found that his eyesight was literally patchy: sometimes he had tunnel vision and at other times there were gaps in the centre of his line of sight. The specialist to whom he was referred diagnosed that the retina of one eye was becoming detached; eye surgery was then fairly primitive and in any case it was too late to save the sight of one eye. Its vision was lost. It was in that summer that Mead, monocular, played his last public cricket. Lady Normanton organised a charity match at Somerley near Ringwood between the police and an XI of professionals. John Arlott, who then represented the police in a welcome interval from his service for the force in war-torn Southampton, described the match in a memorable article in 1967.

The pitch had been used for cricket — in her ladyship's husband's father's time. It presented 'a terrifying aspect'. The opposition included several pre-war county professionals including one Test player: 'Then Philip Mead walked in. He treated someone's presumption that he had come to watch with a contemptuous look. He was playing . . . he was now in his late 50s.' (He was 54.) 'He had lost the sight of one eye and we had thought him deep in retirement. Four byes were the only runs scored when the opener was caught off his glove defending his face and number three had been bowled by a shooter which ricocheted off his ankle.

Philip Mead came in, as always, at number four. He walked out, stirring old nostalgias, drooping-shouldered, wide-hipped with mighty bowed legs, at that strange gait, half roll, half bustle, using his bat as a walking stick. Before he even took guard, he addressed the field quietly but with feeling. 'Ruddy marquee — full of women — nowhere to put your box on — careful where you're bowling, young Eastwood.'

He then took guard and went through the most eccentric ritual ever known in cricket. As he did before every ball he ever received — and any bowler who interrupted him was waved back while Philip began it all again — he touched his cap four times to square leg (no respect intended), tapped his bat four times in the crease and took four tiny steps up to it. Now the bowler might bowl. The first ball whipped back and hit him on the thigh with a sinister sound — both smack and crack. He looked down the pitch in high anger. "That's bust me packet of fags," he said.

The next ball, last of the over, was fast and about a length: he moved forward to it, it lifted, went through — surely an edge to wicket-keeper or slips — but his bat was no longer there. It was not possible to bat on such a pitch; but he did, without a hurried stroke, for almost an hour. He stopped those that kept low, avoided or accepted in the ribs those that lifted: from others he created barely imaginable singles. He lifted one ball: It moved away from the bat and, leaning over, he cuffed it with only a turn of the wrists, and

155

it hummed: a skimmer, one bounce for four. It was picked up beyond the boundary by one of the earlier batsmen, a useful county professional worth 1,500 runs a season. As I ran round from third man, he tossed the ball back to me. The look on his face mixed harsh envy with admiration. "Look at that old so-and-so: he's old enough to be my father; hasn't touched a bat for years, he can't even see and there he is batting better from memory than I shall ever know how to." The estate team (one retired hurt) made 68: Mead 33 not out: otherwise only extras — 18 — reached double figures. When we batted, Philip stood at slip, his body inclined just perceptibly forward from the hips and once, as a snick seemed to have passed him, he absently-minded put out a hand and caught it.

He was not without sympathy; as he walked down the pitch between overs he turned to mutter: "Worse than air raids, ain't it?" We made 31 (two retired hurt), extras 14. It was all over by tea. Then the old man, too great for our congratulations, drew contentedly at a glass of beer and a cigarette and was heard to say "If pitches had been like that, I wouldn't have given up bowling."

In 1942, the other eye showed similar signs of deterioration; he underwent surgery, consisting of stitching of the retina. It was unsuccessful and within a very short time that eye, too, let him down, leaving him with little more than an indication of the difference between light and dark.

He soon learned his way around the house and garden and was able to pick runner beans, even if he could not plant them, but he could no longer go out on his own. To a man who three years before had been playing cricket in the sunshine and touring with a team of young men in East Anglia, enjoying life to the full, his existence had become highly restricted. He had no income apart from a nominal grant and there was, indeed, little money coming into the home — Alfie was a cripple and Frank's working career was spasmodic. Framlingham retained their interest and when, as late as 1944, Philip Mead was unable to accept their invitation to return, it was Frank who took over as coach. The situation was dire. He made a daily venture to Winton Conservative Club. There his reputation and misfortune were willingly and tacitly accepted, and he could talk of cricket and racing among friends. The club allocated a free pint of beer daily and his companions noted with amusement that if his glass was empty, there was a chance that his hand would alight on someone else's.

The loss of sight by a sportsman in his middle 50s is a deep tragedy, but Mead never let on that he viewed his loss in that light. When a cousin commiserated, his only reply was that his blindness resulted from too much play on blinding pitches. He never, ever, complained. He preserved dignity and required little help with such matters as eating, he continued to smoke, with the concession that he no longer smoked in bed! He could still dress up and, when peace arrived, occupy a place at the top table of local club dinners where he was always ready to say a few words.

The war's end found Mead still only 59 years old. Peace brought him welcome change. In 1946, Herbert Sutcliffe, now retired from cricket, learned of Mead's disability and publicly announced his intention of raising a fund for him. Sutcliffe worked with great thoroughness and was well supported. Cricket matches were played, the response was enormous. The case of Leonard Braund was then brought to Sutcliffe's attention: Braund, born in 1875, had played for Surrey and then, memorably, for Somerset between 1896 and 1920 and for England, and remained in cricket until 1939 as a first-class umpire. During the war, he suffered the amputation of both legs. To the surprise of Mead's family, Sutcliffe decided to apportion the fund between the two handicapped men. Fortunately, the total exceeded £8,000. This compares well with the £7,500 raised as an official benefit for Arnold, McCorkell, Herman, Bailey and Hill over the three years 1947, 1948 and 1949, and it brought in a weekly sum which usually paid the rent.

The other major benefit of peace for Mead was the return of first-class cricket. He became a constant visitor to the Hampshire dressing room at Dean Park. In 1946, many of his team mates were still in the side; John Arnold was a familiar and comforting presence until his own retirement in 1950, and McCorkell, Arthur Holt and Gerald Hill, the last of the pre-war players to leave the side as late as 1954, were all pleasant and attentive reminders of happier days. By that time, Mead was a popular figure wih a new generation of Hampshire cricketers who made occasional journeys for his sandwiches and beer. He 'listened' to the sound of bat on ball, correctly judging when a stroke was not played from the middle of the bat, but hardly ever left the bay-windowed dressing room: indeed, his wan complexion suggested that he saw little fresh air. Occasionally, he moved, a slighter figure than in his playing days, more publicly as he was led to a seat in the members' pavilion at Southampton — there were no executive boxes then.

He was fortunate that the County's President, in the years after the war, and the rest of Mead's life, was Harry Altham, player with Mead, administrator and most important, historian, while the captain, Desmond Eagar, also had a keen sense of the past. We have already seen how in 1955, Eagar ensured that Mead shared in the end-of-season celebrations: in the following spring, Altham formally declared open a new office block at the County Ground, Southampton.

After congratulating G. L. Thorne, the Honorary Architect, Mr. Altham went on to refer to 'the presence of that great batsman, Philip Mead, at the ground upon which he scored so many of that astonishing aggregate of 55,000 runs in his great career and on which he made 160 and 33 both not out against the Australians when Hampshire beat them in 1912.' The President, putting his arm through Phil Mead's, ended: "I do not know which I admire more, his batting of yesterday or the cheerfulness and courage with which he triumphs over his infirmity today. Phil, I would like you now to come with me and be associated with the unveiling of this block but first, perhaps, I could persuade you to say one word on your own account." Phil Mead was glad to say that the County's cricket was as good as ever it was and that he was grateful that he had not been forgotten.

He was prepared to venture further afield, visiting the National Sporting Club in 1948, when Bradman's Australians were guests of honour at lunch, and he was photographed there with Lord Tennyson. The next year he was among the first group of former professional cricketers who were admitted to honorary life membership of M.C.C. In September, he was personally congratulated by the Club's President, the Duke of Edinburgh, when he brought an XI to play Hampshire at Dean Park for the benefit of the National Playing Fields Association. It was a source of deep pleasure to Mead to be reminded by the Duke that the honour was restricted 'to the truly great'.

That same year, Mrs. Mead died after a short illness; now Phyllis, aged 24, was responsible for the men of the family. For the rest of her father's life she was his constant support. After Braund's death in 1955, the whole of Sutcliffe's fund was available for Mead and his situation was accordingly more comfortable, but £600 to £700 a year was not the valuable income it had been before the war, and there were still occasional difficulties.

In 1957, he visited Lord's for a reunion of old England cricketers, during the test with Goddard's unsuccessful West Indian tourists, and was photographed with Hobbs, Rhodes, Warner, Woolley and other great veterans.

His general health varied very little, apart from increasing susceptibility to the old athlete's enemy, arthritis. However, in the following spring of 1958 he suffered an internal haemorrhage. Rushed to hospital, he underwent urgent surgery but on 26th March 1958 he died.

ACKNOWLEDGEMENTS

and

FACTS AND FIGURES

ACKNOWLEDGEMENTS

I am indebted to E. F. Hayter, Gerald Hill, Arthur Holt, Dick Moore and Cecil Paris for their memories of Hampshire cricket in the 1930s and to Charles Knott for his assistance. A. F. Baker F.C.A., Chief Executive of Hampshire C.C.C. allowed me access to the County's minutes; Peter Thompson and Mike Newsom of the *Evening News*, Portsmouth, and of Southern Newspapers kindly gave me access to their archives. John Arlott was always encouraging and allowed me to quote freely from his reminiscences of Mead's last match.

I thank Victor Isaacs for the statistics relating to Mead's career.

I am also grateful to the following:

M. J. C. Allom; R. S. Barker (Suffolk County Cricket Association); John Barnes; John Bond; Peter Calson; Miss D. Daniels; Mike Duley (Winton Conservative Club); Ian Dyer; Alan Edwards; D. W. B. Filer; Geoffrey Ford, F.C.A.; Bill Frindall; Norman Gannaway; Leslie Gillett (Framlington College); S. E. A. Green (M.C.C.); Imogen Grosberg; Frank Higgs; A. G. H. House; Gen. Sir Patrick Howard-Dobson (Framlington College); Jean Jones; Jan Kemp; Peter Large (Hon. Librarian, Surrey C.C.C.); John W. Mckenzie; John May, M.P.S.; M. H. May; H. Morgan-Dockrell (Dublin); Major D. C. Nation; M. Newman; Frank K. Pike; A. G. T. Pocock; Alan Rayment; W. J. M. Ricquier; Lorraine Scott-Malcolm; Tony Sheldon (Cricket Memorabilia Society); E. W. Swanton; Arthur Toomer; R. A. Venne; E. M. Wellings; R. C. White and Martin Wood.

Finally, to Phyllis Mead who has taken a constant interest.

N.J.

C. P. MEAD. HIS FIGURES FOR HAMPSHIRE 1905-1936

Opponents:	I	TNO	R	HS	100	50	AVGE
Derbyshire	52	5	1292	227	3	5	27.48
Essex	65	8	3070	207	11	8	53.85
Glamorgan	20	1	867	162	1	6	45.63
Gloucestershire	81	10	3409	187	8	21	48.01
Kent	92	9	4369	198	15	18	52.63
Lancashire	64	5	2335	132*	5	15	39.57
Leicestershire	76	9	3419	159*	13	15	51.02
Middlesex	79	11	2600	179*	5	13	38.23
Northamptonshire	45	7	1463	151*	5	5	38.50
Nottinghamshire	62	11	3010	280*	10	14	59.01
Somerset	86	15	3450	176*	8	21	48.59
Surrey	85	13	3444	179*	8	22	47.83
Sussex	85	11	3633	224	9	16	49.09
Warwickshire	60	12	3319	222	10	14	69.14
Worcestershire	75	13	3391	235	11	11	54.69
Yorkshire	88	17	3197	213	10	12	45.02
	1115	157	46268	280*	132	216	48.29
M.C.C.	8	—	148	37	—	—	18.50
Oxford U.	5	—	285	93	—	2	57.00
Cambridge U.	5	2	457	160*	2	2	152.33
Australians	15	4	705	160*	3	1	64.09
South Africans	9	4	357	77*	—	4	71.40
New Zealanders	3	—	133	99	—	1	44.33
West Indians	7	1	408	132	1	3	68.00
All India	3	2	127	53*	—	2	127.00
Philadelphians	1	—	4	4	—	—	4.00
	56	13	2624	160*	6	15	61.02
	1171	170	48892	280*	138	231	48.84

(H. Morgan-Dockrell)

PHIL MEAD — A STATISTICAL SURVEY by Victor H. Isaacs

Career Record of First-Class Matches — Season by Season

Season	Team(s)	Mat	Inns	No	Runs	HS	Avge	100	50	CT	Runs	Wkts	Avge	5WI	Best
1905	Hampshire	1	2	1	41	41*	41.00	—	—	1	56	2	28.00	—	2/56
1906	Hampshire	21	39	1	1014	132	26.68	2	6	20	778	22	35.36	1	5/62
1907	Hampshire	25	46	1	1190	102	26.44	1	6	24	1109	42	26.40	2	6/55
1908	Hampshire/Hambledon XI	25	43	5	1118	119*	29.42	2	3	31	935	27	34.62	1	7/18
1909	Hampshire/The Rest	24	41	2	1459	114	37.41	1	9	23	815	23	35.43	—	4/38
1910	Hampshire/M.C.C.	27	48	3	1416	111	31.46	1	10	33	495	12	41.25	—	3/22
1911	Hampshire/M.C.C.	29	52	5	2562	223	54.51	9	9	25	713	21	33.95	—	3/44
1911/12	M.C.C. in Australia	13	18	2	531	98	33.18	—	4	4	—	—	—	—	—
1912	Hampshire/M.C.C.	34	52	14	1933	160*	50.86	7	8	26	722	14	51.57	—	3/20
1913	Hampshire/M.C.C.	32	60	8	2627	171*	50.51	9	10	29	442	5	88.40	—	2/25
1913/14	M.C.C. in South Africa	16	19	0	745	145	39.21	3	1	5	35	2	17.50	—	2/35
1914	Hampshire/M.C.C.	31	53	5	2476	213	51.58	7	12	43	185	4	46.25	—	1/13
1919	Hampshire/Players	23	38	7	1720	207	55.48	3	13	22	311	10	31.10	—	4/57
1920	Hampshire/M.C.C.	26	44	6	1887	178*	49.65	6	7	31	540	19	28.42	1	5/13
1921	Hampshire/England	33	52	6	3179	280*	69.10	10	16	27	457	13	35.15	—	2/8
1922	Hampshire/Players	32	50	10	2391	235	59.77	8	8	26	67	3	22.33	—	3/22
1922/23	M.C.C. in South Africa	14	21	2	695	181	36.57	1	3	7	—	—	—	—	—
1923	Hampshire/Players	32	52	8	2604	222	59.18	7	15	41	558	15	37.20	—	2/14
1924	Hampshire/Players	29	45	6	1644	154	42.15	3	10	14	113	3	37.66	—	1/0
1925	Hampshire/Tennyson	29	45	4	1942	213*	47.36	4	10	19	215	9	23.88	—	2/10
1926	Hampshire	29	45	8	2326	177*	62.86	10	8	36	370	8	46.25	—	3/34
1927	Hampshire/Players	28	41	9	2385	200*	74.53	8	10	25	210	5	42.00	—	2/19
1927/28	Tennyson in West Indies	3	5	1	418	151	104.50	3	—	—	65	1	65.00	—	1/53
1928	Hampshire/Players	30	50	10	3027	180	75.67	13	12	32	245	14	17.50	—	3/24
1928/29	M.C.C. in Australia	10	14	3	460	106	41.81	1	4	2	11	0	—	—	—
1929	Hampshire/M.C.C.	21	38	7	1733	233	55.90	5	8	13	57	2	28.50	—	1/2
1930	Hampshire	29	49	5	1305	143	29.65	1	8	26	67	1	67.00	—	1/1
1931	Hampshire	29	46	9	1596	169*	43.13	3	10	16	—	—	—	—	—
1932	Hampshire	27	45	5	1210	121	30.25	3	5	16	7	0	—	—	—
1933	Hampshire	27	44	6	2576	227	67.78	10	9	18	5	0	—	—	—
1934	Hampshire	29	46	8	2011	198	52.92	6	8	25	11	0	—	—	—
1935	Hampshire	30	55	12	1650	151*	38.37	4	6	8	19	0	—	—	—
1936	Hampshire	26	42	6	1190	126	33.05	2	9	3	—	—	—	—	—
TOTALS		814	1340	185	55061	280*	47.67	153	258	671	9613	277	34.70	5	7/18

162

For Hampshire against sides in England

Opponents	Mat	Inns	No	Runs	HS	Avge	100	50	CT	Runs	Wkts	Avge	5WI	Best
Derbyshire	29	52	5	1292	227	27.48	3	5	25	327	7	46.71	—	2/76
Essex	41	65	8	3070	207	53.85	12	7	25	383	11	34.81	—	4/57
Glamorgan	14	20	1	867	162	45.63	1	6	8	55	2	27.50	—	1/7
Gloucestershire	50	81	10	3409	187	48.01	8	20	61	554	29	19.10	1	5/13
Kent	51	92	9	4369	198	52.63	15	18	42	731	11	66.45	—	2/21
Lancashire	36	64	5	2335	132*	39.57	5	15	29	447	12	37.25	—	2/16
Leicestershire	47	76	10	3419	159*	51.80	13	14	37	546	13	42.00	—	3/38
Middlesex	47	79	11	2600	179*	38.23	5	13	44	697	11	63.36	—	2/16
Northamptonshire	31	45	7	1463	151*	38.50	10	5	29	322	21	15.33	1	7/18
Nottinghamshire	35	62	11	3010	280*	59.01	10	14	18	211	4	52.75	—	2/10
Somerset	52	86	15	3450	176*	48.59	8	21	57	740	27	27.40	1	6/55
Surrey	50	85	12	3444	169*	47.17	8	23	45	915	27	33.88	—	4/179
Sussex	49	85	11	3633	224	49.09	9	17	43	692	20	34.60	1	5/49
Warwickshire	40	62	12	3390	222	67.80	9	16	38	672	21	32.00	1	5/62
Worcestershire	46	73	13	3320	213*	55.33	11	10	55	723	16	45.18	—	3/22
Yorkshire	50	88	17	3197	213	45.02	10	12	43	647	21	30.80	—	4/89
Australians	8	15	4	705	160*	64.09	3	1	10	149	3	49.66	—	2/56
Cambridge University	3	5	2	457	160*	152.33	2	2	3	171	1	171.00	—	1/95
Indians	2	3	2	127	53*	127.00	—	2	1	—	—	—	—	—
M.C.C.	4	8	0	148	37	18.50	—	—	3	19	0	—	—	—
New Zealanders	2	3	0	133	99	44.33	—	1	—	—	—	—	—	—
Oxford University	3	5	0	285	93	57.00	—	2	3	62	2	31.00	—	1/23
Philadelphians	1	1	0	4	4	4.00	—	—	2	60	2	30.00	—	2/20
South Africans	5	9	4	357	77*	71.40	—	4	4	100	4	25.00	—	3/63
West Indians	4	7	1	408	132	68.00	1	3	4	29	1	29.00	—	1/9
TOTALS	700	1171	170	48892	280*	48.84	138	231	629	9252	266	34.78	5	7/18

109	Hampshire v Yorkshire	Southampton	1906
132	Hampshire v West Indians	Southampton	1906
102	Hampshire v Warwickshire	Southampton	1907
119*	Hampshire v Leicestershire	Southampton	1908
110	Hampshire v Leicestershire	Leicester	1908
114	Hampshire v Northamptonshire	Northampton	1909
111	Hampshire v Warwickshire	Birmingham	1910
100	Hampshire v Somerset	Southampton	1911
109	Hampshire v Leicestershire	Leicester	1911
127	M.C.C. v Leicestershire	Lord's	1911
100*	Hampshire v Leicestershire	Leicester	1911
223	Players v Gentlemen	Scarborough	1911
101	Rest of England v Warwickshire	The Oval	1911
120*	Hampshire v Yorkshire	Huddersfield	1911
207*	Hampshire v Warwickshire	Southampton	1911
194	Hampshire v Sussex	Portsmouth	1911
111*	Hampshire v Yorkshire	Sheffield	1912
135	Hampshire v Worcestershire	Worcester	1912
106	Hampshire v Kent	Southampton	1912
111	Hampshire v Warwickshire	Coventry	1912
140	Hampshire v Cambridge University	Southampton	1912
160*	Hampshire v Australians	Southampton	1912
109	Hampshire v Essex	Leyton	1912
102	Hampshire v Leicestershire	Southampton	1913
113*	Hampshire v Leicestershire	Southampton	1913
170	Hampshire v Warwickshire	Southampton	1913
116	Hampshire v Surrey	The Oval	1913
160*	Hampshire v Cambridge University	Cambridge	1913
127	Hampshire v Nottinghamshire	Southampton	1913
100*	Hampshire v Nottinghamshire	Nottingham	1913
100	Hampshire v Sussex	Southampton	1913
171*	Hampshire v Gloucestershire	Bournemouth	1913
145	M.C.C. v Transvaal	Pretoria	1913-14
102	England v South Africa	Johannesburg	1913-14
117	England v South Africa	Port Elizabeth	1913-14
213	Hampshire v Yorkshire	Southampton	1914
126	Hampshire v Somerset	Bath	1914
117	Hampshire v Kent	Tonbridge	1914
115	Hampshire v Warwickshire	Birmingham	1914
104*	Hampshire v Gloucestershire	Bristol	1914
158	Hampshire v Somerset	Southampton	1914
128	Hampshire v Kent	Bournemouth	1914
207	Hampshire v Essex	Leyton	1919
122*	Hampshire v Essex	Bournemouth	1919

100*	Hampshire v Yorkshire	Southampton	1919
125	Hampshire v Worcestershire	Worcester	1920
178*	Hampshire v Essex	Colchester	1920
122*	Hampshire v Yorkshire	Leeds	1920
176*	Hampshire v Somerset	Taunton	1920
102*	Hampshire v Warwickshire	Portsmouth	1920
144	Hampshire v Leicestershire	Southampton	1920
103	Hampshire v Somerset	Southampton	1921
129	Hampshire v Australians	Southampton	1921
280*	Hampshire v Nottinghamshire	Southampton	1921
108	Players v Gentlemen	Lord's	1921
113	Hampshire v Sussex	Horsham	1921
224	Hampshire v Sussex	Horsham	1921
182*	England v Australia	The Oval	1921
156	Hampshire v Sussex	Portsmouth	1921
103	Hampshire v Middlesex	Southampton	1921
159*	Hampshire v Leicestershire	Portsmouth	1921
152	Hampshire v Kent	Southampton	1922
235	Hampshire v Worcestershire	Worcester	1922
105	Hampshire v Leicestershire	Southampton	1922
179*	Hampshire v Essex	Leyton	1922
211*	Hampshire v Warwickshire	Southampton	1922
100*	Hampshire v Kent	Canterbury	1922
103	Hampshire v Somerset	Bournemouth	1922
131	Hampshire v Lancashire	Bournemouth	1922
181	England v South Africa	Durban	1922-23
106*	Hampshire v Surrey	The Oval	1923
162	Hampshire v Glamorgan	Southampton	1923
132	Hampshire v Worcestershire	Worcester	1923
222	Hampshire v Warwickshire	Birmingham	1923
147	Hampshire v Sussex	Hove	1923
145	Hampshire v Middlesex	Lord's	1923
123	Hampshire v Yorkshire	Leeds	1923
140	Hampshire v Surrey	The Oval	1924
154	Hampshire v Sussex	Hastings	1924
101	Hampshire v Leicestershire	Southampton	1924
162	Hampshire v Gloucestershire	Southampton	1925
115*	Hampshire v Surrey	Portsmouth	1925
112	Hampshire v Nottinghamshire	Southampton	1925
213*	Hampshire v Worcestershire	Bournemouth	1925
109	Hampshire v Gloucestershire	Gloucester	1926
161	Hampshire v Somerset	Knowle	1926
107	Hampshire v Essex	Southend	1926
132	Hampshire v Nottinghamshire	Southampton	1926
101	Hampshire v Sussex	Hove	1926
103*	Hampshire v Nottinghamshire	Nottingham	1926

175*	Hampshire v Kent	Canterbury	1926
117	Hampshire v Middlesex	Bournemouth	1926
132*	Hampshire v Lancashire	Manchester	1926
177*	Hampshire v Worcestershire	Worcester	1926
187	Hampshire v Gloucestershire	Southampton	1927
108*	Hampshire v Kent	Southampton	1927
200*	Hampshire v Essex	Southampton	1927
183	Hampshire v Yorkshire	Portsmouth	1927
141	Hampshire v Northamptonshire	Southampton	1927
100*	Hampshire v Northamptonshire	Kettering	1927
128	Hampshire v Kent	Canterbury	1927
142	Hampshire v Worcestershire	Bournemouth	1927
103*	Hon. L. H. Tennyson's XI v Jamaica	Kingston	1927-28
117	Hon. L. H. Tennyson's XI v Jamaica	Kingston	1927-28
151	Hon. L. H. Tennyson's XI v Jamaica	Kingston	1927-28
157	Hampshire v Middlesex	Lord's	1928
129	Hampshire v Worcestershire	Southampton	1928
110	Hampshire v Gloucestershire	Southampton	1928
118	Hampshire v Yorkshire	Southampton	1928
130	Hampshire v Surrey	Southampton	1928
156	Hampshire v Essex	Leyton	1928
130	Hampshire v Kent	Southampton	1928
180	Hampshire v Warwickshire	Bournemouth	1928
138	Hampshire v Nottinghamshire	Bournemouth	1928
117	Players v Gentlemen	Bournemouth	1928
117*	Hampshire v Gloucestershire	Bristol	1928
148	Hampshire v Leicestershire	Leicester	1928
103*	Hampshire v Worcestershire	Worcester	1928
106	M.C.C. v Tasmania	Launceston	1928-29
166*	Hampshire v Essex	Leyton	1929
129	Hampshire v Leicestershire	Southampton	1929
120*	Hampshire v Essex	Portsmouth	1929
102*	Hampshire v Kent	Bournemouth	1929
233	M.C.C. Australian Team v Lord Hawke's XI	Scarborough	1929
143	Hampshire v Nottinghamshire	Nottingham	1930
106*	Hampshire v Northamptonshire	Northampton	1931
106*	Hampshire v Sussex	Portsmouth	1931
169*	Hampshire v Surrey	Bournemouth	1931
104*	Hampshire v Derbyshire	Southampton	1932
111	Hampshire v Lancashire	Portsmouth	1932
121	Hampshire v Kent	Dover	1932
109*	Hampshire v Surrey	Southampton	1933
198	Hampshire v Kent	Southampton	1933
150	Hampshire v Leicestershire	Southampton	1933
116	Hampshire v Gloucestershire	Gloucester	1933

114	Hampshire v Lancashire	Bournemouth	1933
135	Hampshire v Kent	Canterbury	1933
152	Hampshire v Nottinghamshire	Southampton	1933
113*	Hampshire v Lancashire	Manchester	1933
227	Hampshire v Derbyshire	Ilkeston	1933
131*	Hampshire v Worcestershire	Bournemouth	1933
179*	Hampshire v Middlesex	Lord's	1934
139	Hampshire v Australians	Southampton	1934
138	Hampshire v Derbyshire	Portsmouth	1934
125*	Hampshire v Worcestershire	Worcester	1934
198	Hampshire v Kent	Folkestone	1934
120*	Hampshire v Yorkshire	Bournemouth	1934
151*	Hampshire v Northamptonshire	Northampton	1935
117*	Hampshire v Nottinghamshire	Nottingham	1935
100*	Hampshire v Somerset	Southampton	1935
116	Hampshire v Surrey	The Oval	1935
126	Hampshire v Kent	Southampton	1936
104	Hampshire v Essex	Southend	1936

PHIL MEAD IN TEST CRICKET

1911-12	v Australia	at Sydney on 15-21 Dec 1911	0 & 25	
	v Australia	at Melbourne on 30 Dec 1911, 1-3 Jan 1912	11	1ct
	v Australia	at Adelaide on 12-17 Jan 1912	46 & 2*	1ct
	v Australia	at Melbourne on 9-13 Feb 1912	21	1ct
1913-14	v South Africa	at Lord's, Durban on 13-17 Dec 1913	41	
	v South Africa	at Johannesburg on 26-30 Dec 1913	102	
	v South Africa	at Johannesburg on 1-5 Jan 1914	0 & 86	
	v South Africa	at Lord's, Durban on 14-18 Feb 1914	31 & 1	
	v South Africa	at Port Elizabeth on 27, 28 Feb, 2, 3 Mar 1914	117	
1921	v Australia	at Manchester on 23-26 Jul 1921	47	
	v Australia	at The Oval on 13-16 Aug 1921	182*	
1922-23	v South Africa	at Johannesburg on 23-28 Dec 1922	1 & 49	
	v South Africa	at Cape Town on 1-4 Jan 1923	21 & 31	
	v South Africa	at Kingsmead, Durban 18-22 Jan 1923	181	
	v South Africa	at Johannesburg on 9-13 Feb 1923	38 & 6	
	v South Africa	at Kingsmead, Durban on 16-22 Feb 1923	66 & 5	1ct
1928-29	v Australia	at Brisbane on 1-5 Dec 1928	8 & 73	

INDEX

Abel, Bobby — 77
Abercombie, C. H. — 34, 38, 47, 49
Aird, Ronald — 122
Akers-Douglas, I. — 141
Alderman (Derbys) — 137
Allen, G.O. — 125
Alletson (Notts) — 20
Allom, M. J. C. — 108, 109
Altham, H. S. — 79, 157
Ames, L. E. G. — 52, 117, 125, 132, 135, 136
Andrews, J. T. (Australia) — 72
Arlott, John — 81, 143, 148, 155
Armstrong, Warren — 10, 26, 31, 63, 65, 67, 69, 74, 75
Arnold, A. C. P. — 47-49
Arnold, John — 2, 121, 127-135, 139, 140, 142, 144-148, 157
Arnott — 110
Ashdown, W. H. — 132, 134, 140, 141
Astill, W. E. — 78, 91, 137

Bacon, F. H. — 9, 48, 50
Badcock, J. R. — 13
Bailey, Sir Abe — 16
Bailey, Jim — 107, 127, 129-136, 157
Baldwin — 10
Bardsley, Warren — 26, 32, 65
Baring, Giles — 128-130, 134-138
Barling, Tom — 132
Barnes, Sydney — 21, 23-26, 31, 42, 44-46
Barratt (Notts) — 68, 97
Barrett, E. I. M. — 29, 32-34, 41, 59, 62
Bates (Warwicks) — 80
Bedser twins — 3, 152
Belle, B. H. (Suffolk) — 153
Bencraft, Sir Russell — 56, 92, 94, 105, 139, 150
Bignall, G. N. (also played under name of G. Newcombe) — 29, 41, 55
Bird, M. C. — 37, 42, 44
Blythe, Colin — 20, 42, 54
Booth, Major (Yorkshire) — 18, 42, 46, 54
Bosanquet, B. J. J. — 11, 23
Bowell, A. — 2, 10-12, 15, 19, 20, 35, 37, 41, 53, 58, 60, 62, 67, 68, 74, 78-80, 89, 93-98, 102, 105, 106, 121
Bowes, Bill — 122, 134, 142
Bowley, E. H. — 3, 97
Boycott, Geoffrey — 4
Boyes, Stuart — 78, 80, 82, 89, 99, 107, 121, 127-135, 142-144, 148
Bradman, Sir Donald — 76, 105, 115, 118, 139
Braund, Leonard — 48, 61, 157, 158
Brearley, Walter — 29
Brockway, Charles — 128
Brodribb, Gerald — 128

Bromley (Australia) — 139
Brown, Bill (Australia) — 139
Brown, George — 2, 17-21, 34, 35, 41, 50, 53-60, 62, 66-72, 78, 80, 82-87, 89, 91-93, 95, 98, 99, 101, 103, 106, 107, 111, 121, 124, 127-138
Brutton, C. P. — 87
Bryan, J. L. — 90
Budgen — 43
Burton (Yorks) — 62
Busk, R. D. — 55

Calthorpe, Hon. F. S. H. — 78-80
Cameron, J. J. — 109
Cardus, Neville — 65
Carr, A. W. — 82, 84, 85, 100
Carter (Australia) — 31
Causton, E. P. G. — 55
Challenor, George (W.I.) — 86, 88
Chapman, A. P. F. — 24, 87, 90, 98-100, 113-119, 125, 132, 134-136, 141
Charlesworth — 23, 29
Chester, F. — 133
Chipperfield (Australia) — 139
Clark, E. W. — 104, 108, 109
Collins, H. L. (Australia) — 56
Compton, Dennis — 106
Constable, Bernard — 152
Constantine, Sir Learie — 86, 111
Cook (Lancs) — 60, 81
Cotter (Australia) — 10
Couteur, P. R. Le — 23
Cowdrey — 106
Cox (Sussex) — 20, 68
Cox, J. L. (South Africa) — 43
Crawford, Rev. J. C. — 7
Crawford, J. N. — 11, 42
Creese, W. L. — 127, 129, 132-135, 137, 140-144, 147

Daley, J. V. (Suffolk) — 153
Dalmeny, Lord — 11
Darling, Joe — 10
Day, S. H. — 49
Day, H. L. V. — 78-80, 98
Dean (Lancs) — 60
Dempster, C. S. — 137
Denton, David — 46
Difford, Ivor — 42, 45
Dipper, Alf — 2, 21, 66
Douglas, J. W. H. T. — 21, 24, 25, 27, 31, 37, 42-46, 55, 58, 65-69, 113
Down, J. H. — 53
Drake, E. J. — 46, 141, 145
Ducat, Andrew — 2, 54

Duckworth, George — 113, 115, 128
Duleepsinjhi — 125
Durham, R. — 155
Durston (Middlesex) — 71

Eagar, Desmond — 1, 48, 157
Eckersley, P. T. — 98, 110
Edinburgh, Duke of — 158
Englefield, Beatrice (Mrs. Philip Mead) — 14, 15
Evans, A. J. — 66

Fagg, A. — 140, 141
Fairservice, C. — 132
Falcon — 21
Farnes, Kenneth — 147
Faulkner, G. A. — 22, 42
Fender, P. G. H. — 71, 72, 75, 79, 82, 97, 108, 129
Fenley, S. — 144
Field, Frank — 20, 23
Fielder — 20
Fleetwood-Smith (Australia) — 139
Forrest, Ted (Suffolk) — 153
Foster, F. R. — 18, 24, 25, 28, 31, 35, 103
Foster, H. K. — 31, 37
Foster, M. K. — 98
Foster, R. E. — 76
Fox (Warwicks) — 80
Freeman, A. P. — 74, 114-119, 123, 125, 132-135, 140, 141
Fry, C.B. — 6, 9, 14, 18-24, 29, 32-34, 42, 45, 47, 51, 61, 66, 67
Fry, Stephen — 129

Geary, George — 78, 86, 114, 118
Gibbons (Hampshire) — 103
Gilligan, A. E. R. — 68, 84, 87, 88, 113
Gilligan, F. W. — 55
Goddard, Tom — 130, 137
Gower, David — 76
Grace, E. M. — 48
Grace, W. G. — 3, 4, 8, 10, 14, 47-49, 102, 104, 106, 112, 129, 138, 147, 154
Gray, J. — 2
Greenidge, Gordon — 1, 2
Gregory, Bob (Surrey) — 97
Gregory, J. M. (Australia) — 56, 65-67, 71, 72, 75, 115
Gregory, Syd (Australia) — 10
Greig, Col. J. G. — 16, 47, 53, 59, 67, 68, 93, 94
Griffiths (W.I.) — 132
Grimmett, C. V. (Australia) — 51, 114-116
Gross, F. A. — 103
Gunn, George — 21, 24, 25, 28, 51

Haig (Middlesex) — 125
Haig-Smith, H. A. — 53
Haigh, Schofield — 11, 31
Hall, P. M. — 55
Hallows, Charles — 51, 75, 82, 87, 98, 113
Hammond, W. R. — 4, 7, 87, 102, 110, 114-118, 122, 127, 128, 138
Hands, P. A. M. — 45
Hands, W. C. — 36
Hardstaff, Joe — 138
Hardstaff, Senr. — 133
Hardinge, H. T. W. — 2, 68, 98, 133-136
Harfield, I. — 107, 124
Harris, Lord — 47, 113, 118
Harrison, G. C. — 46, 62
Hartley, A. — 19
Hawke, Lord — 19, 47
Hayes, Ernest — 11, 29, 31
Hayward, Tom — 11, 14, 23, 51, 54, 77, 104, 112
Headley, George (W.I.) — 109
Heath, George — 145
Hendry (Australia) — 67, 72
Henley, H. J. — 113
Herman, O. W. (Lofty) — 121, 127, 132, 133, 136, 141-145, 157
Heseltine, Colonel — 97
Hesketh-Pritchard — 35
Hearne, J. W. — 18, 21, 23-27, 43, 46, 47, 54, 55, 61, 63, 71, 88, 100
Hendren, E. (Patsy) — 2, 3, 18, 51, 54, 55, 61-64, 82, 86-88, 90, 99, 100, 113-119, 125, 128, 145
Hill, A. J. L. — 11, 61
Hill, Clem — 10, 26, 28, 31, 64
Hill, Gerald — 136, 137, 141, 142, 145, 148, 157
Hirst — 11, 23, 46
Hitch, W. — 21, 24, 47, 63, 75, 141
Hoare, Capt. C. A. R. — 9
Hobbs, Jack (Sir) — 2-4, 11, 14, 16, 19, 23-28, 31, 38, 40-47, 50, 51, 61, 63, 65, 69, 86, 90, 91, 97, 99, 100, 104, 113-119, 127, 138, 145, 158
Holmes, Percy — 51, 60-66, 82, 87, 103, 111, 113
Holt, Arthur — 123, 144, 157
Holt, J. K. — 109
Hopkins (Australia) — 10
Hopkins, Jesse — 50
Hordern, H. V. (Australia) — 24
Hornby, A. H. — 37
Horton, H. — 2
Hosie, A. I. — 68, 69, 107, 110-112, 143
Howell, Harry — 62, 66, 79, 86
Humphreys, E. (Kent) — 47
Hutchings, K. L. — 54

Hutton, Sir Leonard — 76, 106, 138
Hyman, W. — 48

Ingle (Somerset) — 144
Iremonger, James — 21
Ironmonger (Australia) — 115, 116

Jackson, A. (Australia) — 118
Jackson, F. S. (Sir Stanley) — 47, 150
Jaimes, C. L. R. — 149
Jameson, T. O. — 55, 112
Jaques, A. — 35, 38, 47, 48, 49, 50, 53, 54, 59
Jardine, D. R. — 87, 113, 114, 115, 116, 117, 118
Jeeves (Essex) — 49
Jephson, Rev. W. V. — 32, 35, 41
Jessop, Gilbert — 11, 19, 20, 37, 42, 45, 54
Jessop, G. L. O. — 138
Jesty, Trevor — 2
Johnson, P. R. (Somerset) — 38, 121
Johnston, A. C. — 16, 20, 29, 33, 34
Judd, A. K. (Hampshire) — 98, 107, 133, 138, 144
Jupp, V. W. C. — 20, 66, 82, 104, 125

Kellaway (Australia) — 115
Kemp-Welch — 110
Kennedy, A. S. — 2, 11, 14, 16, 17, 32-34, 38, 41, 47-50, 54-56, 60, 62, 63, 68-70, 74, 77-80, 82-88, 91-99, 102-107, 111, 121-124, 127-130, 132-138, 140, 142, 147
Kenyon, Donald — 1
Khan, Jahangir — 147
Killick, E. H. — 12
Kilner, Roy — 46, 60, 61, 81, 86, 91, 94, 100
Kingsley, P. G. T. — 125
Kinneir, S. P. — 21, 23, 25
Kippax, Alan (Australia) — 139
Knight, A. E. — 19
Knight, D. J. — 66

Lacey, Sir Francis — 150
Langford — 10, 15
Larter, J. D. F. — 151
Larwood, Harold — 97, 113-118, 128, 136, 144
Laver (Australia) — 31
Lawson, H. M. — 147
Lee, Frank — 121
Lee, Harry — 2
Lee, G. M. — 108, 110
Levett, W. H. V. — 133, 141
Leveson-Gower, H. D. G. — 42, 113, 150
Lewis, C. (Kent) — 140, 141

Leyland, Maurice — 87, 113, 115, 117, 118
Lilley, A. A. — 21
Littlejohn, A. R. — 18
Livsey — 17, 49, 53, 59, 67, 68, 74, 78, 80-83, 92, 97-99, 106, 107, 121, 122, 125
Louden, G. M. — 55
Lovegrove, E. W. (Suffolk) — 153
Lowndes, W. G. L. F. — 138-140, 143

Maartensz, S. G. A. — 55
Macartney (Australia) — 29, 65-67
Macaulay, G. G. — 103, 134
MacBryan, J. C. W. — 61, 74, 86, 91
MacLaren, A. C. — 77
McBride — 98
McCabe, Stanley — 139
McCorkell, N. — 2, 127, 132-137, 140, 142, 144, 145, 147, 148
McDonald, E. A. — 27, 65-67, 71, 72, 75, 104
McDonnell, H. C. (Twyford School) — 38, 48, 49
McGahey, C. P. — 49
McIntyre, A. S. — 68, 80, 152
McLaren, J. W. — 25
McLeod, Alistair — 48, 144
McLeod, K. G. — 19
Mailey, Arthur — 67, 75, 76
Makepeace, Harry — 63, 64, 86-88, 98
Mann, F. T. — 82, 84, 85, 113
Mannors, J. E. — 147
Marriott, C. S. — 135
Marshall, Roy — 1, 149
Martindale (W.I.) — 132
Mead, Frankie — 129
Mills, Percy — 61
Minnett (Australia) — 32
Moberly, J. C. — 9
Moore, R. H. — 56, 121, 122, 137, 140, 142-144, 147, 148
Morant, E. J. — 12
Morris, H. M. — 102
Morrison, Sir William — 109
Murphy, Patrick — 4, 122, 123, 148

Newcombe, G. (see Bignell) — 55
Newman, J. A. — 1, 11, 15-17, 21, 29, 34-38, 41, 46, 48-50, 53, 54, 59, 62, 67-69, 74,
    77, 80, 81, 87-89, 92, 93, 98, 99, 102, 107, 111, 112, 121, 128
Nichol, Maurice (Worcs) — 137
Nichols, M. S. (Essex) — 102, 103, 127, 147
Noble, M. A. — 10
Normanton, Lord — 155
Nourse, D. — 32, 84

Oates (Norfolk) — 68, 73
Oldfield, W. A. — 67

O'Reilly, Bill — 139

Palmer (Hampshire) — 135
Pardon, Sydney ('Wisden') — 28, 76
Paris, C. G. A. — 122, 123, 140, 143, 145, 147, 148
Parker, Charlie — 58, 72, 75, 128, 130
Parker, J. P. — 98, 102, 103
Parkin, Cecil — 72, 81, 122
Payne, M. W. — 34
Peach, Alan — 125
Pearce, W. K. — 87, 96
Pearson, Fred — 59
Pearsse, W. — 10, 50
Peebles, Ian — 123
Perkins, C. (Suffolk) — 153, 154
Pentelow, J. N. — 14
Perrin, P. (Essex) — 11, 23
Pierpoint, Fred — 152
Porter, Dr. H. (Suffolk) — 153
Ponsford, W. — 116, 139
Pothecary, A. E. — 127, 129, 132-137, 140-147
Pothecary, S. — 55
Powell, A. G. (Suffolk) — 153, 154

Quaife, W.G. — 51, 80

Ranjitsinghi, Prince — 18
Ransford (Australia) — 31
Redman, E. C. — 147
Relf, Albert — 68
Relf, Robert — 18, 20, 31, 42, 44, 154
Remnant, E. — 35, 41, 46, 54, 68, 121
Rhodes, Wilfred — 11, 14, 21, 23-27, 31, 33, 46, 47, 56, 60, 63, 66, 100, 103, 125, 158
Richards, Barry — 1
Richmond (Notts) — 66, 67
Robertson-Glasgow, R. C. — 51, 108
Robey, George — 121
Robinson, D. C. — 42, 43
Robinson, Emmot — 56, 60
Robson, Charles — 17
Robson, Frank — 61
Rogers, Neville — 2
Root, Fred — 98, 110
Royal Family, members of — 46, 47, 123
Russell, C. A. G. — 63, 64, 71, 82, 84, 85, 87, 102
Russell, J. — 2
Rutherford, J. S. — 35, 36
Ryan, Frank — 55, 56, 59, 60
Ryder, J. (Australia) — 67

Sandham, A. — 75, 82, 84, 88, 90, 97, 125, 129, 130, 138, 149
Sangster, Murray (Suffolk) — 153
Santall, F. R. — 80
Santall, Sidney — 23
Scott, J. D. — 114
Scott, O. C. — 109
Scott, W. E. N. — 103
Seabrook, F. J. — 110
Sellars, Brian — 134
Sharp, A. T. (Leics) — 48
Sharp (Lancs) — 14
Sharpe, Jack — 19
Sheffield, E. J. — 133
Shipley, W. R. de la C. — 78, 80, 87, 89
Shipman, Alan — 78
Shuter, John — 31
Skelding, Alec — 78
Smart, G. — 80
Smart, J. — 80
Smith, C. L. — 1
Smith, Denis (Derbys) — 137
Smith, E. J. (Tiger) — 21, 24, 26, 31, 42
Smith, Peter (Essex) — 147
Smith, R. A. — 1
Smith, S. G. — 47
Soar, Tom — 9, 10
Spooner, R. H. — 19, 21-24, 29, 31, 45
Sprot, E. M. — 2, 10-13, 17, 32, 36, 41
Staples, Sam — 97, 114, 117, 130
Stevens, G. T. S. — 100
Stocks, F. W. — 151
Stone, J. — 10-12, 16, 35, 37, 41, 49, 53, 87, 121
Street, A. E. — 135, 141
Streeton, Richard — 129
Strudwick — 21, 23, 24, 31, 42, 65
Studd, Sir Kynaston — 118, 125
Sullivan (Surrey) — 108
Surridge, Stuart — 3, 152
Sutcliffe, Herbert — 2, 4, 60, 62, 82, 86-88, 90, 91, 99, 100, 103, 113-115, 117-119, 122, 128, 130, 157, 158
Swartz, R. O. — 11

Tarbox, C. V. (Worcs) — 110, 123
Tarrant, Frank — 23, 46, 54
Tate, Maurice — 68, 69, 78, 81, 86, 87, 91, 97, 100, 113, 116, 117, 125, 128, 149
Taylor, H. W. (South Africa) — 44, 82, 84, 85
Taylor, J. M. (Australia) — 66
Tennyson, Lionel (later Lord) — 2, 17, 34, 38, 42, 44, 45, 47, 49, 55, 59, 62, 66, 68-75, 77, 80, 81, 87, 88, 91, 92, 95, 102-104, 107-109, 121, 124, 127-129, 138, 142-144, 148

Thomas, 'Taffy' — 104
Thompson, G. J. — 23
Thornton, C. L. — 82
Thwaites, Alderman and Mrs. (Mayor and Mayoress of Bournemouth) — 104
Timms, J. E. — 104
Todd, L. J. — 132, 134-136, 140, 141
Toomer, Arthur — 40
Toomer, Walter — 40, 57, 108
Toone, Sir F. C. — 117
Trumper, Victor — 10, 19, 51
Turner, D. R. — 2
Tyldesley, Ernest — 2, 51, 66, 72, 82, 87, 90, 99, 100, 108, 109, 113, 115, 117, 118, 138
Tyldesley, J. T. — 11, 19, 51
Tyldesley, Richard — 81, 104, 128

Utley, R. P. H. — 111

Valentine, B. H. — 132, 135, 136, 141
Verity — 134
Vine, J. — 20, 21, 28
Voce, Bill — 130, 141
Vogler, A. E. — 11

Waddington (Yorks) — 56, 60, 81
Waddy, Rev. K. F. — 80
Walden, F. — 135
Walker, Donald — 148
Wall, Tim — 114
Walters, C. F. — 137
Warner, P. F. — 11, 18, 19, 21, 24, 25, 31, 42, 56, 100, 113, 150, 158
Washbrook, Cyril — 138
Watt, A. E. — 133-136, 141
Waugh, P. (Suffolk) — 153
Weigall, G. J. V. — 109, 113
Webster, Tom (cartoonist) — 64, 79
White, G. C. — 11
White, J. C. — 58, 61, 71, 113, 115-118, 144
Whysall (Notts) — 2, 68, 90, 91, 106, 125
Wilson, E. Rockley — 56, 62
Winning, C. S. — 56
Woolley, Frank — 2-4, 19, 21, 23-26, 28, 31, 33, 36, 42, 45, 51, 65, 71, 72, 82, 86-88, 90, 91, 100, 108, 112, 113, 118, 127, 134, 135, 141, 158
Worthington (Derbys) — 137